CLARK CO. LIBRARY  P9-DDS-933

AUG - - 2008

LAS VEGAS-CLARK COUNTY
LIBRARY DISTRICT
833 LAS VEGAS BLVD. N.
LAS VEGAS, NEVADA 89101

MY *three* FATHERS

MY *three* FATHERS

AND THE ELEGANT DECEPTIONS OF MY MOTHER, SUSAN MARY ALSOP

William S. Patten

PUBLICAFFAIRS
New York

Copyright © 2008 by William S. Patten

Published in the United States by PublicAffairs™, a member of the Perseus Books Group.

All rights reserved.
Printed in the United States of America.

This book contains excerpts from a number of letters and diary entries, most of which belong to the author's mother or family members. In the case that an excerpt did not belong to the author or his family, he has made an effort in good faith to find and contact the owners, their surviving family members, or their estates. In some cases, no rights holder could be found or the rights holders had not yet, at the time of publication, responded to the author's query.

All photographs in the book are courtesy of the author unless otherwise noted.

The excerpt from Derek Walcott's poem "Love After Love" appears in Farrar, Straus, and Giroux's edition of a Derek Walcott anthology titled *Collected Poems 1948–1984*. The excerpt appears courtesy of the publisher.

No part of this book may be reproduced in any manner whatsoever without written permission except in the case of brief quotations embodied in critical articles and reviews. For information, address PublicAffairs, 250 West 57th Street, Suite 1321, New York, NY 10107.

PublicAffairs books are available at special discounts for bulk purchases in the U.S. by corporations, institutions, and other organizations. For more information, please contact the Special Markets Department at the Perseus Books Group, 2300 Chestnut Street, Suite 200, Philadelphia, PA 19103, call (800) 810-4145, ext. 5000, or e-mail special.markets@perseusbooks.com.

Designed by Pauline Brown
Text set in 11.5 point Garamond

Patten, William.
  My three fathers : and the elegant deceptions of my mother, Susan Mary Alsop / William S. Patten. — 1st ed.
      p.   cm.
  Includes bibliographical references and index.
  ISBN 978-1-58648-555-9
  1. Patten, William—Family. 2. Patten, William, d. 1960. 3. Alsop, Joseph, 1910-1989. 4. Cooper, Duff, Viscount Norwich, 1890-1954. 5. Children of celebrities—United States—Biography. I. Title.
  CT275.P415A3 2008
  920.073—dc22

2008002882

First Edition

10 9 8 7 6 5 4 3 2 1

For Sydney

contents

Family Trees   ix
Introduction   xiii

1. The Butler of St. Mary's   1

2. Yankees at the Court   21

3. An Incident at Sea   43

4. The Smell of Fear   51

5. The Making of a Warrior   67

6. Dangerous Liaisons   79

7. Standing Up to Hitler   97

8. Keeping the Fire Lit   115

9. The Sad Brave Smile   139

10. Nabbing My Mother   167

11. In Camelot's Court   193

12. Making the Club   213

13. Launched by Joe   231

Contents

14. Mother Breaks Away   255

15. Facing Demons   271

16. A Partnership Restored   289

17. Leaving Lotus Land   303

18. The Long Good-bye   315

19. Looking at the Box   331

20. Meeting the Stranger   339

     Notes   *349*
     Acknowledgments   *363*
     Index   *367*

DESCENDANTS OF

John Jay

Peter Augustus Jay ═ Josephine Pearson
(1821–1855) (1829–1852)

Augustus Jay ═ Emily Kane
(1850–1919) (1854–1932)

Peter A. Jay ═ Susan Alexander McCook
(1877–1933) (1879–1978)

Delancey Kane Jay ═ Elizabeth Morgan
(1881–1910) (1889–1976)

Kane Jay Susan Mary Jay ═ William S. Patten
(–1926) (1918–2004) (1909–1960)

— Elizabeth Morgan Jay
— Peter Jay
— Sybil Kane Jay
— Theodora Morgan Jay
— Augusta Jay
— Katharine Jay ═ Robert Bacon

— William S. Patten ═
(1948–
— Anne Emily Patten
(1950–

— Katharine Bacon
— Sarah Bacon
— Charlotte Bacon
— Elizabeth Bacon
— Susan Bacon
— Robert Bacon

n S. Patten Elizabeth Anne Patten Sybil Alexandra Patten
1971– (1974– (1978–

Elizabeth,

6TH CHILD OF MRS. JORDAN
AND THE DUKE OF CLARENCE
(LATER KING WILLIAM IV)

George	Sophia	Henry	Mary
EARL OF	1795–1837	1797–1817	1798–1864
MUNSTER			

*I*n 1791 Prince William, Duke of Clarence (the third son of George III), fell in love with a leading actress at Drury Lane known as Dora Jordan. For more than twenty years, despite attacks from the press, Dora was his loyal partner, helping him pay his debts out of her earnings as an actress, and bearing him ten (illegitimate) children, known as the Fitzclarences. Under pressure from the royal family, William eventually abandoned her. Four years later, in 1816, Dora died alone and destitute outside Paris. In 1818 William married Princess Adelaide of Saxe-Meiningen. After William succeeded his older brother George IV and took the throne in 1830 as William IV, he legitimized the Fitzclarences.

Elizabeth, the sixth child of William and Dora, married the Earl of Errol. They had four children, and in 1846 their second daughter, Agnes, married James Duff, who later succeeded his uncle as fifth Earl Fife. Their wedding took place in the British Embassy in Paris, where, exactly a hundred years later, their grandson Duff Cooper served as Ambassador.

Lord and Lady Fife spent much of their time at Duff House, near Banff, and at Mar Lodge in Scotland. The Prince of Wales, later Edward VII, was a frequent guest at Mar Lodge, and in 1889 his eldest daughter, Princess Louise, married the Fife's only son, Alexander. Alexander was then made the first Duke of Fife. His sister, Agnes, eloped twice before she settled down with Duff's father in 1882.

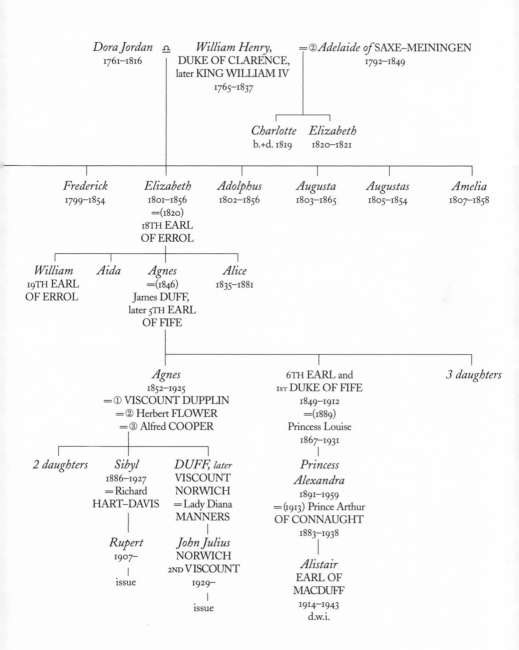

Dora Jordan ⚭ William Henry, =②Adelaide of SAXE–MEININGEN
1761–1816   DUKE OF CLARENCE,   1792–1849
later KING WILLIAM IV
1765–1837

Charlotte   Elizabeth
b.+d. 1819   1820–1821

Frederick   Elizabeth   Adolphus   Augusta   Augustas   Amelia
1799–1854   1801–1856   1802–1856   1803–1865   1805–1854   1807–1858
=(1820)
18TH EARL
OF ERROL

William   Aida   Agnes   Alice
19TH EARL   =(1846)   1835–1881
OF ERROL   James DUFF,
later 5TH EARL
OF FIFE

Agnes   6TH EARL and   3 daughters
1852–1925   1ST DUKE OF FIFE
=① VISCOUNT DUPPLIN   1849–1912
=② Herbert FLOWER   =(1889)
=③ Alfred COOPER   Princess Louise
1867–1931

2 daughters   Sibyl   DUFF, later   Princess
1886–1927   VISCOUNT   Alexandra
=Richard   NORWICH   1891–1959
HART–DAVIS   =Lady Diana   =(1913) Prince Arthur
MANNERS   OF CONNAUGHT
1883–1938

Rupert   John Julius
1907–   NORWICH   Alistair
| 2ND VISCOUNT   EARL OF
issue   1929–   MACDUFF
| 1914–1943
issue   d.w.i.

Family tree adapted from Claire Tomalin's *Mrs. Jordan's Profession: The Actress and the Prince* (New York: Knopf, 1995), 394–395.

— introduction —

A number of people suggested I write about my mother and my three fathers. It is the story of a rarified world that seems far away today. Writing about it has been like putting together an old jigsaw puzzle with some of the pieces faded beyond recognition or missing.

The story is offered in five parts: my mother's John Jay background and her upbringing, my English father's Edwardian background and career, my American father's life and our family life in Paris in the 1950s, my stepfather's life and our family life in Washington in the 1960s and '70s, and the last thirty years of my mother's life. My own story weaves in and out of these parts.

The big transition in my upbringing occurred shortly after the death of my American father, Bill Patten, in 1960. At the end of that year my mother, as described in chapter 10, agreed to marry Joseph Alsop. The following year my sister and I moved to the United States and, with our mother, took up residence in Joe's home in Washington, D.C.

People have asked me whether I truly didn't know about my connection to Duff Cooper during my adolescence. I did not, at least not consciously. But as this book illustrates, during most of my life I was constantly probing this kaleidoscope of fact and fiction. My memory bounces back and forth between images of Paris in the 1950s and facts I have gathered since then from shelf loads of biographies, memoirs, and letters. The workings of memory are illusive, however, and ten years from now I might have a different answer about Duff.

I suppose I grew up in a privileged world, but it has taken half a century for me to appreciate it. When I look at the lovely photos my mother took of my sister and me in Paris, I wonder who *is* that little boy? My mother's first book, *To Marietta from Paris, 1945–1960,* describing our glamorous lives in Paris in the 1950s, felt so fictional that it was painful for me to read it.

Parts of this chronicle will also seem fictional. Memory is imperfect and the past can resurface at unpredictable times. I began writing this book in 2004, the year my mother died, and in the fall of 2007 I received an unexpected package of letters from England. This apparently unopened envelope contained what appeared to be a complete collection of my mother's love letters to an English diplomat I last saw at my father Bill Patten's funeral in 1960. It included a cover letter from this man's literary executor explaining why he was sending me the letters. I had heard vague reports of this affair but had never imagined finding any evidence of it.

Father number one, Bill Patten, was the father I grew up with in Paris until he died in 1960, when he was only fifty-two. Bill had been stationed in Paris as a diplomat right after World War II, and he died when I was twelve. No one knows for sure if he knew I was not his son.

Father number two, Joseph W. Alsop, my stepfather, was a nationally syndicated columnist, a classmate of Bill Patten's, and the man my mother married the year after Bill died. We returned to the United States, and Joe took my sister and me under his formidable wing. He guided me with special attention through my adolescent and college years until I married my first wife in 1970. He died in 1989, and my memories of him are vivid.

Father number three is Duff Cooper, my biological father, an Englishman born in 1890. He became famous for his solitary stand against Hitler in 1938, having already distinguished himself as a young officer in the Great War of 1914–1918. Duff was the ambassador to Paris when my parents arrived there in 1944. I do not remember ever meeting Duff; he feels as distant to me as my grandfather Peter A. Jay, who was only a few years older and was also a diplomat in Paris in the early 1900s.

On a historic level, both Joe and Duff were worldly men and confidantes of national figures like Winston Churchill and Edward VIII in England or American presidents John F. Kennedy and Lyndon Johnson and other world leaders. Their robust advice grew out of their knowledge of history and their hands-on involvement in politics. They were both superb writers who combined genuine scholarship with a bent for the rough-and-tumble of daily politics.

Bill, a much gentler and less ambitious man, was not involved in power politics but managed small things with great grace. In his background role he was in fact the key link in this small male triangle. Though Bill was never a major player, I suspect that Duff admired him, and I know Joe loved him.

Though the two Americans, Bill and Joe, were almost twenty years younger than the Englishman, all three fathers knew one another. Bill and Joe even shared an apartment as young bachelors in New York in the thirties. It was mainly through Bill's marriage to my mother and their close relationship to Duff and Diana Cooper in Paris that Joe later became a friend of the Coopers.

Though it did not start out that way, my mother has emerged as the pivotal figure of this story. I was never close to her in the visceral way one hopes most children feel about their mothers, but I profoundly admired her. This distance between us has no doubt made me yearn, throughout my life, to make connections with others.

Telling this story has rekindled my sense of awe at my mother's intense energy, self-discipline, and talent. Susan Mary Alsop is more than the linchpin of this story; she is the most extraordinary of its figures and the most daunting of its driving forces.

Susan Mary Patten with "Charlus," Clos St. Nicholas, Senlis, June 1947

one

The Butler
of St. Mary's

"Can't we tell the servants not to feed her
[Lady Leone]?" "They don't.
Mildred brings her food, like a raven."
"The one with the picnic basket?"
"We could stop her from coming—tell the
concierge not to let her in?"

—*DON'T TELL ALFRED*, NANCY MITFORD

OUR INTERVENTION WITH my mother took place during duck-hunting season. I flew down to Washington, D.C., from Portland, Maine, in late October 1995. At the time, I was running a newspaper in Camden and driving each week to the Bangor Theological Seminary, where I was studying for a master's degree in divinity.

Soon after arriving in Georgetown, I realized that I had left my suitcase in my car at the Portland International Jetport. I was happy to have an excuse to buy some new clothes, but a familiar alarm began to ring somewhere deep in my brain—one that sounded whenever I was about to see my mother.

My mother was Susan Mary Alsop, the surname acquired from her second husband, newspaper columnist Joseph W. Alsop.

She had divorced Joe more than twenty years earlier and moved back into a house her mother owned on Twenty-ninth Street. It was a drab beige house that she livened up inside with bright colors and Louis XVI furniture.

Susan Mary, or Mother, as I usually called her, was seventy-seven in the fall of 1995. After leaving Joe, she had made a name for herself as an author and hostess. Leafing through *Spade and Archer's 50 Maps of Washington, D.C.* several years ago, I was surprised to find a section titled "Susan Mary Alsop's Georgetown" replete with a map of one of my mother's favorite walks. On another page she was included on a short list of the city's "Grande Dames and Power Hostesses."

Susan Mary Alsop drove a small Honda and was generally frugal, so her elevated status had crept up on me. Perhaps I'd been living in Maine too long. During the past half century she had established a reputation in high places for her discretion and her capacity to connect powerful people. I guess I had not quite realized how far her gift for maintaining emotional boundaries had catapulted her into stardom.

She combined an inner steeliness with the subdued elegance of a Jamesian—or perhaps Merchant Ivory Productions—heroine. As more than one reviewer observed about my mother's historical portraits, including *Yankees at the Court* or *The Congress Dances,* she belonged in the stories she wrote about. Power, diplomacy, and elegance were fused together both in her books and in the life she led.

Mother's two leather address books—one for America, one for Europe—were prima facie evidence that she was a very busy woman. Reading through them, one sees the outline of her three "careers"—the diplomat's wife in Paris, the journalist's wife in Washington, and, toward the end of her life, a successful writer. The names and addresses give credence to the assertion she once made to a journalist that she was not interested in living what she referred to as an "ordinary life." This was a brazen statement, one she would not have shared with me, but borne out by the life she led.

My mother's stoicism was an asset in her dazzling world of artists and statesmen, intellectuals and diplomats. Her elegance was appreciated by most, but less by me. I thought of her as a brave little soldier, and I was always surprised when my friends told me how warm and engaging she had been with them. Her flair for attracting friends and offering her services to others was legendary. I think it was a well-honed survival skill—an idea she would have laughed at politely and then dismissed as pop psychology. Her friend columnist Edwin Yoder wrote after her death in 2004, "Readers of the recent obituaries for Susan Mary Alsop could feast on colorful reports of a fairy-tale life among the high and mighty and elegant . . . But the woman I knew was a gritty survivor."

Until my stepfather, Joe Alsop, died in 1989, few of us had seriously worried about my mother's deepening alcoholism. Mostly our concerns focused on Joe's drinking. Although Joe and Susan Mary had divorced fifteen years earlier and lived separately, they remained a pair. They went to parties together, went on walks together, and focused on their grandchildren together.

My mother had tightly controlled her drinking for years, but after Joe's death my sister, Anne (who is two years younger than I am), and I could sense her deep loneliness and had become increasingly concerned. We saw it from different angles—Anne from Utah, where she lived, and me from Maine—but we concurred that the problem was serious. When I sat down alone with my mother after lunch one time and told her that I thought she needed help controlling her alcohol, she thanked me icily and got up and left the room. My letters to her were similarly cast aside.

The alcohol intervention we had planned for Susan Mary had been triggered by my sister's ambitious plan to relocate her to a neighboring house in Salt Lake City, where Anne lived with her husband, John Milliken, and their two daughters. Most friends thought that uprooting my mother from Washington was a crazy idea but appreciated that Anne was taking some initiative. And no one liked to confront my sister when she had put her mind to something.

In the early part of the summer of 1995, Anne and John drove down the coast from Northeast Harbor with my mother to visit me in Camden. My daughter Sybil and I prepared lunch for them, and we ate outside in my garden. My mother's move to Utah seemed decided without much discussion. But when I visited her alone in Northeast Harbor later in the summer, I could tell she was terrified by the idea.

I had been pushing for an intervention for some time. Anne herself began to have doubts when she returned from Maine to Utah in August and heard firsthand reports of Mother passing out at our summerhouse in Northeast Harbor. As my sister began to realize how disturbing our mother's alcoholism would likely be for her own family, especially her two little girls, she called me at my newspaper office in Camden late that summer, and we agreed to try an intervention.

My sister is not afraid of confrontations; on the contrary, we are both impatient with half-truths and pretentiousness. Anne likes to say that life is "white-water," a feeling that lay just below the surface of our upbringing. She once told a reporter that growing up in Washington we expected "the roof to come crashing down at any time." In fact, we are both so viscerally conditioned to the idea of Armageddon that I sometimes wonder if we don't invite it.

We both have an unusual aptitude for bilateral vision. When Anne and I are in a restaurant, we're instinctively aware of the people around us; like camp survivors, we tend to be always on our toes, looking around corners. The center of the action always tends to be somewhere else; certainly it was never us.

Ever since I left home at the age of nine, Anne and I have been geographically separated, and during holidays we have both been too preoccupied to get together—except during times of crisis. Then we rally to the occasion. Anne is strong willed, sometimes a little scatterbrained, and fiercely loyal. Our mother's prolonged death brought us closer together.

I felt relieved when in the 1980s Anne embraced our childhood friend John Milliken as her second husband. She had finally found a safe harbor, and in a way had returned to the home-centered values that our father, Bill Patten, had instilled in us. John brought stability, and together they have raised four beautiful daughters.

In August 1995 I referred Anne to the Freedom Institute, a respected substance-abuse center in Manhattan that I had contacted a few years earlier concerning a friend. Anne called the director and liked her. The show was on. Like most things in our family, once the plans started moving, the pace was dizzying. Anne took on the job of recruiting three of my mother's close friends to join us for the intervention.

When Anne and I arrived in Washington, Mother assumed we had come to divide up the furnishings of her Georgetown house, which was being readied for sale before her presumed move to Utah. I sensed that the move to Utah terrified her and that she was doing it in large part to please Anne. The evening before the intervention, Anne and I went through the downstairs dividing up furniture with yellow stickers. We laughed self-consciously as we moved about the house.

When we were finished, my mother took us out to dinner at a fancy restaurant in the refurbished Mayflower Hotel with some friends, a younger couple who were devoted to her. The atmosphere seemed showy and claustrophobic. As I watched people drink their wine and martinis, I wondered how my mother would look at a meeting of Alcoholics Anonymous.

Charles Whitehouse and Duff Cooper, picnic at
Chateau St. Firmin outside Paris, August 1947

The "chain of love," as the group of interveners is sometimes
called, gathered in a hotel room off Connecticut Avenue the following morning. We were evenly divided between friends and
family. Anne and I were joined by two strong women who were
among my mother's oldest friends: Nancy Pierrepont, a New
York interior decorator who had helped my mother redo her house
in Georgetown, and Polly Fritchey, another of Washington's
power hostesses. Anne had also invited Charles Whitehouse, a
retired career ambassador and a cousin of my mother's. He represented the U.S. Foreign Service, which was an essential con-
stituency in my mother's life, effectively her spiritual home.
I remembered Charlie from one of his Christmas cards, a color

photo of him dressed in his foxhunting attire astride a horse. But when we saw him in the parking lot of the hotel that morning, this veteran diplomat of Laos and Thailand, and an ex-Marine to boot, was looking quite pale.

The other half of our group was family: Anne's husband, John, and my daughter Eliza. Eliza would be a special surprise for my mother, as she was in the middle of fall term at Stanford University. But she had visited Mother that summer in Maine and, like Nancy Pierrepont, had seen her lying on the floor drunk and spent a long night helping the Filipino nurses watch over her.

The initial goal of an intervention is to convince the alcoholic to accept treatment for his or her "disease," as alcoholism has finally been classified by the American Medical Association. The likelihood that an intervention will succeed depends largely on the cohesiveness of the participants and on having well-orchestrated timing that catches the alcoholic off guard.

What gave our group an edge in dealing with my mother was that her own close friends were involved. They were breaking the cardinal WASP rule against talking openly and calmly about an embarrassing personal secret. The friends present were her real family. Indeed, when it came to important decisions, my mother depended far more on her friends than on her family. The fact that both friends and family were solidly united now amounted to a palace coup.

Whatever personal qualms Mother's friends may have had about Alcoholics Anonymous, they had immediately agreed to step forward and confront her. They did so because they were far more down-to-earth than she was and had no illusions about the seriousness of the situation. Behind the pinstriped suits and elegant clothes, they understood the perils of substance abuse and had seen the consequences of Susan Mary's heavy drinking firsthand. Like my mother, they were intensely loyal.

My brother-in-law, John, escorted my mother to the hotel in a chauffeured limousine on the pretext that she was needed for a family meeting. She walked into the sitting room wearing a beige raincoat and a Tyrolean hat. She looked surprisingly dowdy, especially compared to Connie Murray, the counselor from the Freedom Institute, who had a buttoned-down Park Avenue look.

It was impossible to gauge my mother's reaction to seeing us all there. Her good manners camouflaged her real feelings. She sat down and waited with a benign smile to see what was going to happen next.

We had all been instructed to use non-accusatory language. Each of us expressed our love for Susan Mary and then detailed specific examples of alcoholic behavior that caused us concern. "Love" is probably the wrong word for what we were expressing; in light of our controlled behavior, it was more devotion and loyalty that were palpable in that meeting. Either way, the counselor gently guided the conversation as we took turns telling our stories.

The most troubling instances were the most recent, particularly events that Eliza and others had witnessed at the end of the summer. One example involved Mrs. Pierrepont arranging for an ambulance to take my mother to the Mount Desert Island Hospital after she had passed out on the floor of her house. Fortunately, Polly Fritchey had been visiting Northeast Harbor that August and had witnessed Susan Mary's fall into the bushes after a cocktail party given by their friend Brooke Astor. They delicately corroborated the facts.

Anne and I were the last to speak. Anne was the only one to show her feelings with real passion and tears. "Mummy," she said, "I adore you, but I can't put my daughters at risk by having you live next door if you're going to keep up the smoking and drinking!"

I empathized with Anne's pain, but it also scared me a little. Her heroic efforts to save our mother would only work if Susan Mary wanted to save herself, something we had no control over. Anne desperately wanted her mother close to her but knew she had to draw a sharp line when it came to protecting her own children. She also clung to the naïve hope that Mother would respond positively to the threat of not being allowed to move next door to them in Utah.

Finally I spoke. I was actually surprised that the others seemed interested in what I had to say. I had been in encounter groups of this type before, but with my mother and sister both in the room I felt insecure and on uneven footing. It felt almost reassuring to notice that Mother was clearly not interested in what I was saying, and, not surprisingly, I can't remember a word of what I said. I knew she realized that this gathering wasn't about words; her mind was racing ahead to anticipate our agenda. The moment was simply another of the many dances we had done all of our lives. She was pretending to listen attentively, but her mind was calculating the best escape route.

After each of us had spoken, my mother asked in a puzzled tone what we wanted her to do about it. Connie Murray, the counselor from the Freedom Institute, had the answer. She told my mother that we had found a highly regarded program, the Chemical Dependence Family Program at St. Mary's Hospital, which had a good reputation for the treatment of older people with addiction problems. There was a room available. Although Susan Mary was shocked to hear that the hospital was in Minnesota and that we had booked a flight for her that very afternoon, I knew she was relieved that a plan of action was in place. She was never one for indecision.

I was fairly sure that my mother would accept our suggestion that she seek help—at least temporarily. We were too unified in our approach and our language was too direct for her to dismiss us outright. She hated public scenes and was accustomed to using courtesy as a weapon to buy time on the rare occasions when she was cornered by circumstance. I also knew she could not abide waiting around.

Although Mother expressed concern about outstanding commitments, such as an upcoming dinner party she was hosting for *Architectural Digest,* she did not belabor the point. It was not in her nature to be ungrateful when special efforts were made on her behalf, and there was no way she could understand our carefully plotted intervention as anything but a special effort. My mother was momentarily trapped by her own unforgiving code of good manners.

The maids had my mother's bags packed when we returned to Twenty-ninth Street. Soon I was alone with my mother in a taxi headed for Washington National Airport. She fumbled through her handbag checking for phone messages she might have missed that morning. She had several messages, including one from Yitzhak Rabin's wife and one from General Colin Powell's wife.*

As the taxi drove along the edge of the Potomac River, it struck me that although she had traveled from the Great Wall of China to the great tombs of Egypt, my mother had never been to the American Midwest. She was born in Rome and as a little girl lived in Romania and Argentina. She had visited Europe's most beautiful cathedrals, walked around Vienna and St. Petersburg, danced under the chandeliers at Versailles, and floated down the Grand Canal to Venetian costume balls. She had dined privately with presidents Kennedy, Johnson, and Nixon in the White House. Yet she had never been to the American heartland, never eaten a Big Mac, and had probably never even heard of the Mall of America.

---

* Prime Minister Rabin was assassinated a few days later in Israel, on November 4.

A central tenet of Alcoholics Anonymous is that social status is irrelevant, a phony impediment to the raw honesty needed to address the pains and fears of alcoholism. Facing the disease takes a special kind of courage, a willingness to expose your deepest vulnerabilities rather than disguising them with sophistication and wit. My mother was courageous, but she always devoted her strength to covering up pain, not revealing it to strangers—or friends and family, for that matter.

Alcoholics Anonymous assumes that we all share certain basic feelings, that we are far more alike than we are different. My mother's life, however, was predicated on an entirely different principle. She reveled in her own uniqueness. On a certain level, she had a point. Susan Mary had not only outlived most of her contemporaries, but she had also begun to blossom as an author of well-received historical biographies and architectural essays at a time when many of her remaining peers were preparing to retire. In seventy years she had crafted a distinctive life in Paris and then in Washington. In her own mind, she had done this essentially by herself. Her sense of uniqueness was well earned, but it had come at a higher price than any of us really knew.

Using a well-developed veil of self-effacement and exquisite manners, Susan Mary almost always got her own way. She cleverly orchestrated everyone around her. She had a diplomatic knack for making people believe she was truly fascinated by them, even when she was inwardly itching for them to leave. She was intellectually redoubtable. She was also physically resilient, having conquered colon cancer and lived for more than half a century as an indomitable cigarette-smoking anorexic. So who was going to convince her that something as familiar as booze was stronger than she was?

Sitting next to her on our interminable flight to Minnesota, I recalled many memorable flights from my childhood. Beginning when I was nine, I had been shipped off each year from Paris to

Beachborough, an English boarding school outside of Oxford. At thirteen I was sent from Washington to Groton School, a boarding school in Massachusetts, where I spent the next five years. During one Thanksgiving vacation, which started in New York, I mistakenly took a shuttle headed back to Boston instead of to Washington, where I was expected for the holiday.

Exile is a familiar experience for me. It began well before my first trip to Beachborough. When I was four I had been sent from our house in Paris to a French school. I remember the first day especially well, because I vomited all over my desk in the classroom. That earned me a yearlong reprieve from school. In my experience, the void of being abandoned is registered most acutely in the stomach.

Now it was my mother who was being exiled, and it was she who was having "tummy problems" as she called them. She rose from her seat several times on the flight to go to the toilet. At one point she leaned a little toward me and conceded, "I don't think I've ever felt so depressed in my life." I could not think of anything worth saying in response. A little later she promised, "Don't worry . . . I'll behave." I felt embarrassed for both of us.

Well into the four-hour flight I noticed Senator Paul Wellstone working the aisles on a routine trip back to his home state. I marveled at his energy but was relieved that my mother did not recognize the disheveled liberal from Minnesota as he moved down the aisle fishing for eye contact. Unlike generals Powell or Rabin, he had never made the guest list at Mother's home on Twenty-ninth Street.

Finally landing, we were met at the gate by a thin blonde wearing a chauffeur's hat and holding a sign that read "Alsop." A stretch limousine had been ordered for us at the Minneapolis airport. Our driver was supposed to take us directly to Fairview Riverside Hospital, where the St. Mary's program was located, but she was new to her job and got lost. My mother and I gazed dully out the window like two lost sheep as the large limousine meandered through downtown Minneapolis. For once, my mother did not seem impatient to get where she was going.

When we finally reached the hospital, I noticed that our chauffeur had inadvertently driven up on the curb in front of the entrance. It was late afternoon. The place seemed very quiet. I brought my mother up to the third floor, where the "seniors" stayed. The ward seemed calm, and I was pleased that Mother had a private room.

I felt there was no point lingering around the ward. In our family, good-byes are abrupt, and this was no exception. I left my mother with the nurses and returned to Maine for nearly two weeks. I wrote her several letters, our customary way of communicating. (My stepfather, Joe Alsop, had even proposed marriage to my mother using airline stationery.)

A couple of days after I got back to Maine, I drove to see my younger daughter, Sybil, perform in a play at her school, Proctor Academy, in New Hampshire. Somewhat appropriately, she was playing the role of Helen Keller's mother in *The Miracle Worker*. The play opened with Sybil on an upper balcony nursing a baby in her arms, two young boys on either side of her, and as the lights dimmed I heard Sybil's voice scream, "She can't see, can't hear you!"

In my diary that night I wrote: "Feeling drained tonight, gnawing sadness at the thought of that thin, waiflike creature I left at an AA meeting in the chapel at St. Mary's last night. She left both meetings to go back to her room to get her dark glasses and then returned. Must be like a bad movie she finds herself in, degraded, scared, depressed, angry etc."

Looking back on the trip to Minneapolis, I felt that I myself had been playing some kind of understudy role in a grade-B movie. The next morning, on my way home, I contested a speeding ticket in Franklin, New Hampshire, and the judge gave me a break.

Ordinarily I would have been exultant, but as I walked out of the court, facing the long drive back to Camden, I was struck by how limited my relief felt.

Back in Maine, I wrote my mother several letters. I tried to explain how we were trapped in our family by words, by our addiction to writing, by our tendency to intellectualize. Although I wrote, "the program seems so bloody simple that it almost demeans us," I found myself employing the simplistic bromides of the rehabilitation program itself. I even resorted to old clichés from my upbringing, patronizing phrases like "I'm so proud of you" and bloodless pronouncements like "You will, of course, make up your mind about the length of treatment after the evaluation is completed."

I cringe today when I reread these letters. "Try to realize," I wrote her, "that whatever you do or say, you are and have been forever a real success in my eyes." Why couldn't I tell her that in some ways she was a success, but that she had never been a good mother to me? I had fallen into the same saccharine trap I had warned her about. Though I genuinely hoped I would somehow connect with her, I could not divorce myself from the fear that this was still one more charade.

Before returning to St. Mary's for the family week, Anne and I had a conference call with our mother and Kal, her counselor. Susan Mary explained coolly that she would be leaving the program early, as she had committed to host a dinner for *Architectural Digest* in Washington. Anne's voice rose and faltered as she reminded Mother that she had promised to complete the program in order to move out next to Anne's family in Utah. "Oh, but I thought you knew, I have no intention of moving to Utah!" my mother responded calmly.

About ten days later I flew back to Minneapolis to join Anne and John in the Seniors Family Program, an opportunity for us to address the issues of alcoholism as a family in a neutral environment. I stayed at the Nicollet Island Inn, a limestone 1893 factory overlooking the Mississippi River that had been renovated into a four-story Victorian inn.

When I saw my mother, one of the first things I noticed without surprise was how much she was trying to take care of the staff. She was constantly complimenting the counselors and commenting on how tired they must be. Kal told us how impressed he was by my mother's diplomatic skills.

Anne, John, and I were grouped together with a few other families who had come to support the identified alcoholic. My instinct was to connect with some of these people having already actively supported another family member in a similar program. In fact, I stayed in touch with one woman whose alcoholic husband killed himself after leaving the program.

On October 31, a date marked in my diary, I headed for the hospital cafeteria, where I saw Fran, our family counselor, walking out with some people. As she passed by, she gave me an unusual look. There was tenderness in her eyes, and none of the clinical detachment that most counselors maintain. I was feeling raw from a verbal attack from Anne earlier that morning in our family counseling session, so this compassionate glance left me unnerved.

Anne had flared up at me as we waited for the elevator in the hallway of our Washington hotel after the intervention. I was accustomed to her angry blasts from our childhood together, but I couldn't understand what was happening now. I knew she had big resentments against me from the past, but during this period I can't even remember the specific issues that triggered her. We had fought as kids, but what I felt bad about most was not being there for her during hard times in her first marriage. I was baffled at her behavior now and felt alone.

All of a sudden I realized that some kind of secret was being kept from me. The combination of my sister's flare-ups and Fran's unexpectedly tender glance told me in a flash that there was something else—something major—going on.

When Anne, John, and I reconvened at St. Mary's with Kal and Fran after lunch, I told the group—looking mainly at my sister—that I could smell a rat and that I was leaving on the next plane home unless someone told me what was up. The counselors nodded, and without much discussion we retreated to another conference room, where my mother soon joined us. Apparently, Kal and Fran had already persuaded the group that it would be a good idea to tell the truth.

It was a small room. I don't think Fran joined us. The room felt like a large closet; it had one window and was just big enough for the five of us. Not looking at anyone in particular, my mother started by telling the story of Duff Cooper's death in 1954.

Duff Cooper was a familiar name. I knew he was the only cabinet minister in Neville Chamberlain's government to resign over the Munich Pact of 1938 and the British ambassador to Paris after the war. I had also learned about a decade before by reading John Charmley's biography of him that Duff had had an affair with my mother, but I had never talked with her about it. I had read Duff's biography of the French diplomat Charles Maurice de Talleyrand before even knowing of their affair, and possibly another one of his books, *Operation Heartbreak*. My main impression of Duff Cooper was as a quasi-literary figure.

Most of my mother's recitation focused on Duff's wife, Lady Diana Cooper. Mother explained how his body had been taken off the ship on which he had died and had been brought back to Paris. Lady Diana, she said, "was so brave." She had asked my mother to accompany her on the special train that would be taking her husband's body back to London and the service at Westminster Abbey. I had no idea why Mother was talking about an event that had happened almost fifty years earlier. Perhaps she was going to make an esoteric connection with Duff's legendary drinking problems?

After a while Kal nudged my mother gently. She looked up as if suddenly remembering, placing her palm on her forehead, and said, "Oh, yes, of course, and he's your father," as if I'd known this for a long time. Anne later confessed that Mother had shared the "big secret" with her several years earlier, after they had had several drinks. In the sober light of that hospital room, my mother made her admission seem akin to being forced to say, "My name is Susan Mary Alsop, and I'm an alcoholic."

Images of my father—or the man I had always *believed* was my father, Bill Patten—flashed through my mind, especially the moment when I heard he had died. My English headmaster at Beachborough, whom we called Froggy, had opened the door of my classroom in 1960 to tell me that my mother was waiting to see me. He led me through the front parlor of my prep school and into his private sitting room. There I saw my mother and her friend Marina Sulzberger sitting on his sofa, and I knew instantly why they were there. Kal's gentle face reminded me now of Froggy.

I broke down in tears, and without saying a word I left the conference room. I strolled in the corridor with the image of Bill Patten broken into pieces once again. John joined me and put his arm over my shoulder. When we returned, I was still too shocked to say much of anything. I recall noting to myself that I had read several of Duff's books, which somehow made him feel a bit more real.

The most obvious tension in the room when I returned was between my mother and Anne. My sister claims that I asked my mother why she had not told me before and that she said something to the effect that I was "too pathetic." My sister may be right, but I have no recollection whatsoever of asking the question, and I certainly don't recall my mother saying those words about me.

I suppose it felt better to have a First Lord of Admiralty as my dad rather than the milkman, but as I returned to my hotel room later, I began to feel very sad for Bill Patten and a little sad for myself. Writing some notes in my diary that evening in the Nicollet Island Inn, I realized it was Halloween.

As the evening progressed, the world ground to a halt. I recalled that Marvin Ellison, an ethics professor at Bangor Theological Seminary, had warned me about family interventions: "Watch out, the shit will fly in all directions." I thought about Duff and wondered whether he liked sailing boats as much as I did.

The following day the weather was freezing, but the hospital allowed my mother to take a brief outing around the city. I started sorting things out in my room at the Nicollet Island Inn.

That evening I scribbled in my diary: "How fascinating! Yesterday, Halloween eve, I learn at age 47 that I'm illegitimate, a word I can barely spell correctly. I'm at the Nicollet Island Inn today. My mother has been given the day off from St. Mary's, so Anne and John are taking her on a tour of a local museum. What kind of *museum* have we as a family just escaped from?"

Despite our entreaties, my mother decided to terminate her treatment early, declaring victory over us once again. At the end of the family weekend, the patients and their families in our group stood in a circle and said good-bye to one another.

Before I left, a truck driver whose husky forearms were covered with tattoos, and who had been in the same program as my mother, came over to me and said, "Hey, Bill, I hope you won't be offended if I say this, but I remember the day Susan arrived here. I was looking out the window with Jim, and we saw your limousine arrive outside. We saw little Susan get out and then this guy holding the door for her and carrying her suitcase. I said to Jim, 'Hey, I bet that's her butler!'"

My mother and I never talked about St. Mary's again. She hated being cared for and treated the St. Mary's experience as if it had been an alien happening. If I had not kept a diary of the events leading up to the intervention, the whole experience might have faded away like a surrealistic dream—my mother kidnapped and shipped away to a distant planet. It wasn't hard for her to convince herself and some of her Georgetown friends that it had all been an embarrassing mistake.

Some of her Georgetown friends have told me that she made light of the whole episode. What none of us, including her lawyer, knew until after she died nine years later is that she had signed a contract to sell her Georgetown house in anticipation of moving to Salt Lake City before we left for St. Mary's. Fortunately, the real estate broker found a way of nullifying the terms of the contract. After my mother died, that broker was able to bring back the same buyers, who chose once again to buy her house.

Although it took a little longer, within a couple of years Mother had also slipped out of the agreements she had made to sobriety at St. Mary's. She may have controlled her drinking more carefully, but my mother continued to smoke and drink until her death. What saddened me more than her actual drinking was the battered hope that I could ever really connect with her.

Emily Astor Kane Jay between her two sons, Peter A. Jay and DeLancey K. Jay, circa 1896

two

Yankees
at the Court

I wish to goodness we could go back
to the old Therapia days!

—LETTER TO PETER A. JAY FROM A DIPLOMATIC COLLEAGUE

IN MONTEVIDEO IN 1925 ABOUT THEIR POLO CLUB

IN CAIRO BEFORE WORLD WAR I

$\mathbf{M}$Y MOTHER'S ROOTS lay among the Louis Vuitton trunks stacked on shelves in the cellar at 1611 Twenty-ninth Street, her home in Washington. My mother moved into this house after her mother died in 1977. Some of the Vuitton suitcases had SMJ, for Susan Mary Jay, embossed on top. They lay there for more than fifty years like coffins, gathering dust, while my grandmother Susan Jay lived on and on, defying her doctors and sipping her one little daiquiri each evening, usually alone.

I visited Twenty-ninth Street regularly as a child; my grandmother rarely had other visitors. Her stories about the Jay family and their Huguenot ancestry somehow never caught my imagination. I sensed that they were worthy and industrious people, but there was a Puritan quality about them that somehow made me feel distanced from them.

My grandmother Susan Alexander Jay was a solid, sedentary woman with a round face and blue eyes. She was five feet seven inches when my mother was born, and she moved slowly and deliberately. She seemed to be very fond of me, and I listened to her stories until she was in her late nineties. But in my adulthood, when I became aware of how demanding she had been on my mother, I realized that maybe she was not as sweet as she looked. My grandmother was physically resilient, and my mother inherited this quality. Both my grandmother and my mother survived colon cancer, both after major operations. When my mother was in her late sixties, she also survived a misdiagnosis that the cancer had returned.

My grandmother knew a great deal about our family ancestry, and what I know comes mostly from materials I collected from her basement. She was the eldest daughter of Colonel John J. McCook, a well-known corporate lawyer in New York. As a young girl, she accompanied her father in Moscow when he attended the coronation of Nicholas II, the last czar of Russia, in the spring of 1896. It seemed to me as if her life since then had been mainly a steady downhill slide. One of her favorite expressions was *"Plus ça change, plus c'est la même chose!"* (The more things change, the more they are the same!)

She had seven uncles, each of whom fought for the Union in the Civil War. They were known as the Fighting McCooks, famous in the annals of the Civil War. The clan consisted of "the tribe of Dan" and his eight sons, and "the tribe of John," Dan's brother, and his five sons—altogether fifteen men of Ohio. The two youngest, including my great-grandfather John, were students at Kenyon College in Gambier, Ohio, when the war began, and John was not allowed by their mother to enlist for two years. His best friend was his brother Charlie, who ran away to enlist. Charlie died in his father's arms after the Battle of Bull Run. By the summer of 1862 John had turned seventeen, and his mother could no longer stop him from enlisting.

Major Daniel McCook with his Henry rifle (from collection of Mrs. Peter A. Jay)

John McCook began as an aide-de-camp to his older brother Dan Jr. in the 52nd Ohio Volunteer Infantry. After two years of fighting, he was wounded in the back at Shady Grove. After thirty-seven surgeries on his back he was told he could not return to active duty.

My grandmother also inherited a Presbyterian legacy through her mother's father, Henry Alexander, son of Dr. Archibald Alexander, the first professor of Princeton Seminary—a "commonsensical Calvinist" as *Time* described him. Her father,

John McCook, had joined the law firm of his father-in-law and married Henry's only daughter, Janetta.

The man Susan married, my grandfather Peter Jay, was the great-great-grandson of John Jay, best known as our country's first chief justice of the Supreme Court. But he was also president of the Second Continental Congress, secretary of foreign affairs of the Confederation, and governor of the state of New York. According to John Adams, writing in 1815, he had "as much influence in digestion of the Constitution, and obtaining its adoption, as any man in the nation." But it was his extensive role as one of our nation's first diplomats, starting in 1779 at age thirty-three as minister to Spain, that probably influenced my mother more than anything.

In 1782, together with Benjamin Franklin and John Adams, John Jay traveled to Paris and negotiated the settlement of America's Revolutionary War. Though these early Americans were rarely mentioned to me in my early childhood, the Treaty of Paris is commemorated by a small plaque on a building on the Left Bank in Paris, which my mother must have passed many times during the fifteen years she lived there.

Professor Richard B. Morris has written, "Jay's diplomatic achievements in Paris still stand unrivalled in the annals of American diplomacy." He was diligent and cautious. Twelve years later he negotiated the Jay Treaty, which in Washington's view "bought time" and postponed another war until 1812, when America would be better prepared for battle.

In a book on the first Peter A. Jay, the oldest son of John Jay, one of his descendants records a revealing comparison between Alexander Hamilton and John Jay: "With Hamilton it was sentiment, with Jay a principle; with Hamilton enthusiastic passion, with Jay duty as well as love . . . Either would have gone through fire and water to do his country service . . . Hamilton with the roused rage of a lion, Jay with the calm friendliness of a man; or, rather, Hamilton's courage would have been that of a soldier, Jay's that of a Christian."

This tradition of conscience was reflected in the steps that the various Jays took to end slavery. Judge William Jay, son of the chief justice, was "one of the most prolific pamphleteers of the abolitionist movement," and his son, William Jay Jr., forwarded fugitives out of New York City while he was a student at Columbia University.

My stepfather, Joe Alsop, would caustically observe that the only reason the Jays could afford public service was because they married the daughters of wealthy Dutch merchants along the Hudson River. Joe had a point. The first American Jay, Augustus, Justice John Jay's grandfather, married Anna Maria Bayard, whose paternal grandmother was Anna Stuyvesant, Peter Stuyvesant's sister. John Jay married Sarah Livingston, and subsequent generations married Van Cortlandts and Van Rennselaers. Further confirming Joe's claim, I found a parchment letter that notes Peter Jay's starting salary as twelve hundred dollars a year. Even in 1902, that would have done little to cover the expenses of a man who spent much of the diplomatic year playing polo and touring the world with friends.

The Jays' frugality is reflected in a description Peter, the son of the chief justice, provides of his wife Josephine Pearson's setting up a new house "& now wants to complete my ruin by embellishments, etc. etc. We will have a mighty small establishment altogether, first of all both Josie and I are pretty thin specimens of humanity, rather of the bean pole order . . . the house chimneys & all will go in your drawing room & have plenty of space left."

My grandmother was far more focused on the subject of money than her husband was, and much of my mother's seventy years of correspondence with her deals with issues of money. My grandmother once sent me a 1792 letter from Alexander Hamilton to John Jay's wife, Sarah, apologizing that he had misplaced

Portrait of young Peter A. Jay by John Singer Sargent, painted in Paris in 1880

some "Certificates," presumably some bonds. Hamilton then declared, "Of all delinquencies, those towards the ladies I find the most inexcusable and hold myself bound by all the laws of chivalry to make the most ample reparation possible in any mode you shall find preferable. You will, of course, recollect that I am a married man!"

The Jays were generally more preoccupied with how to save money rather than with how to make it. This prudence about money is reflected half a century later in my grandfather's letters from Eton to his mother, which often refer to saving up his allowance. Peter, who was in his early teens, writes his mother: "I am taking great care of my money. You will be astonished to see how much I will bring back. Papa, you may remember, wanted you to give me my 10 shillings a week in a lump sum at the beginning of the term, I did not want it."

Peter A. Jay and his brother DeLancey K. Jay with
a dog, circa 1897

When I was growing up, no one in the Jay family, including my
mother and grandmother, had much to say about Peter. According to my cousin Peter Jay, a Maryland horse farmer and publisher, the same was true on his side of the family. His namesake,
my grandfather, was a largely forgotten man. My grandmother
told many stories about the past, but her husband rarely figured
in them.

I never knew either Peter or his brother, DeLancey Jay. Born
respectively in 1877 and 1881, they both died before I was born.
Their parents, Augustus Jay and Emily Astor Kane Jay, lived in
Paris during the late nineteenth century while Augustus was
serving in the American embassy. The two boys were sent to
Eton at an early age. I have a packet of letters from them mostly
addressed deferentially to their mother, who was living on the
Avenue Marceau in Paris.

"Dear Mummy," sixteen-year-old Peter writes from Eton, "I find that I have only 2 pairs of drawers; also I find I have a thin pair of trousers, summer ones. I have ordered a suit of tails as you told me to; also I have had my town coat well pressed and kept at the tailors." He then mentions only briefly in closing, "I am going to the doctor this afternoon," and signs off without indicating why he needed to see the doctor.

To my surprise, Peter was allowed to keep a pet squirrel, which, he tells his mother, eventually escaped or was killed by rats. Peter evidently found solace in little animals: "I have sold my guinea pigs—six of them—as well as six white rats I bought. You will be pleased to hear that I am tired of them, so I will not want them in Paris."

Peter's letters to his parents are predictably uncomplaining. "I am very well, and only cough when I run up stairs fast," he writes. He tells in passing about two Eton boys who tried to run away, but both were caught. One was expelled and the other "only got another swishing."

Peter's "Mummy," Emily Astor Kane, is known in the family as "The Black Pearl." She had a lively appetite for Parisian pleasures, and—like my mother—was popular with French aristocrats. In the living room of the Antoine de Noailleses (Antoine was one of my childhood friends), I remember seeing a photograph of Emily skating in the Bois de Boulogne with Antoine's Mouchy ancestors. Antoine's grandparents, Henri and Marie, and his parents, Philippe and Diane, were close friends of my parents. Henri reminded my mother when they met in 1945 "not to believe for a second that the French are hospitable; they are simply bored with four years of their own society." Like their British counterparts, the noble Mouchys boosted their flagging fortunes by befriending and occasionally marrying American heiresses. Emily made quite an impression. In my mother's obituary the English papers claimed that her grandmother Emily used to rouge her nipples.

Emily Astor Kane Jay (center) skating in the Bois de Boulogne with French friends: Bonnie de Castellane (far right) and the Comte and Comtess de Ganay, circa 1890

My grandfather Peter went from Eton to Harvard, graduating in 1900. Right up until his last post in Argentina he was concerned about paying his dues to the Old Etonian Association. Class notes from Harvard indicate that he stuttered slightly whenever he became animated. Soon after graduating, Peter continued a long family tradition by joining the Foreign Service. A newspaper clipping about his wedding nine years later reported: "Mr. Jay will probably remain a diplomat, for he has the rare qualities that make a man well fitted for this life. These qualities are his by inheritance. Perhaps the Jay family is the only one in this country, every generation of which for several centuries has produced the inborn talents of a diplomat."

President Theodore Roosevelt, a family friend, had a more skeptical view of inherited privilege. Writing to Peter's father, whom he addressed as "Gussie," in October 1902, the president

T^{he} Outlook
287 Fourth Avenue
New York

Office of
Theodore Roosevelt

March 10th 1909.

My dear Jay:

I am so pleased to hear of your
engagement, especially to so sweet a
girl as I know Miss Mc Cook to be. Will
you give her my warm regards, and her
father also! You and I think alike on
the really vital things, my dear fellow.
With all good wishes,

Sincerely yours,

Theodore Roosevelt

Mr Peter A. Jay,
Knickerbocker Club,
New York.

Letter from President Theodore Roosevelt to
Peter A. Jay

Peter A. Jay lying in a boat on the Nile, circa 1905

noted, "[I]t was a great pleasure to appoint your son," but cautioned, "I want him to take his duties very seriously and above all to remember all the time that his usefulness is conditioned upon his remaining genuinely American and realizing that his duty is to his countrymen, wholly irrespective of their social condition."

Roosevelt may have had the exhibitionist "Black Pearl" in mind when he wrote this. However, he would have been sympathetic to the challenges of controlling strong-willed females, as he himself had little control over his oldest child, Alice Lee Longworth. "I can run the country or I can control Alice, but I can't do both!" he reportedly once replied to a cabinet minister who complained to him about his daughter.

When my grandparents had to leave Paris, Grandmother Jay was not happy. As their ship entered New York Harbor and Peter remarked how welcoming the Statue of Liberty looked, she supposedly replied tartly, "They should have given it back to the Indians!"

Despite Roosevelt's democratic ambitions, his friends' daily life in the Foreign Service resembled a first-class compartment on the Orient Express filled with familiar faces from social clubs at Eton and Harvard. Polo matches around the world and private cabins on steamships were de rigueur. Peter's old friend Hugh Gibson wrote from the U.S. Legation in Warsaw in 1922 half seriously of the "appalling eventuality" he had just heard that "the service will be put on a merit basis." He stressed, however, that "we are getting enthusiastic here over the prospects of polo for next spring and summer. I have some ponies in mind that can be trained during the winter."

Another diplomatic friend called Buck complained from Montevideo in 1925 that the Communists were trying to recruit his chauffeur, and "the cooks are forming a league against the house-maid-keeper who works with no reference of holidays . . . one of them knocked over ten dishes the other day before I had her fired after a right royal row in the kitchen. I wish to goodness we could go back to the old Therapia days. There was no such trouble then."

Horses played a big role in the Jay family. I suspect that my grandfather's happiest days were spent on horseback before he got married. After his first year at Harvard he traveled around the world with two classmates, Francis Lee Higginson and William A. M. Burden. They were in a party that "American patrols at Tien-Tien" reported was "fired upon," but "nobody was hurt." A few years later Peter explored Persia on horseback and took a leisurely trip going down the Nile.

But Peter's bachelor days were numbered. After being posted to Asia, he wrote to an old friend, saying that he did not enjoy Japan. Undoubtedly, the loneliness of his distant post influenced his decision to get married.

In her trunks my grandmother kept a thick envelope with newspaper clippings describing her wedding to Peter Jay in 1909. The ceremony took place at the Fifth Avenue Presbyterian Church with her uncle the Rev. Dr. Maitland Alexander officiating. Peter had eleven ushers. As reported in the papers, the guest list boasted many notable New Yorkers, including Mr. and Mrs. John D. Rockefeller I and the city's mayor, George McClellan.

The McCooks' home-state paper, the *Ohio State Journal,* was far more lavish in its coverage of the event. It devoted a full page to the wedding under the heading "Cherry Blossom Honeymoon" and featured original portraits of the couple. Perhaps thinking the angle exotic, the *Journal* emphasized that the couple would be heading to Japan after the wedding. First Lady Helen H. Taft wrote Peter a personal note of congratulations on White House stationery two days after her husband's inauguration, noting that his new father-in-law, Colonel McCook, "has been well known to both of us for a long time." She also sent a handwritten note of congratulations to my grandmother on her marriage.

Polo game at Therapia Club, Cairo, Egypt, circa 1905

As it turned out, the young Jays were not in Japan for more than a year. Nevertheless, it was a memorable experience for my grandmother. She used to tell me about meeting General Aritomo Yamagata, the nationalistic warlord who reveled in the Japanese victories during the recently concluded Russo-Japanese War. When it came to venerating military figures, my grandmother was uncommonly ecumenical.

While my grandmother was no fan of the Roosevelt family—their brashness and impetuosity offended her sense of decorum—she and Peter did their best to promote President Roosevelt's Christian mission to secure world order. As a friend of Roosevelt, but now professionally beholden to Taft, Peter Jay needed to be careful.

In 1910 Peter was instructed by President Taft to leave Japan and assume the position of consul general in Cairo. My grandmother later remembered the prewar years in Cairo as the liveliest period of her life. She may have romanticized her life in Egypt, but as an Anglophile she reveled in the final throes of its Kiplingesque world.

When World War I began, Peter was assigned to Rome. He wrote his wife a letter describing days spent introducing General John Pershing to the Italians who were petitioning America for aid. Peter compared Pershing to the British general Lord Herbert Kitchener, with whom they had become friendly in Cairo several years earlier: "He is a fine soldierly looking man, but *entre nous* I did not find much magnetism or profound intelligence. He seemed to me more military (in the Prussian officer style) than had K." Lord Kitchener was the much admired hero who avenged the honor of the British Empire in 1895 after the Madhi killed General Charles Gordon in Khartoum.

I have a newspaper photograph of my grandfather Peter at the time of his appointment to Rome. He is a serious-looking man with a high forehead and an intense look in his eyes. His diplomatic passport records that he was thirty-eight years old, six feet one inch tall, with a "prominent" chin, an "oval medium full" face, and a "healthy" complexion. My grandmother joined Peter in Rome in 1915. Signed by the American ambassador Thomas Nelson Page, her passport shows her wearing a hat with flowers and a lace-trimmed dress with a small brooch at the top of its cleavage. The passport indicates that she was accompanied by her little daughter, my mother's older sister, Emily.

My grandparents and their daughter Emily spent most of the First World War in Rome, where my mother, Susan Mary Jay, was born on June 19, 1918, the last year of the war. There was strangely little I could find in the old trunks about the Jay family's years in Rome. Though they lived in a rented palazzo at the time my mother was born, they were almost within earshot of the front. The absence of documents may stem from the fact that the crisis atmosphere reduced the tendency to memorialize events in letters. Undoubtedly, the family was more focused on DeLancey Jay, who went into the trenches and was critically wounded (but perhaps I simply did not find the right trunk).

During the war DeLancey's elbow was torn apart by machine-gun fire. It happened on a wet October day in the Argonne while he was leading his men to try to rescue the "Lost Battalion" of 550 men who had strayed into a small valley encircled by Germans. In *Ultimate Sacrifice* by Kevin Coyne, the wounded Jay, who was later awarded the Distinguished Service Cross, passed on his command to Eddie Grant, the baseball star, who had also joined in what was known as the Plattsburg movement under another Harvard man, General Leonard Wood. One third of the 1,200 men who attended the first Plattsburg camp were from Harvard.

Following DeLancey's death in the spring of 1941, another World War I veteran, Grenville Clark, a noted peace advocate, wrote that DeLancey had "an almost uniquely high sense of obligation. Without even knowing it, his standard was that of conduct over and beyond the call of duty, not only in his army service, but in all relationships of his life."

The two Jay boys married very different women. DeLancey's wife, Elizabeth Morgan, was a gentle, warmhearted woman who loved animals. I remember last seeing her at her small house in Windsor, Vermont. In her father Edwin Denison Morgan's *Recollections for My Family* one sees the relaxed, untidy happiness of a family-centered world. Family in the Morgan household meant everything, and money was there to be spent with a delightful lack of guilt.

The bulk of Morgan's recollections revolve around hunting in England and Ireland or cruising around the world on one of his yachts. He was best known for having organized and partially financed the successful defense of the America's Cup, first against both Lord Dunraven's challenges in the 1890s and then against Sir Thomas Lipton's challenge in 1901.

Morgan built houses—Beacon Rock on the ocean in Newport and Wheatly in Westbury, Long Island—with the same energy he built boats. He tried to get his neighbors to invest in an electric plant (later the Long Island Lighting Company) once it dawned on him that maintaining sixty-five gas lamps at Wheatly each day proved to be "a serious and unsatisfactory arrangement."

What stands out most vividly for me is the family's love of animals, whether breeding dogs or horses. My stepfather remembers being a young man visiting the Morgans at Wheatly, and all the small dogs in the living room made him think the carpet was moving. For my mother, these visits to her cousins' home must have offered a welcome contrast to her parents' empty house, with the barking of dogs replacing the sound of her father's asthmatic coughing in another room.

During the summer of 1920, a gravely ill President Woodrow Wilson congratulated Peter on his appointment as minister to San Salvador. However, considering what a minor posting it was, and spending hours in discussion with his wife and getting the advice of his colleagues, Peter had accepted the appointment with major reservations, and only as an interim position.

Nevertheless, he arrived in San Salvador in 1921 in time for a revolutionary uprising. He reported home that casualties were limited and that he had met with students and workers to warn them against illegal violence. He made his disdain for such behavior clear: "During the height of the rioting all the Legations & Consulates, except ours, hoisted and kept flying their flags, but as I have such a deep contempt for these people, I declined to dignify the trouble by allowing our flag to be used."

He also reported meeting with President Jorge Melendez, whom he felt was too conciliatory with the insurgents and thus would not last long. We have photographs showing Peter and his

American staff dressed in white linen suits holding pet dogs on their laps, looking somewhat out of place.

Later that same year, Senator Henry Cabot Lodge wrote my grandmother a polite note describing his efforts to expedite Peter's Senate confirmation as minister to Romania. "Only three days before I went with Senator [Le Baron Bradford] Colt, who was most cordial about it, to the White House and the President approved it at once . . . It has been a great pleasure to me to be of service to you and your husband, whose father and mother are old friends of mine and his father was in my class in college and we were always very close friends." Despite Theodore Roosevelt's attempt to democratize the Foreign Service, the diplomatic corps remained something of an old boy's club, with posts in Western Europe most in demand. Most diplomats shared the prevailing Eurocentric attitude about the Hispanics as "really impossible people," as Peter put it in a letter to his mother sent from San Salvador.

Settling into Romania must have been a sharp contrast to the tropics of Central America. Peter's initial role was to promote mining and oil rights for international companies, an initiative that no doubt bored him. The Romanian court life tested his patience as well. In June 1924 he wrote his wife about the annual public buffet at the racecourse:

> I sat by the Queen of Greece who is, as you know, very unresponsive, and so had a very stupid time compared to last year. She [Elisabetha, who had married King George of Greece three years earlier, who was now living back in Romania in exile] scarcely spoke to anyone at the table except myself who managed to occasionally stimulate her to some slight conversation. They—K&Q of Greece—left yesterday for Paris and London to take cures, a fat reducing one for her."

Queen Marie of Romania in peasant costume, a gift
"with warm memories" to Peter A. Jay, circa 1925

Fortunately, Elisabetha's mother, known as the Queen
Mother of the Balkans, was one of the most extraordinary
women in Europe. She offered a delightful consolation for Peter
largely based on their shared love of riding. Born in England,
Queen Marie was the granddaughter of Queen Victoria and Tsar
Alexander II of Russia. Considered to be a future consort for
Prince George, later King George V, she was shipped off instead
by her mother at seventeen to marry Prince Ferdinand, the heir
to the Romanian throne.

Having established herself with her fairly weak and socially
inept husband, who was also notoriously clumsy on horseback,
Marie was in her late forties and the mother of six children when
the Jays arrived in Bucharest: "In Sinaia Marie led her family,

guests, and a pack of Russian wolfhounds on long tramps through the woods; in Bucharest she paid frequent visits to the Cismigiu Gardens, rising as early as 4.30 A.M. to catch the roses and peonies at their freshest . . . she still galloped her horses nearly every day, accompanied by whatever members of the younger generation could keep up with her."

My grandmother kept the personal invitations Peter received to join the queen on her morning rides, as well as numerous signed photographs of her, often dressed in peasant clothes, some with wolfhounds at her side and some dedicated to "my friend." In her biography of the queen, *The Last Romantic,* Hannah Pakula writes suggestively about Marie and Peter: "Both men and women became infatuated with Marie and had to be eased gently and smilingly out of her life. There was Peter Jay, the American Ambassador to Roumania; only his good manners saved them both from an embarrassing diplomatic situation."

Because of her beauty and charisma, Marie became, according to Pakula, the target of unfounded rumors, especially among "the Roumanians for whom infidelity was a way of life." One suspected lover was another American and a cousin of Peter's, the handsome Waldorf Astor, who twenty years earlier had counseled the queen on how to approach her own people and had encouraged her to learn their language. When in 1906 Waldorf married an American, Nancy Langhorne Shaw, Marie continued to write many letters to maintain contact with the couple.

Several photos of my mother in Romania show a round-faced five-year-old with big brown eyes, dressed in furs and standing next to her friends, each with a toboggan. Looking today at the exotic costumes of Queen Marie's oldest son, Carol II, and his father, King Ferdinand, with their Tyrolean-like plumed hats and medal-emblazoned uniforms, and the queen's assortment of mink-lined coats and tiaras and long-veiled robes, there must have been a fairy-tale quality to my mother's surroundings. In one photograph of Peter in a parade on his way to putting the Congressional Medal on the Unknown Soldier's grave, my grandfather stands out as remarkably unadorned in his top hat and dark suit.

There was also something Spartan about his account to his mother in July 1923 of his "stupid" brush with death on a runaway horse going through "some rather wild and woody country." He explains that "though I ran him through a marshy ground some two or three feet deep to slow him down[,] I could not check him and could only spend my time avoiding hitting big trees." Peter escaped with a broken right forearm and bruises.

Not surprisingly, there is a faintly weary tone to Peter's long letter to his brother, "Lanny," the following month reminiscing on their times together traveling from Bucharest to Constantinople in 1905. "It made me feel very old when I remembered that it was 20 years ago—September, 1903—that I became 1st Secretary [at Therapia], having already been 3rd Secretary in Paris and 2nd Secretary in Constantinople." This time he describes having requested a destroyer with a crew of 127 to transport them from Bucharest to Constantinople, and how Susan became seasick on board because of the rough weather. Peter also concurs with DeLancey's decision not to send his son Peter off to school at Eton.

My mother wrote an essay at Foxcroft about meeting the queen and refusing to recite a text she had been told to memorize for the occasion. This unusual act of social defiance stayed in Romania and surfaced only when I came across the essay as I dug through the Louis Vuitton trunks eighty years later.

My mother admits her ambivalent view of her Jay lineage in an amusing anecdote in her book *To Marietta from Paris, 1945–1960*: "Asked about myself by the Chinese in Peking a few years ago, I said that my ancestors were simple people who had felt deeply about their religion during the Ming Dynasty and fled their native country, France, because of it. The Chinese warmed to this and asked respectfully if on arrival in America they had tilled the soil. I felt rather ashamed, in the People's Republic, that I had never heard of much soil tilling."

Peter's final diplomatic post was as ambassador to Argentina. It is not clear how the Jays felt about accepting this assignment, but what is clear from the letters are the priorities he was assigned: "The importance of the Argentine as a field of commercial expansion cannot be overestimated[,] and the Secretary of State desires that nothing be left undone to cultivate and foster American trade throughout Latin America especially," wrote his old friend Joseph C. Grew, the undersecretary of state. Peter's answer was "*qui s'excuse s'accuse,*" which suggests that the chamber-of-commerce aspect of his duties did not thrill him.

Ironically, perhaps, Peter's arrival in Buenos Aires in the spring of 1926 not only coincided with the notorious Sacco-Vanzetti trial but also was followed by a bomb attack in the city. Undaunted by the anticapitalist undertones of the event, Peter was the featured speaker at the U.S. Chamber of Commerce's annual banquet at the Plaza Hotel in June. Peter wrote his old colleague William R. Castle a couple of days later that Nicola Sacco and Bartolomeo Vanzetti were "of course swine who should have been executed long ago as common murderers" and were certainly not the "victims of cruel North American capitalism," as elements of the press had suggested.

Given the significant amount of trade between the two countries, Argentina was a major post for an up-and-coming diplomat. Yet there is something in the tone of Peter's letters that suggests a lack of excitement about his daily work. Within the year, my grandfather Peter Jay and his own family were to become victims themselves of a domestic tragedy that was a turning point in my mother's life—one that would profoundly affect her future.

Susan Mary and Emily Jay in Romania, circa 1922

three

An Incident at Sea

[D]eath . . . has robbed her parents of all the joy of living.
—THE *AMERICAN WEEKLY OF BUENOS AIRES*, DECEMBER 25, 1926

M Y MOTHER SOMETIMES told us, usually after a meal or late in the evening, how her parents had hidden the death of her sister from her for several weeks, until her father had finally revealed the truth to her on board the ship that brought the Jay family back to the States from Argentina in January 1927. She never dwelled at length on the story, and some of the key details will always be a mystery.

I have tried to fill in the blanks by reading Argentine newspaper accounts and finding photos of the converted freighter, the *Pan America*, that brought them back. The ship belonged to the Munson line and carried heavy steel masts of the foredeck. It must have felt like a dressed-up tramp steamer when compared with the elegant Cunard liners on which the Jays were used to crossing the Atlantic.

My mother was eight and her sister, Emily, was fourteen when they arrived in Argentina early in 1926. Though my mother talked of Emily as a blonde beauty, photos of the period

COPYRIGHT 1925 BY
THE CHRISTIAN SCIENCE PUBLISHING SOCIETY   Twenty-T

JAY IS NAMED AMBASSADOR TO THE ARGENTINE

Envoy to Argentina

Elevated by President Coolidge From Post in Rumania

MINISTER TO CHINA YET TO BE NAMED

Senate Approves Mr. Philip for Persia—Kreeck Named to Paraguay

PETER AUGUSTUS JAY

Special from Monitor Bureau

WASHINGTON, March 18 — Changes in the United States Foreign Service continue to be made, for the most part with an eye to the utilization and promotion of career men for the greater efficiency of the service.

Peter Augustus Jay, whose nomination as Ambassador to Argentina to succeed John W. Riddle, has been sent to the Senate, is a conspicuous example. Of a distinguished Newport, R. I., family, he entered the service soon after his graduation from Harvard in 1900 and has been continuously active in it, having served as third and second secretary at Paris, secretary at Constantinople and at Tokyo, diplomatic agent and consular representative at Cairo, secretary and later counsellor to the Embassy in Rome, minister to Salvador and more recently to Rumania, where he has had the responsibility of protecting American rights under the changed mining laws of Rumania.

LABOR TO RAISE PROTOCOL ISSUE

Motion to Be Introduced in British Parliament by Ramsay MacDonald

By Cable from Monitor Bureau.

LONDON, March 18—The whole question of Austen Chamberlain's Geneva mission is to be debated in the House of Commons on Tuesday upon a Labor motion which is published today which declares that the peace protocol is the "only practical plan" for "disarmament and the

Clipping of Peter A. Jay's appointment to Argentina as U.S. ambassador from the Christian Science Publishing Society, March 1925

show a lovely dark-haired girl playing the piano and smiling warmly at the camera.

Although Mother never talked much about her, it is easy to imagine that Emily had been her confidante in San Salvador and Romania, her best friend as they traveled the oceans, and an indispensable link between her and the rather rigid adult world the two sisters inhabited. Emily was old enough in Buenos Aires to accompany her father on his morning horse rides.

It was early December, and Christmas must have been on the girls' minds. My mother remembered how Emily had complained of stomach pains one evening, but that since their parents were entertaining, my grandmother had told Emily to go back to bed. (This initial event does not appear in my grandmother's correspondence about this period.)

Argentine newspaper accounts then tell how the now fifteen-year-old Emily was taken to a hospital for a stomach operation, probably appendicitis, and how an infection had started there. Dr. Mariano R. Castex is quoted as saying it was poison in the intestines; others, however, talked of morning sickness.

In a long letter to her mother, my grandmother described in detail how Emily was brought home to the embassy after the operation, still conscious but in great discomfort, and how a contingent of nurses and volunteers looked after her for three or four days while her mother sat by her bedside. The letter was written while Emily still lived, and her mother wanted to get the letter on the next boat back to the States.

My mother never made any reference to the charges of medical incompetence against Dr. Castex that were trumpeted in the headlines of the local newspapers: *"Un Error Científico Habría Causado la Muerte de la Hija del Embajador Americano."* Although she had been operated on for an attack of acute appendicitis, Emily died in the early evening of December 20 from what papers called encephalitis lethargica, a brain infection.

The Jay tradition of good manners and discretion assumed control, and no official investigation was requested by my grandparents. Newspaper accounts suggest that Peter was visibly upset, but the potential controversy was soon squashed under the more pressing need to maintain smooth political relations with Argentina.

Particularly since there was a private service for Emily at the embassy on December 22 and it was requested that flowers be

American Embassy in Buenos Aires, 1920s

sent, it boggles the mind to imagine the elaborate lies her parents must have had to invent to tell my mother. Why was her sister suddenly absent during the Christmas holidays? It is inconceivable that this bright little girl did not detect something amiss in the long faces and subdued gloom that no doubt enveloped the premises over Christmas. So it may even have been something of a relief when her parents told her they would soon be going back to the United States. She may have dreamed that Emily was waiting for her in New York.

In one of my mother's accounts of this episode, she did describe hearing the noises of a procession passing by the front of the embassy and asking about it. She said that her English nanny, Miss Edwards, told her it was some kind of parade going by—when in fact it was her sister's funeral.

My mother never saw the story that ran in the Buenos Aires American paper shortly after Christmas. The newspaper accounts recounted the barest facts:

And as the passing on of Emily Kane Jay has robbed her parents of all the joy of living, so it has visited upon the American community of Argentina a very real material loss, for Ambassador Jay has cabled to President Coolidge his definite resignation from the diplomatic service and he and Mrs. Jay, with their younger daughter, are sailing by the S.S. Pan America next Thursday to accompany back to the United States the body that served as the brief home on Earth of the soul that was Emily Kane Jay.

Her father's parting letter to the American colony in the *American Weekly of Buenos Aires* had been brief but adequate, as everyone already knew about the tragedy the Jays had experienced. A little more than a month earlier, Peter had read President Coolidge's Thanksgiving proclamation at the First Methodist Episcopal Church in Buenos Aires. But now he was done, his diplomatic career finished. At the age of forty-nine, Peter Augustus Jay was a beaten man. The ache in his chest was not from his riding accident in Romania. It was a new pain, a far deeper one that would never leave him.

During the two- or three-week voyage from Buenos Aires to New York, my grandmother apparently confined herself to her cabin, for, according to my mother, my mother was vaguely told that she was "resting" and could not be disturbed. My mother was never explicit about how much this bothered her or how bizarre it must have seemed. I always felt hesitant to probe when Mother launched into this extraordinarily intimate story, perhaps paralyzed by the power of the revelation and in some way afraid that my questions would be an excuse for her to close down.

One of the most enduring and sepulchral images of my mother's story was her reference to the flags on the boat being flown at half-mast. This always seemed to me quite plausible, given my grandfather's rank as ambassador. In one version of her story it was Miss Edwards's inability to think of an excuse to give the young Susan Mary for her question about why the flags were at half-mast that prompted her father to tell her the truth. In another version it was as the ship approached New York City after its long voyage that my mother's father took her on his knee and told her the truth. It would have been January 18. Either way, Peter finally told my mother.

I believe it was this trauma that catapulted my mother into adulthood—way ahead of her years. The photos show my mother becoming progressively anorexic as she moved through adolescence in the 1930s. I also have the feeling that on some level my mother grew to believe that *she* should have died instead of Emily, and that much of her life involved trying in different ways to compensate.

Calvin Coolidge replied to Peter's letter of resignation, saying: "I can ill afford to lose men of your experience and record in so many foreign capitals. I can well understand, however, your desire to have the opportunity of caring for your personal affairs after 25 years devoted to your Country."

The family never recovered from Emily's death. My grandfather continued to struggle with his asthma and led the life of a

Susan Mary and Emily Jay holding a guitar, Argentina, 1926

semi-invalid without any serious occupations or interests. My grandmother became something of a recluse, and from an early age my mother found solace with her aunts and uncles and friends outside the house. In all the many years I knew her, my grandmother never talked to me about Emily. My mother continued all her life—wherever she was living at the time—to make sure that Grandmother Jay was kept informed and comfortable. My mother's childhood was over at the age of nine.

Breakwater, on the Shore Path, Bar Harbor, Maine

four

The Smell of Fear

The smell of stale face powder in this
ladies' room is the smell of fear.
—MARIETTA PEABODY TO SUSAN MARY JAY
AT THE BAR HARBOR CLUB, 1933

MY GRANDFATHER PETER Jay's decision to retire and return
home may also have been influenced by the fact that just before
Emily died he had inherited a shorefront estate called Breakwater in Bar Harbor, Maine, from his great-aunt Annie Kane.
Her husband, John Innes Kane, had died in 1913, and Annie
may have felt that her great-nephew deserved a proper refuge after spending so many years serving his country abroad.

Breakwater had been constructed in 1903 toward the end of
the Gilded Era on what is known as the Shore Path in Bar Harbor. Built on massive square granite blocks, the heavy Tudor-
style structure, which still stands, once had a sizable carriage
house at the entrance. There was a secret passageway from the
billiard room to the second floor, and most of the windows had
small diamond-shaped glass panes.

During my mother's adolescence in the late 1920s and 1930s,
Bar Harbor was making a slow transition from an extravagant
summer playground for the very rich to a busy holiday town

Susan Mary Jay as an adolescent

serving tourists who were visiting Acadia National Park, then the only national park on the East Coast.

Life at Breakwater in its heyday was quite formal. I remember a story about my grandmother scolding her butler, Johnny Parascan, because a tradesman's car was parked at the front door. Johnny, who never seemed to get things quite right, must have enjoyed telling Mrs. Jay that the old car belonged to a gentleman named John D. Rockefeller Jr., who was waiting to speak to her in the front parlor.

It is easy to imagine my mother as a lonely nine-year-old girl wandering around at the base of Breakwater's twenty-foot-wide main staircase, trying not to think of her sister, and looking toward the musician's gallery for melodies that never came. She was very conscious of the lack of music in her childhood—and she apologized to me near the end of her life for never having brought music into our lives.

Although there was no music to speak of, the library at Breakwater brimmed with serious history books. The featured categories were American diplomatic history, biographies of the Jays and their commercial treaties, and a colorful collection of Victorian diplomatic memoirs. In 1922 Peter gave his wife the two-volume *Life of Robert, Marquis of Salisbury*, by Lady Gwendolen Cecil. It sat beside a three-volume *Life of Lord Curzon, Viceroy of India*, who was a close friend of the Jays' Cairo acquaintance Lord Kitchener.

Leafing through Lord Edward Cecil's memoir, *The Leisure of an Egyptian Official*, I was impressed that he opened with Rudyard Kipling's lament, "Here lies a fool who tried to hustle the East." Some of these English diplomats had been contemporaries of Peter's at Eton. These books channeled the Victorian-era ethos of British imperialism with which my mother grew up.

The solemn architectural interior at Breakwater had a sharp foil in the natural magnificence just outside. When Susan Mary drew her bedroom curtains in the morning, she could see the sun rising across Frenchman's Bay. She had a view of the plump Porcupine Islands at the entrance to Bar Harbor. At the lower edge of Breakwater's lawns lay the famous Shore Path that ran—as it still does today—from downtown Bar Harbor north and south along the coastline in front of the summer estates. For an adolescent, this offered a natural route of escape. Susan Mary could head north toward the commercial center of town and the tennis and swimming club or head south away from people along an increasingly rugged coastline that now constitutes Ocean Drive.

In addition to participating in social activities at the Bar Harbor Club, my mother and her friends could take long hikes along mountain trails, swimming at remote ponds and picnicking

Marietta Peabody and Elise Dix at the Bar Harbor
Club, circa 1934

on lookouts with sweeping views of the Atlantic. She was a lifelong hiker and often found solace walking along the trails of
Mount Desert. Hiking appealed to her because it is one of the
few sporting activities that can be done in total solitude, a condition she knew well and often preferred.

But my mother's real life went far beyond her own home;
from an early age she nurtured her relationships with the extended family. At the nucleus of this group were her mother's
sisters, particularly Martha Cross, and her real family grew to include her energetic first cousins, Mrs. Winthrop Aldrich, Mrs.
Arnold Whitridge, and Mrs. Sheldon Whitehouse, the daughters of Mrs. Charles B. Alexander, and other cousins who in
some senses replaced my mother's own mother.

From 1900 Q Street in Washington, D.C., my ten-year-old
mother writes: "Dear Mama, I am now at Mamaly's [Mrs.

Alexander], where you remember I'm staying to lunch. Janetta [Mrs. Whitridge], and Mamaly and I went to see the last of the cherry-blossoms." This habit of letter writing evolved at an early age. Her large, roundish, rather easy-to-read scrawl offered the footprints upon which much of this present book was written. Writing an essay titled "3 O'Clock in the Afternoon" at the age of eight, my mother's imagination was being taken with the need to keep moving. She describes a group of children who are suddenly told by their mother: "We are going in an airoplane to France in an hour and a half, get your trunks packed, and Miss Skeleton if you don't get my imitation chinchilla coat out of the cellar it will be the worse for you."

Muffy Brandon Cabot, a perceptive friend of my mother's, who helped her move out of my stepfather's house in the early seventies, recalled noticing my mother's "aloneness." She said it was as if "there was always a lonely little girl beating inside of her." Muffy reflected recently that "structure was so important to her because of the anxiety inside . . . she wasn't free to be a rebel."

After returning from Argentina in 1927, Susan Mary's anxiety was as tightly controlled as her anorexic figure. Until the end of her life, the only physical ailment I remember her complaining about were occasional references to "tummy problems." Such complaints also appear occasionally in her letters from Paris. Seeing her eat a meal reminded me of someone tiptoeing through a minefield, all the while praising the lovely landscape. In restaurants when we were alone or with the children, she could not wait to get the bill, as if the sooner this ordeal was over, the better.

When she was fourteen my mother was sent to Foxcroft, a boarding school near Middleburg, Virginia. She applied herself diligently at Foxcroft, graduating in 1935 with honor grades and a comment from Charlotte H. Noland, the headmistress, saying,

Susan Mary Jay and Elise Dix on a ranch, circa 1934

"This shows hard work." In 1933, while she was at school, her father died. It was the year that Franklin Delano Roosevelt boldly asserted, "The only thing we have to fear is fear itself." My mother quotes her closest friend, Marietta Peabody, who, as they brushed their hair before stepping out onto the ballroom floor of the Bar Harbor Club one summer, observed, "The smell of stale face powder in this ladies room is the smell of fear."

After divorcing her first husband, Desmond FitzGerald, in 1947, Marietta had married Ronald Tree, a wealthy American with a taste for beautiful houses like Ditchley in England, which he soon sold, and a Palladian pavillion he built at Heron Bay in Barbados. Their house staff in New York included Collins, the butler Tree brought with him from England; Mabel, the governess for their daughter Penelope; and Alice, the Tree family's maid.

One night when I was in college and staying with Marietta Peabody Tree, who was also my godmother, in New York, I came home to her house on Seventy-ninth Street heartbroken after splitting up with a girlfriend. Marietta was reading in bed. When I told her, in tears, what had happened, she said to me rather briskly that this was the kind of experience that would make me stronger and bid me good night. I got more comfort from talking to Alice than anyone else. I could never completely escape the feeling of being a little boy in my godmother's august presence.

Being dumped by a boyfriend at the Bar Harbor Club was not likely to have been one of my mother's or Marietta's big fears—they were both too beautiful and spirited. Susan Mary was not quite as tall as Marietta, but she was slimmer and had big brown eyes and dark hair. Though she did not enjoy horses, she had a graceful stroke on the tennis court. As far as my mother and Marietta were concerned, the rituals of the summer colony were prime bulwarks of the patriarchal WASP culture that they would politely undermine for the better parts of their lives. They had more important things to think about than whether a boy would dance with them.

My mother's childhood friend Bill Blair described at her funeral how she and Marietta were always discussing world politics on Bar Harbor's Shore Path while the rest of their friends talked of tennis and sailing. For the two young women, it was their repugnance for provincial complacency and the threat of being locked into it forever that the "stale smell of face powder" really evoked.

Still, some of my mother's young suitors worked hard to pierce her veil of seriousness. Perhaps the most humorous admirer during the late 1930s was twenty-three-year-old John Alsop, my future stepfather's youngest brother, who in a summer of 1938 letter addressed my mother as "my darling little black-eyed daisy." A slew of lengthy epistles filled with fantasy escapades and trivia came streaming from his office at Smith Barney & Co. These letters pursued her at the Asticou Inn and at Breakwater in Maine and in Boca Grande, Florida.

Alsop masked his seriousness by posing as one of the Tarleton brothers questing for Scarlett O'Hara and was often outraged at Susan Mary's aloofness: "I am sick and tired of getting stood up by you. Who do you think you are anyhow—Marie of Rumania with your experience? You ought to realize by now that it is not done, to treat an Alsop and particularly the younger (and superior) Alsop in this offhand way!"

When he hears about her engagement to Bill Patten in the summer of 1939, he writes: "That puts the 1, 2, 3 on me. I find myself amazed but delighted. However, the constant shocks are getting me down . . . I've always regarded Brother Patten with great reverence and affection, and am pleased to find that his taste is as excellent as his other qualities—even if he has played Hell with my weekend!"

Both of John's older brothers, Joe and Stewart, also wrote notes of congratulation but in more restrained tones. Joe could not resist adding: "You are my favorite young lady; Bill is almost my oldest friend." Their mother's brother, their uncle Monroe Robinson Douglas, an unpredictable character, wrote: "I could kill my two nephews for having let such a prize as you slip through their fingers."

According to my mother, it was their Harvard friend Desmond FitzGerald, then married to Marietta Peabody, who in the spring of 1939 introduced my mother to Bill Patten. They were at the Maisonette Russe, a restaurant in the St. Regis Hotel. As she described in her book *To Marietta from Paris*, "It was the summer of the New York World's Fair, and I spent many an evening out at Flushing, sometimes professionally as a model for *Vogue*. One particular evening sticks in my mind. There was a parachute thing, from which Babe [then Cushing, later Paley] and I floated again and again in evening dresses until the photographers were satisfied."

Bill Patten had been raised under the powerful umbrella of his mother's Thayer family, the scions of Lancaster, Massachusetts, a village they had largely dominated—first theologically then financially—since the early nineteenth century. Lancaster is located a few miles west of Groton School, which both Bill and his friend Joe Alsop attended. Groton was a small boarding school for boys that was modeled on the British system of senior prefects having authority over the younger classes. It was founded by the Episcopalian minister Endicott Peabody, known as "the Rector," and had mandatory morning chapel services each weekday as well as morning and evening services on Sundays.

From the time of his arrival at Groton in 1923, Bill struggled not only physically but academically as well. He took a year off at Manter Hall in Cambridge in 1925 to "develop intellectual ambition," as the Rector put it, before resuming his fourth form year. Though his "examination marks [were] not up to the required standard," it would only "seem fair to the boy," given his "great diligence," to allow him back, the Rector wrote.

Both of Bill's parents lobbied hard on his behalf, stressing to the Rector how they had hired special tutors for Bill over the holidays. They seemed to have a personal relationship with the Rector, who signed his letters to them "Affectionately Yours," and at times seemed almost defensive, writing back that "we have no established machinery for carrying on a case as Bill's, which is practically unique." Because of his ongoing struggles with asthma, Bill did not graduate with his Groton class but spent his last year of pre-college schooling in Arizona, which was judged to be a healthier climate for him. He rejoined his Groton classmates at Harvard but was initally accepted only on a probationary basis.

Anna Thayer Patten reading to her son Bill
Patten, circa 1914

Even in the fairly terse comments of his teachers at Groton one can detect a certain kind of exceptional grace in a boy who evidently was already struggling with his health. Bill had suffered from asthma ever since he was a little boy. He is "a very attractive lad—more so than most boys," reported teacher F. C. Staples. Although "he is not rugged," wrote the school's physical education director, J. L. Strickland, he is "a well bred boy and thoroughly honest."

My father's letters from his father are warm and intimate; they describe his visits to the Thayer compound in Lancaster and talk about horses and dogs on the estate and the various caretakers and chauffeurs who kept it running. Sadly, Bill's father died in 1927 at the age of fifty-four, just before Bill entered Harvard.

Bill's Harvard experience pivoted around the Porcellian Club, one of the college's most elite social clubs. Over the next thirty or so years remaining in Bill's life, his Harvard friends—especially his fellow club mates—formed a remarkably close bond. Impressed as much by their loyalty and genuine warmth toward one another as by their professional accomplishments, my mother often referred to Bill's college friends as that "exceptional class of 1932." The photographs taken around Boston during this period by their classmate Charles F. Adams show Bill surrounded by his friends, including both my mother and Marietta, with the only overweight, and usually overdressed, figure standing out in the group being Joe Alsop.

During the seven years between his graduation from Harvard in 1932 and his marriage to my mother, the same names reappear year after year in Bill's little blue Smthyson appointment book for dinners, weekends, dances, and other social events: Charles Devens and Charlie Adams; a dance given by R. T. Lyman; squash at the Racquet and Tennis Club with a Hamlin; lunch with the Bacons (my future in-laws) at Piping

Friends on North Shore of Boston; sitting in front, Desmond Fitzgerald (left) and Bill Patten (right); standing, Joe Alsop (third from right); circa 1936 (photo by Charles F. Adams)

Rock; outings with friends named Hallowell, Coolidge, Forbes, Sears, and Phillips. He records a "Grand Dinner at the PC," the Porcellian Club, and a visit to his cousin Prissy Thayer in Lancaster, fall duck shooting at Merrymeeting Bay, and the Harvard–Yale football game. In 1936 the only entry for New Year's Day is "Dinner at Catlin's."

My mother recounted in detail for her mother her first visit to Bill's family in Lenox:

> I was shivering with fear by the time we drew up at the house in Lenox, & my fright was not soothed by my first view of Mrs. Davies [by this time the widow of Bishop Davies, her second husband after my grandfather William S. Patten]. She is about six foot one, I should say, & wears blackish glowing garments which made her look like the Fall of the House of Usher. She greeted me with the warmth of an iceberg and I went up to dress for dinner.

The atmosphere later improved.

> Mrs. D. loosened up after a cocktail and told a story over the vichysoisse (they live darn well, incidentally, & not a trace of matting-on-the-floor Bostonish atmosphere) about her older sister's coming out party to which she was allowed to come down to shaking with excitement and the first person to dance with her was that dashing Harvard senior Guss Jay. Thank God for Papa's sense of duty, I thought gratefully.

This was an artful way of framing her father's beautiful manners as a sophisticated New Yorker kindly putting to ease a more provincial New Englander's social trepidations.

My mother ends this long letter by writing: "I am more maudlin than ever over Bill, in spite of the poodles etc.! He is a very complicated character, & utterly fascinating to me." It is the only time I ever saw her refer to Bill as "complicated."

Bill proposed to my mother in the summer of 1939. My mother received a flurry of letters once news of the engagement got out. Her uncle, DeLancey Jay, noted that both of his sons-in-law, Chauncey Stillman and Frankie Kinnicutt, were "enthusiastic" when they heard the news and hoped that "Bill reciprocates to a certain extent Frankie's and Chauncey's feelings," adding that "Bill's father was a fine chap—quite one of the best."

In the same letter DeLancey apologizes for not having been able to speak to Susan Mary directly, because when he called on the phone "your mother seemed to be in a bit of a hurry (probably with a view to saving money)," which was typical of my grandmother. She would hang up on people while they were still trying to say good-bye, a habit I remember vividly.

My mother was drawn to her aunts in part because of their warm and supportive nature. She received an intimate letter from her aunt Martha giving advice "which probably isn't at all necessary" about how to go very slow with her sister Susan (my grandmother) and "include her just as much as you can at this stage in your plans or discussions."

Susan Mary followed her aunt Martha's advice and resigned from her job at *Vogue* to devote time to planning the wedding. It had been her first job and her first experience as a professional writer as well as a model. Albert Kornfield from *Vogue* wrote saying how much she would be missed at the magazine. He had his own way of describing her famous tact, writing: "I will miss you more than others because of your fine spy work. I shall recommend you to a friend in Washington in case the espionage runs short of undercover agents!"

My grandmother's friends, including the Boston banker Charles Stockton, had warned my mother against marrying someone in such poor health as Bill Patten. But I suspect that it was precisely Bill's asthma, the very same illness her father had struggled with, that attracted my mother. What she, as opposed

Bill Patten with (left to right) Marietta Tree, Nan Crocker, and Susan Mary Jay, circa 1936 (photo by Charles F. Adams)

to most others, saw as "a very complicated character" offered the kind of challenge she had been unconsciously seeking.

The bridal dinner was held at Breakwater, and in late October 1939 Bill and Susan Mary were married in the chapel of the DeLancey Jay estate, Wheatly, in Westbury, Long Island. My mother wore a gown of white satin and a tulle veil trimmed with orange blossoms, and carried an old-fashioned bouquet of white flowers. Her uncle, DeLancey Jay, gave her away, and her cousin Mrs. Francis P. Kinnicutt, the former Sybil Kane Jay, was her maid of honor.

During the first three years of their marriage it is likely my mother felt some tinges of déjà vu living in the socially insular North Shore world. Bill's jobs from 1937 to 1942 ranged from working as a stock salesman for H. C. Wainwright & Co. to fund-raising for the Greater Boston Community Fund until he became an administrative assistant to the Massachusetts Committee on Public Safety in the civilian defense field. It was no doubt a milieu he would have been content staying in if it had worked out that way.

But during the summer of 1944 a happy coincidence in Bar Harbor opened much wider doors for Bill and Susan Mary. Sumner Welles, Roosevelt's undersecretary of state and an old family friend, was strolling along the Shore Path in front of Breakwater while my parents were visiting. An austere man who was much kinder than he let on, Welles could—as my mother later wrote—"hardly avoid coming up the lawn, panama in hand, for he had worked for my father in earlier years." After some polite discussion between Mr. Welles, my grandmother, mother, and Bill over tea on the lawn, the conversation turned to Bill's uncertain career. It is not clear who exactly led the conversation, but the results of this impromptu tea party opened the door to the young Patten's future.

In late November 1944 Bill received a letter from the Department of State offering him the position of "Economic Analyst in the American Foreign Service Auxiliary with salary of $3,800 per annum." The letter stated that "the Department expects appointees to be in excellent physical condition," which Bill was not, so it would appear that the intervention of someone with Welles's rank must have prompted them to make an exception.

With Bill's first assignment being in Paris, my mother was well on her way to her great escape back to Europe and headed toward a life far beyond the Shore Path and the powder room of the Bar Harbor Club. She was being reintroduced to the world of her childhood and the world of her forebears in exactly the same place where three previous generations of Jays had launched their diplomatic careers. And this trip was part of a serious mission—a whole war-torn continent was waiting.

The unrelenting urge to cheer up the world that sprang out of "the lonely little girl beating inside of her" had finally found a broad and magnificent focus. Susan Mary now had a chance to breathe new life into those heavy diplomatic tomes that had stared down at her from the shelves of the library at Breakwater.

Duff Cooper, First Lord of the Admiralty, at Naval Inspection, 1937 (Corbis)

five

The Making of a Warrior

You are quite unlike ordinary people—
you are the heroines of Greece and the popular novels.
—LETTER FROM VIOLA TREE TO LADY DIANA MANNERS
(IN PHILIP ZIEGLER'S BIOGRAPHY OF LADY DIANA)

MY PARENTS, BILL and Susan Mary Patten, had met Duff and Lady Diana Cooper soon after they arrived in Paris at the end of World War II. Though my parents were almost twenty years younger than the Coopers, they became close friends, and my mother, in particular, was chagrined when Duff was recalled to England at the end of 1947. Predictably, the farewell ball for them in December (which Winston Churchill traveled to Paris to attend) was a magnificent occasion. Writing to Marietta a few days later, my mother described it in vivid terms:

We stayed at the party till 5 AM and it seemed too soon to leave that beautiful house, every candle lighted, every piece of the historic gilt services gleaming on the tables, Diana in a pale blue dress of satin with lots of tulle the same color, making the most elegant young Frenchwoman look like nothing beside her. As you wrote, when you first met Diana, she is the only really glamorous woman one had ever met. She and Duff have been so beloved that the party was bittersweet as it meant farewell, but the guests outdid themselves to live up to the occasion. Every man who had an order of decoration wore it, even the most dismal prince appeared dazzling in the Saint-Esprit and the dimmest Spanish first secretary of the Embassy seemed like something out of the *Merry Widow.* The women's dresses were wonderful, all enormous except for a few short Dior ones which looked ridiculous on the dance floor. I wore a Schiaparelli dress made of stripes of mauve satin and heavy ivory grosgrain, with an enormous bustle, very *Lady Windermere's Fan.* Monsieur Christian Dior bowed to me and said, "That is one of the greatest dresses I have ever seen, and I wish it were mine," which made me feel badly, as he has been so generous to me.

The Coopers' departure from the leading foreign embassy in Paris after World War II marked the end of a thrilling period of ascendancy in my mother's life. In her adoration of Lady Diana and her affair with Diana's husband, Duff, she had been catapulted into one of the most glamorous households in Europe.

I was forty-seven years old when I learned that Bill Patten was not my biological father. My mother had long vacillated about whether or not to reveal the truth about Duff to me. Judging from her letters alone, even during my upbringing there were moments when the coincidences of life startled her. Either she glimpsed traits of Duff in me, or I might be drawn to a topic that had also interested Duff.

She could only share her ambivalence about me with old friends like Marietta Tree. When I was two she reported to my godmother, "Billy looks like me but in character is so much like his father that it makes me laugh." When I was in my last year at Groton School, she wrote Marietta: "The history master expects Billy to take honors at Harvard—he got a 94 on his final exam & 96 for a term paper on Talleyrand. Yes, I said Talleyrand!"

What I absorbed as a child was a combination of legend, fact, and whispers that would only later be filled in by history books and biographies. I knew that Duff had been the British ambassador to France when my parents lived in Paris; that he had served as the First Lord of the Admiralty in Neville Chamberlain's cabinet; that he had opposed Chamberlain's appeasement at Munich and had famously been the only member of his cabinet to resign in protest over it; that he was married to Diana, the Lady Di of the interwar years; and that he must have been a monumental figure, especially in the context of the Cold War, because my mother and Joe kept talking about him even though he had been dead for decades.

What I didn't know at the time was that he had been something of a war hero; that he was descended from King William IV; that he was a man of affairs in every sense of the word; that he published a book on Shakespeare and a book of poetry; that he seems to have had a lonely childhood, but blossomed in school at Eton and Oxford; that he was a close friend to many great men of the day, including Winston Churchill and Herbert H. Asquith; that his grandfather, a nephew, and his wife were also "illegitimate" like me; and that he was a remarkable rogue, at least in terms of social propriety.

As a starting point, I tracked Duff's ancestry. His father, Sir Alfred Cooper, was a highly regarded society doctor who had effectively rescued his social outcast wife-to-be, the aristocratically born but martially scandalous Lady Agnes Cecil Emiline Duff, from near destitution.

Lady Agnes was the third child of Lady Agnes Hay and the fifth Earl of Fife. Her grandfather was the Duke of Clarence, later King William IV, and her grandmother was the great Irish comedic actress Dorothea Bland, whose stage name was Mrs. Jordan. Paving the way for Queen Victoria, the eventual king produced no adult heir with Princess Adelaide, but prolifically parented ten illegitimate children with Mrs. Jordan. One of these, Duff's great-grandmother Elizabeth, married William George Hay, the eighteenth Earl of Erroll. King

William IV formally legitimized all ten children well before he died in 1837.

Despite this distinguished ancestry—or perhaps because she inherited what was known as the licentious "Jordan blood"— Duff's mother had led a socially precarious life before she met Sir Alfred. At nineteen she eloped with Viscount Dupplin, the dashing heir to the Earldom of Kinnoull. Two years later, in 1873, they had a daughter. Two years after that, Lady Agnes ran off again, this time with a man named Herbert Flower. He died four years later, by which time Lady Agnes's family had turned their backs on her.

Duff's mother had then been ostracized by British upper-class society. Duff's father—"a classic Victorian success story," in the words of the historian John Charmley—stepped into the breach when he noticed the disgraced Lady Agnes "scrubbing the floor" in a London hospital, as the story goes. Sir Alfred, who specialized in bronchial and venereal disease—the latter being the original basis for his friendship with the Prince of Wales—was well positioned to offer Lady Agnes the safe port she was missing. By all accounts, the marriage to Alfred Cooper was a long and stable one. Lady Agnes produced three more daughters in the 1880s and finally a son, an "adored fair-haired, blue-eyed infant"—my biological father, Duff—in 1890.

The "riotous Jordan blood" did not vanish entirely when Lady Agnes married Sir Alfred. Writing about his mother, Sybil—Duff's closest sister—in his graceful memoir, *The Arms of Time,* the publisher Rupert Hart-Davis speculates about his own legitimacy. Sybil endured a painful marriage and died at forty-one after converting to Catholicism, and Duff's sister Mione suffered a complete mental breakdown in 1923. Duff's diary suggests that he did not feel terrible anguish over the early death of his older two sisters, the other one, Steffie, having died in 1918.

In his memoirs Duff observes that his earliest years were not his happiest. His mother was still largely estranged from her own family—so much so that King Edward VII went so far as to remind his son-in-law, the Duke of Fife, not to snub Lady Agnes. There were few relations on the Cooper side to compensate, so Duff was relatively isolated until he went off to Eton and, later, Oxford, where he made friendships that lasted the better part of his life.

The majestic British Empire was at its peak when Queen Victoria died in 1901, and Duff was just eleven. Of course, the empire's sweep concentrated its bounty on a hereditary elite whose "we happy few" self-regard was legendary. Viola Tree, famed illustrator Max Beerbohm's niece and a friend of Duff's future wife, Lady Diana Manners, breathlessly captures it in a letter to Diana describing a prewar house party: "I've just been to Rowsley where I've had God's own time. I swear that all of you are without doubt the 'Superior People' of history. It is almost too exciting; you are quite unlike ordinary people—you are the heroines of Greece and the popular novels. England can never sink while we've got a king like good King E and while it is inhabited by a few such as us."

As a child, Duff was on the periphery of the elite, the inner core of England's self-satisfied greatness. His mother had the right hereditary connections to let him peek inside this select group, but she was behaviorally suspect. Sir Alfred was an accomplished professional, a very good but not quite eminent Victorian physician, whose role was to serve the aristocratic elite, but who was not himself a member of it.

Indeed, Duff seems to have had mixed feelings about his father, especially compared with the unalloyed affection he showed for his wilder mother. Duff acknowledged that his father had always been good to him, but he admits in his memoirs that standing by Sir Alfred's deathbed at the age of eighteen, he felt "no great sorrow." This initially puzzled me, even in that Victorian stiff-upper-lip world, but the more I learned about Duff, the more I realized that routine and risk aversion were alien to him. Duff's father was cautious and restrained, whereas Duff came alive when the challenges were extreme. He needed to distance himself from his father and bourgeois values.

This may explain Duff's lifelong fascination with Charles James Fox, the roguish Whig firebrand who stood up against King George III in favor of the American colonies and later supported the French Revolution. Like Fox, Duff disdained commerce and had an aristocratic disregard for money that only the rich can afford. Unfortunately, Duff was never rich, so he often had problems with his bank manager, and Fox gambled away a fortune.

The three institutions that liberated Duff from his father's bourgeois world were Eton, Oxford, and the army—more specifically, the Grenadier Guards in the trenches of World War I. Starting at Eton, Duff acquired an elite group of friends to whom he became deeply attached over the rest of his life. More than a few of that group would die young in the war—losses that only deepened the intimacy of those who survived. In his memoirs he said going off to war was as natural as giving up one's seat to a woman on the tramway. The war was a turning point, in many ways a transforming experience, in Duff's life, as it was for British society in general.

According to some historians World War I was the last chapter in what has been called the age of chivalry. During this war, England's warrior princes—her "best and brightest"— fought in the bloody muck of the trenches and paid dearly for it. In total contrast with America's recent wars, the British class system in this great conflict worked against the privileged. Thirty-four British generals were killed by artillery fire during World War I, and twenty-four died by small-arms fire. Many came from elite schools, and virtually all were from elite families.

In *The Return to Camelot: Chivalry and the English Gentleman,* Mark Girouard uses photos of some of Duff's closest school friends—John Manners as a little boy on horseback;

Julian and Billy Grenfell from their mother Lady Desborough's family journal—as exemplars of aristocratic chivalry. He explains that the code of chivalry—inculcated in Edwardian boys from the nursery to the fabled "playing fields of Eton"—made the opportunity to "fight in a just cause . . . one of the most desirable and honorable activities open to man."

Today it is a stretch to comprehend the scope of human carnage that began in 1914. During one day in the summer of 1916—a year before Duff went to war—the British lost more men than America lost during the whole Vietnam War, and this in a population a fifth the size of the United States. The impact on European society was devastating and far-reaching. The marble obelisk in front of our village train station in the Pyrenees, where we have a summerhouse, lists the names of four local men who perished in World War II, compared with thirty-five names of men who died in World War I.

One day recently as I was going to visit the British embassy in Paris, where Duff had been the ambassador after World War II, I noticed a building on a small street nearby, the Rue d'Aguesseau. The building had been dedicated in 1921 to the soldiers of 1914–1918 with serious facial injuries, "*Les Gueules Cassées.*" In addition to the earthy slang of "*gueule,*" what struck me was that the association's mission statement, etched on the front of the building, was "*Sourire quand même,*" or "Smile Anyway." These were Duff's peers, but the image of a facially disfigured man trying to smile reminded me more of my American father, Bill Patten, than of Duff Cooper.

Duff had studied French in Paris before taking his Foreign Office exams, and he developed a lifelong affection for the country, no doubt reinforced by having a brief love affair with an older French countess. Duff was seventeen when he had a fling with the more experienced Comtesse d'Aulby. According to John Charmley, the comtesse told Duff that he made her wish she "were twenty years younger . . . all sorts of impossible things were possible!!!"

By 1916 Duff was a junior member of the Foreign Office and on friendly terms with prime minister Herbert Henry Asquith's family. He had befriended the prime minister's eldest son, Raymond, through the Coterie, an informal group of aristocrats with bohemian habits and a tendency to live on the edge. Duff's future wife, Lady Diana, was one of the most colorful members of this group and was not above laughing at the novelist Maurice Baring when he set his hair on fire or sliced his fingers to amuse her.

Duff's energetic social life propelled him from the heights of frivolity one minute to matters of state the next. One evening at 10 Downing Street, Lord Robert Crewe and Lord Robert Cecil invited him to join Prime Minister Asquith to make a fourth at bridge after dinner. As Duff records in his diaries, the conversation ranged from the campaign in Mesopotamia, to the attempted capture of Baghdad, to the evacuation of Gallipoli and private criticisms of Lord Kitchener. This must have been heady stuff for a twenty-six-year-old.

As the war progressed—or as it dragged into a fatal gridlock—Duff readied himself to join the battle. By 1916 the naïve notion that war was a chivalrous sport had given way to harder-headed realism, even cynicism. Raymond Asquith was mortally wounded on the Somme River that September. Earlier in the year, Asquith had written his wife, "I agree with you about the utter senselessness of war. The suggestion that it elevates the character is hideous." Duff later recalled how "keenly wretched" and depressed he felt about the war, particularly about the deaths of so many close friends.

There was almost relief when the time came to enlist, and in 1917 Duff joined the Grenadier Guards. As he tried to explain to Diana, it was not beating the Germans that called to him but "the vague regret one feels when not invited to a ball even though it be a ball that one hardly would have hoped to enjoy." Indeed, the most tiresome part of his service was being forced to adapt to the regimental training and routine of living with others.

Duff noted in his memoirs that he had "lived very comfortably all my life" and had been accustomed to "having the best of everything." He candidly describes having to make his own bed and mix with "another class" during his training at Bushey Park as leaving him "more utterly wretched" than any time before in his life: "The man who finds himself suddenly thrown into another class is ill at ease, whether he be a peasant in a palace, or a prince in a pot-house." But he found a good hotel nearby with a library and where the wine was very cheap. He takes a moment in his memoirs to honor his "firm friend and wise counselor," wine, and recites the first lines of Hilaire Belloc's "great poem on wine which I am proud should have been dedicated to me."

The June when my mother was born in Rome was the same month that Duff later called his favorite of the six months he spent in the trenches of northern France. Quartered "in a vast farm," Duff and his battalion were resting at the time. Rather than share a bedroom in the farmhouse, which was his due as an officer, and in the absence of a private palazzo, the twenty-eight-year-old chose to live in a tent: "I am not one who enjoys life under canvas but I have always preferred privacy to chance companionship." Indeed it was his lifelong need for female companionship that eventually led to my being conceived.

In addition to writing letters, when he was not in action Duff was constantly reading poetry, novels like Balzac's, detective stories, and some history. On May 23, 1918, he wrote: "I am reading Doctor Thorne now, the sequel to Barchester Towers. I have discovered that the edition of Gibbon I have with me omits the indecent Latin quotations in the notes. Isn't that a shame? I hardly care to go on with it."

His letters to Diana were witty and lighthearted. On August 14 he wrote her: "[R]eading about Rupert Brooke makes one half in love with easeful death. It is very becoming to die young, but to be on the safe side you need a background of sea and mountains and isles of Greece."

In the early morning of August 21, 1918, a machine-gun nest pinned down Duff's company. The commander told Duff to deal with it, which he immediately set out to do. Visibility was poor in the morning mist, and Duff soon found himself separated from his company by enemy fire. He "took a shot at" one of the enemy soldiers and knew enough German to authoritatively command the others to surrender. Much to his surprise, eighteen unarmed German soldiers emerged with their hands up. Thinking they were outnumbered, they must have been astonished to find themselves facing "a rather undersized Second Lieutenant," as Duff's biographer Charmley described him. This earned Duff the Distinguished Service Order, Britain's second-highest military honor.

In a letter to Diana dated August 25, Duff described the attack in strangely elegant prose: "My platoon of 30 was then reduced to 10—and at the last minute as we were forming up for the attack I discovered that my sergeant was blind drunk—a dreadful moment. But it was followed by some of the most glorious in my life. A full moon, a star to guide us—a long line of cheering men, an artillery barrage as beautiful as any fireworks creeping on before us—a feeling of wild and savage joy."

Unlike many soldiers who want to banish brutal images of war, Duff seems to have been fascinated by the emotional power of his memories. It was probably more than fascination, more like falling into a self-protective kind of insanity, as no one who fought in those trenches could fully comprehend the scope of the new killing culture that had been unleashed around them.*

In addition to his social ambitions, perhaps Duff needed to separate himself from other men because on some level that he could not adequately put into words he felt revolted by humankind. On the other hand, he was also a proponent of the

---

* See *Dynamic of Destruction: Culture and Mass Killing in the First World War* by Alan Kramer (Oxford: Oxford University Press, 2007).

class system that propelled his career in London to such a degree that he later accepted an offer to write a laudatory biography of General Douglas Haig, whose tactics, particularly in the Battle of the Somme in 1916, have been seen as incurring unnecessarily large numbers of casualties for little tactical gain, earning him the nickname "Butcher of the Somme."

No one will ever know for sure. But a letter of August 11 to Diana describing "an arm sticking out of the earth" shows the strong connection between death and beauty in my young father's mind, balancing the frozen rituals of death with the lively affectations of a dinner party. In the first part of the letter he pictures a recent dinner she attended:

> Birrell fingering his port . . . Venetia fingering her hair . . . you leaning forward and side to side like the conductor of an orchestra calling at will for the right sound from each instrument, yourself bright and animated and beautiful as the Mother of Love.
>
> This afternoon in lovely sunlight and heat I went for a little crawl by myself and had rather fun. I found an arm sticking out of the earth. I don't know what impulse made me take off the glove. The arm had been there a long time and there was little left but the bones. The hand was beautiful—thin and delicate like the hand of a woman and the nails had grown long and even like a Mandarin's nails. How much the flesh may have once hidden the beauty of the framework you couldn't tell, but it must have been a small hand and I think the owner must have been proud of it because gloves are not usually worn at the war. It gave me no feeling of disgust or uneasiness but rather content that the beauty can still hang about the bones, surviving the corruption of the flesh, and staying with the body until the bitter end of complete annihilation. The hand was raised and the fingers curved in rather an affected gesture. I wish I could have kept the glove. My brother officers were amazed at my lack of squeamishness—and yet they would think nothing of treading on a beetle. How different we are. Thank God we are not as other men.

Lady Diana Manners, 1916 (Corbis)

six

Dangerous Liaisons

an orchid among cowslips,
a black tulip in a garden of cucumbers
—RAYMOND ASQUITH DESCRIBING LADY DIANA MANNERS

W̲E WENT TO a party given by Frieda which I enjoyed. I danced with Poppy Baring who is a very attractive girl. The Prince of Wales was there and was rather in wine. He was staying at Windsor for Ascot and had come up clandestinely with Prince George (Duke of Kent) after the rest of the party had gone to bed. He gave an amusing account of poker in the royal circle. Daisy and Fred (Cripps) left soon to go on to Rectors but later I got a message from Daisy to go and pick her up at her house. It was about half past three. I went trembling with hope. As I turned the corner into Stratton Street I saw Reggie who had very shortly before left the party with Lois getting out of a taxi at the corner. As it is a cul de sac there was no escape so I drove on to the end, rang the bell, the door was opened by Daisy. I explained to her quickly what had happened and bolted into the cellars where I remained until all was quiet above when I slipped out.

—DUFF COOPER'S DIARY ENTRY OF JUNE 18, 1923

Duff was one of the lucky ones. He returned to London physically intact and a decorated war hero. But any celebration was muted. He had lost a huge number of his closest friends. His best friend at Eton, John Manners, had been killed early on. Another close friend, Hugo Charteris, a brother-in-law of Lady Diana, was killed in the spring of 1916. Hugo's brother, Yvo, was also dead.

Imperfect as it is, our grasp today of the psychological trauma caused by war is excellent compared to what it was in World War I. John Keegan, a leading military historian, has observed that during the First World War, "men whose symptoms we can now recognize as those of a true psychiatric breakdown were shot for desertion." It is impossible to know how many severe psychiatric casualties were sustained between 1914 and 1918. The British upper class needed all of their rich supply of denial and stoicism.

For Duff the death toll among his close friends was staggering. Looking back in 1918 on a trip to Venice he had taken before the war, of the original four who motored out there together, Denny Anson, Billy Grenfell, George Vernon, and Edward Horner, "not one remains. The most precious guests were Raymond Asquith and Charles [Lister], both dead."

On January 4, 1918, Duff writes in his diary that Lady Desborough—already having lost both "Julian, brilliant athlete and memorable poet, and Billy, who equaled his brother in athletics and surpassed him in scholarship"—came down to breakfast "holding the table as gallantly as ever. A pleasant morning spent playing with ponies and donkeys and sitting about." The day before, she had heard that her son's—and Duff's—great friend Patrick Shaw-Stewart, a poet and banker whom "she had loved and helped in his career," had been killed on the front.

Despite and probably because of these losses, the war drew Duff closer to one of the great beauties of the day, Lady Diana

Manners. Duff had met Diana, who was only two years younger than he was, in the spring of 1913 in London and then again in Venice that summer. Duff had been visiting Raymond and Katharine Asquith. Diana was staying in a nearby villa with the senior Asquiths and Lady Emerald Cunard, mother of the notorious Nancy Cunard. Raymond, who would be killed at the Somme three years later, once described Diana memorably as "an orchid among cowslips, a black tulip in a garden of cucumbers, nightshade in the day nursery."

Diana's beauty was less evident as a child. She was born with a small bump on her forehead that the family called "the unicorn's horn." Diana's mother, Violet, was a granddaughter of the 24th Earl of Crawford. Officially, her father was the 8th Duke of Rutland, but her biological father was most likely Henry Cust, a handsome journalist and member of Parliament. Diana's official father was chiefly interested in "fly-fishing and fornication," according to the biographer Philip Ziegler, and therefore he could hardly complain about his wife's infidelities.

Diana wrote, "[Duff] grew into my life, as I grew into his." The relationship between them that had started before the war developed and deepened as the fighting continued beyond anyone's expectations. During Duff's five months of fighting in France, he received forty-five letters from Diana along with bottles of port to fortify him and nineteenth-century French novels to remind him, as she said, that the local landscape was worth the fight. He responded in kind, but the joking coded language was a thin veil disguising their shared terror at the appalling odds against survival. Before an upcoming advance attack Duff wrote reassuringly in a letter dated "1 am 23rd of August 1918": "I adore you. *Don't worry*. Probably shan't be able to write tomorrow. The Germans are charming and always surrender. Duff."

When Duff returned to London, his pursuit of Diana became more concerted and more plausible. The membership of the Coterie, already discriminatingly small, was ravaged by the war. Duff was one of very few remaining in the Edwardian elite with whom they had grown up; the security of their prewar life had been pulverized and its remnants were dissolving all around them.

Courting Diana Manners was an uphill challenge. Wooed by some of the most powerful men of the day—including press baron Max Beaverbrook and friend Prime Minister Asquith—Diana was well accustomed to being the center of attention. Her beauty was captivating. Winston Churchill remarked, "Was this the face that launched a thousand ships?" The novelist Mrs. Hwfa Williams called Diana the "White Baby" because of her "extraordinary white skin and beautiful blue eyes."

Diana is one of the major luminaries in Juliet Nicolson's *The Perfect Summer,* a social chronicle of England in the summer of 1911: "Diana was the golden girl of the summer, and as far as an infatuated press was concerned she could do no wrong." Her need to stand out was epitomized by arriving at an "all-white" dress party dressed as a black swan, much to the disapproval of Lady Sheffield, the hostess, and her irreverence was exemplified by shouting at former prime minister Arthur Balfour during a parlor game, "Use your brain, Mr. Balfour, use your *brain!*"

Diana's mother naturally had higher aspirations for her daughter than seeing her marry a hard-drinking young gambler with no money. But Diana casually turned down marriage offers from magnates and politicians. Her reaction to her mother's efforts to get her interested in the Prince of Wales, the heir to the throne, was to call him a "sniveling cub."

In her early years Diana ran with a fast crowd of promiscuous and rebellious women that included Nancy Cunard, about whom Margot Asquith once remarked, "What's Nancy up to now? Is it dope, drink or niggers?" But though she enjoyed flying close to the flame, Diana herself was relatively indifferent to sex.

She met her physical needs strictly on her own terms. In 1917 she accepted the expensive gifts of the wealthy Ivor Guest, Lord Wimborne, who was used to buying what he could not otherwise obtain. But despite avoiding most personal confrontations, Diana energetically resisted several of Ivor's onslaughts both verbally and physically.

She once admitted that her ambivalence about men's carnal needs grew in part from a "fear of losing my pedestal of ice." Her need to be worshipped was far stronger than any desire for physical intimacy. "You beautiful, blond, white-breasted bitch. How desperately people adore you," Duff wrote her during their courtship. She likened Duff's early attentions to a "rainbowed ornamental fountain" and compared them with "that vile torrent of gravy and steaming, stupefying blood," as she described the passionate advances of a wealthy American she referred to as the "ghastly" George Moore. Years later, when the king of Spain let his hands get a little carried away over Diana, Duff and Diana could only chuckle over his buffoonlike attempts.

The essence of their relationship, however, largely finessed the issue of sex. Most of the time Duff lied about his affairs, and he claims in his diary that he felt horribly guilty about the lying—but not guilty enough to slow down. In fact, he admits quite often that the "intrigues" surrounding the affairs added to and even created their appeal. Though more jealous in the early days, Diana seems largely to have grown to accept Duff's infidelities. Daisy Fellowes, an heiress and "destroyer of many a happy home," as Duff called her in 1919, was a friend of the Coopers for over thirty years. When he met her in 1919, Duff said he "got on well with her especially when we reached the subject of pornography." According to his diary, Daisy was a part-time lover of his until at least 1938.

What replaced sex for Duff and Diana was a vibrant feeling of companionship. Thirty years later Diana had become accustomed

Lady Diana and Duff Cooper, 1931 (Corbis)

to playing a role at the heart of some of Duff's affairs. The French socialite and poet Louise Levêque de Vilmorin temporarily lived with the Coopers in the British embassy. Her biographer, Jean de Bothorel, wrote: "The three of them [Duff, Diana, and Louise] were bound together in a strange harmony, mysterious, and incomprehensible to all their friends . . . When Duff was absent, Diana was the only person Louise wanted to be with." Likewise the

Duchess of Windsor once observed that the main drawback of having an affair with Duff was that when it was over, one would usually have to be comforted by his wife.

Though Diana seems to have taken few sexual risks, drugs—mostly morphine—were another matter, especially during the war, when many of her childhood friends were being killed. Duff, however, was not drawn to drugs. In 1925 he documented "a reaction of disgust" after sleeping with a girlfriend who had just smoked opium after having a fight with her husband. Duff also expressed concern about Diana, writing in his diary, "I hope she doesn't become a morphineuse. It would spoil her looks." After a night of "debauch" in the winter of 1919, Duff warned her "how ugly it made her look. Fear of ugliness is I think the best preventive."

As a good Edwardian, Duff made a distinction between a fleeting appetite and a more enduring need for intimacy. He wrote in his diary, "My infidelities are entirely of the flesh. I feel guilty of no faithlessness, only of filthiness." Filthiness, of course, covered a range of other, more destructive weaknesses from drinking to gambling.

His diary suggests that he relished the draw of playing with fire, as in 1924 in his affair with Lady Warrender, known as Dollie. They met at one of Lady Curzon's parties: "[T]he stately rooms of Carlton House Terrace looked more like a Montmartre restaurant, littered with confetti, masks, streamers, celluloid balls etc. I wore a skeleton mask in which nobody recognized me and I had the greatest fun." Duff talked with Dollie and "thought her perfect."

But later on, as the affair with Dollie evolved, Duff admitted: "Before the conquest was completed there was glamour and romance about the matter that made it seem too [much] like real love and real love for another is the only crime against Diana I could never forgive myself and that she could never forgive me.

But with the flight of that illusion the wrong that I do Dollie grows greater."

Although he once said he hoped neither Diana nor his son would ever read his diary, he was equivocal about others reading it. Profoundly affected by surviving the trenches in 1918, he told his nephew Rupert Hart-Davis that "perhaps the answer is that people who love life as much as I do want to keep some record of it—because it is all that they can keep." There are moments in his diary when he seems to be flaunting his weaknesses. While his attempts and failures to control his drinking seem transparent, his repeated amazement that women should fall for him is somewhat disingenuous.

Duff understood better than most the costs and trade-offs of passion. On the Grand Canal in Venice after dinner with the American songwriter and composer Cole Porter and his wife, Linda, Duff lectured Diana, saying, "[H]appiness and romance don't go together. Romance cannot survive without difficulties and dangers." Even floating down the Grand Canal, Duff remained far more a romantic pragmatist than a pragmatic romanticist.

The stories in Duff's diaries confirm what his biographer had already noticed about his trysts: that they were neither predatory nor exploitive. He was more addicted to romance than to sex, writing in his diary in 1920, "I love romance and intrigue and cannot do without them." Even twenty-six years later, at the age of fifty-six, he wrote poetically about his brief affair with Gloria Rubio, who was then engaged to Ahmed, son of the Egyptian minister Fakhri Pasha. He slipped out late one afternoon to meet Gloria before an embassy dinner with Julian Huxley and Evelyn Waugh. "It was a lovely evening, having rained all day. The view from her window of the Sacre Coeur with the sunset rays on it was memorable—very memorable to me."

Duff had a habit of seizing an opportunity on the spur of the moment when it presented itself. As ambassador to France in early November 1944, after a dinner in Paris with Lady Diana, Cecil Beaton, and various French friends, Duff received an urgent message to call Prime Minister Churchill. His hostess, Louise de Vilmorin, escorted him to the door, where, Duff reports, he "found myself kissing her and falling in love. She returned my kisses." This must have offset his disappointment when he discovered that Churchill had "nothing to say at all; the call was quite unnecessary."

Throughout Duff's mature life, it was equally the companionship and human qualities of the woman, couched in all the ups and downs and subterfuges of the relationship, that enticed him. He wrote in his diary about his possibly unconsummated love affair and long friendship with the lovely Lady Cranborn, the wife of Robert Cecil, Lord Salisbury, starting in the early 1930s. He notes in his diary, "I only wanted her to know that I loved her." His old friend Cynthia Asquith, the daughter-in-law of the prime minister, had already noted in her diary before the Great War: "Under the Coterie crust I think he [Duff] is really a dear." Women could see the sweetness and vulnerability behind his bravura façade.

While he seems to never have been attracted to recreational morphine, Duff had more control over his love life than he did over alcohol. My mother used to tell me in an admiring way, "All upper-class Englishmen drink a lot." Duff and his good friend Winston Churchill were exemplars of the type. In his diaries and memoirs Duff acknowledges that he drank more than was good for him. While he admits that booze often led him astray, I suspect he would have had a hard time conceding that he was physically dependent on what William Styron called his "mood bath." The truth is that it contributed to his early death.

In 2005 my half brother, John Julius (he was Duff Cooper's son), published Duff's private diaries. They show something more of the daily human struggle that is absent from Duff's memoirs. At one point Duff constructs a little formula to control his drinking, "based on the division of days with five categories," as follows.

A = No drink until dinner, then only one sort

B = Either only one sort at luncheon and dinner or nothing until dinner then more sorts than one

C = More sorts both at luncheon and dinner but nothing between

D = No restrictions but no excess

E = Excess

This little list may have been inspired by a troubling comment that he also recorded that day in his diary. He had heard that "the Queen, who is my friend, has said that I couldn't be a successful Minister if I burnt the candle at both ends." But the diaries suggest that Duff never put this scheme to use. He makes no further mention of any effort to control his drinking.

When Duff first mentioned his intention to marry Diana to her mother at the Victory Ball in London in December 1918, the duchess reacted as if he were joking. Though she knew Duff was talented, she also knew him to be something of a cad. Besides, she had her eyes on the Prince of Wales as a better catch for her family, if not for her daughter. But Duff persisted, won the duchess over, and then—with her help—gained the consent of the Duke of Rutland, a man who may have admired Duff for his extracurricular prowess.

Duff and Lady Diana were married in June 1919. Partly to help with domestic finances, Diana took up acting in silent films, playing the lead role in 1922's *The Glorious Adventure,* directed by the American J. Stuart Blackton, and playing Queen Elizabeth I in an "inartistic lark," as she called 1923's *The Virgin Queen.* Also in 1923 the Austrian director Max Reinhardt offered Diana the part of the Madonna in the Broadway mime

Lady Diana and her mother, Duchess of Rutland, 1924 (Corbis)

play *The Miracle*, the story of a wonder-working statue of the Virgin in a great cathedral. Over the next three years Diana played this role in New York and most major American cities. In 1927 it toured Europe, keeping the Coopers separate for much of the time.

Letter writing, which had kept Duff and Diana close during the First War, continued throughout their married life. Even in the middle of an affair in 1924, Duff took out Diana's "war letters," rearranged them, and compared them with her current ones. "They are as full of love as the old ones," he noted appreciatively. She, in turn, wrote in the mock-childish tone that reflected the coded language of their class. Writing from Antibes in the spring of 1928, Diana scolds "Duffy," her "darling beloved baby," with a motherly kind of affection: "Dear good Duffy. It was naughty not to tell me about Biddy—when you lie you encourage me to [worry], and also I can't trust you at other times. If there is nothing in the Biddy thing, why not tell me outright about a Paris date. If there's nothing in it you bet she thinks there is and is crowing. Still you must do as you like because you're a good boy and because I do love you, almost whatever you do."

Although Duff notes in his diary in 1922 that he doesn't mind—"except for her sake"—when Diana's doctor tells her that her chances of having a child are slim, the Coopers eventually had their only child, John Julius, ten years into their marriage.

Though not wealthy, the Coopers reveled in an almost unimaginably glamorous and entitled life. Their nonstop social whirl, mixing European royalty with artistic and literary celebrities during weekend house parties, gambling, costume balls at the Carlton House Terrace, and trips around Europe and America, led the playwright Noel Coward to use the Coopers as a model for some of his best social satires. The guest list at their country house in Chantilly outside Paris ranged from Ingrid Bergman to Charlie Chaplin, from Princess Margaret and the Duke of Windsor to Ian Fleming and Isaiah Berlin.

Diana possessed a carelessness that often comes with privilege. She was famous for her reckless driving. Her first crash, in a car Max Beaverbrook had given to her and Duff, was into a milk cart in 1919, which resulted in the street being flooded. Her second crash occurred in 1920 when "Diana forgot to steer and before we knew what had happened the car was on its side in the ditch." In 1951, while dining on Daisy Fellowes's yacht off Monaco, their car slipped into the sea, as Diana "had left the brakes off." Between Diana's crashing into milk trucks and unwittingly hijacking the future king of England's (George VI) car after a small dance, she and Duff occasionally had abrasive encounters with unruly members of the lower class. Duff was almost arrested by a French policeman in 1923 in the Ventimiglia train station when he spat at "the man behind the *guichet* who . . . had imitated Diana's bad Italian and excited gestures to her face in the most insolent way." It is hardly surprising that Duff was blackballed by London's Turf Club.

Occasionally this behavior provoked disapproval from the serious politicians with whom Duff worked. As Duff writes, when British foreign minister Lord Curzon returned to London in October 1922 after negotiating with French president Raymond Poincaré in Paris, his "first action was to ring up Crowe [Duff's immediate boss] and say he thought I was having too much leave . . . I told him I was intending to go away for three days' shooting at Belvoire." Despite such occasional complaints, Duff worked effectively as private secretary to the parliamentary undersecretary of state for two years, saying in retrospect that "having served three masters, a Liberal, a Conservative, and a Labor Member . . . I am glad to think that I got on well with all three."

Duff's political career began in 1924 when he was elected as the Conservative member of Parliament (MP) from Oldham. He admits that the Lancashire cotton mills held no particular appeal for him, and that he did not enjoy the electoral process. In 1928 Prime Minister Stanley Baldwin appointed him to the position of financial secretary to the War Office, and the following year Duff lost his MP seat in Oldham. He was reelected to another seat in 1931 in a by-election. Over the next four years he combined his work as a junior minister with his talent and enthusiasm for writing. He wrote his acclaimed biography of the great French diplomat Talleyrand in 1932 and an authorized biography of British field marshal Douglas Haig in 1934.

In November 1935 Prime Minister Baldwin invited Duff to join his cabinet as secretary of state for war. Duff admits, "I acquired little credit during my tenure of the War Office. With the means at my disposal there was little to be done." Though Duff expected to be without a job when Baldwin handed over his leadership to Neville Chamberlain in 1937, he was happily surprised when Chamberlain appointed him as First Lord of the Admiralty.

In his memoirs Duff notes that Winston Churchill's obstinate stand against his party's moves to grant India self-government in 1930 and his consequent "impotence for the next 10 years" was "the most unfortunate event that occurred between the wars." On the other hand, it opened the door for Duff to take the stand that would define him in the history books, ushering his old friend Churchill back to power.

Duff and Winston had a long and sometimes intense friendship, beginning in 1914 when Duff had just been admitted into the Foreign Office and was invited to join Churchill for dinner at Admiralty House. They played card games and socialized often, the older Churchill often confiding in the younger Cooper, reflecting an instinctive trust and affection for each other. Yet there were also moments when Winston puzzled Duff. In December 1916 Duff was writing in his diary when Winston dragged him off to a Turkish bath, where, "lying on couches like Romans after a good dinner with champagne," Winston talked about his past failures and said "he would take any job offered him at the present time. He is a strange creature." It was a lifelong friendship, and in 1954 Churchill cried as he listened to the eulogy at his younger friend's funeral.

Worldly and nonjudgmental when it came to romantic affairs, Duff was also a natural confidante to both Prime Minister

Baldwin and the Prince of Wales, later King Edward VIII, who became the Duke of Windsor after relinquishing his throne to marry the American divorcée Wallis Simpson. Before the abdication crisis in the fall of 1936, Duff and Diana took some criticism for joining the king and Mrs. Simpson on a Mediterranean cruise on the king's chartered yacht, the *Nahlin*.

As they cruised up the Dalmatian coast, the men in the group launched on childish escapades like breaking into Empress Elizabeth's villa in Corfu with the help of a pair of pliers. In her memoirs Diana mentions what fun it was to also have the king of Greece on board: "Two kings tomorrow night for dinner. It's all a great treat. I think I'm enjoying it as much as (No! more, much more than) anyone else on board."

The fact that Edward VIII was clearly under the sway of the mannish-looking, twice-divorced American woman didn't seem to bother anyone on board, but it had created a political crisis for Baldwin's government in London. The prime minister stayed in touch with Duff, knowing that the king would later ask for his advice. At the king's request, Duff spent an hour alone with him on November 16 to discuss various options. The king told him, "[I]f I can stay and marry Wallis she is going to be Queen or nothing."

Duff avoided as best he could arguments the king had heard before and suggested that perhaps a one-year separation might bolster his cause with the public, but the king "was not responsive to the idea." A couple of days later Duff spent a few minutes alone with Wallis Simpson advancing the same idea, recognizing "that she could persuade him to do anything," but she told Duff that "if she went he [the king] would follow her."

The Coopers' enjoyment of royalty led them to stay supportive of the Windsors, despite Edward's pro-Nazi sympathies, right through to their final assignment in Paris after World War II. Duff found King Edward to have "exceptional charm" when

John and Gussy Alsop, Paris, 1947

they lunched together in 1920, though he admitted in his diary that there is "a leaven of snobbery, or I should prefer to call it loyalty, which magnifies the emotion one feels about him." But by November 1945, Duff, as ambassador to France, and Churchill, as prime minister, were happy to see the Windsors go live in the United States.

Viewed by Americans, however, the Coopers' famous charm was not always so compelling. On a honeymoon trip in 1947, Joe Alsop's brother John and his wife, Gussy, met Duff at a lunch given by my mother. Gussy remembers her impression of him as "a fat old man" who went to sleep in the living room after lunch. Tired from their trip, the Alsops got up to say good-bye when my mother rushed over and told them they needed to stay until "the ambassador" woke up.

Joe's brother Stewart wrote to his mother recommending Duff's "really fascinating biography" of King David but viewed Diana less favorably. He summed up the couple, whom he had just met in Algiers, by noting that Duff "seems to be a trifle stuffy but nice, but she [Diana] irritated me intensely with her dyed hair, her air of languid superiority and her pre-war snobberies."

It is hardly surprising that this daughter of great privilege, accustomed to men throwing themselves at her feet, would have such innate airs of entitlement. Behind this demeanor, however, lay numerous insecurities. Diana always believed that she had some incurable disease, and she held on to a desperate desire to look young. Observing a typical bout of her depression in 1950, Duff noted in his diary, "the fact is that she needs excitement, as she admits . . . She has no intellectual occupation."

Duff and Diana enjoyed an unusual but functional relationship at the center of an extraordinary world of celebrities, writers, and intellectuals. While they were often apart, pursuing their own careers and respective private relationships, the two adored each other and supported each other in a remarkable "live and let live" context. They shared a passion for beauty in art and literature, an almost childish need for excitement and gratification in relationships, and in the end they effectively embodied the idea that "living well is the best revenge."

The foundation of this partnership may have been in their common roots, reaching back into the horrors of the First World War. Compared with what they had experienced between 1914 and 1918, they had been endowed with a second lease on life. What to us may look like living on the edge was their feeling that they had earned the right to enjoy the choicest sweets of life—both together and independently. Shortly before Diana died, John Julius Cooper asked his mother how she had managed to be so devoid of jealousy. "Oh," she said, "they were all the flowers. I knew I was the tree."

Winston Churchill and Duff Cooper at Ditchley Park, 1937 (Courtesy of the Ditchley Foundation)

seven

Standing Up to Hitler

That is fine of him. He has no money and
gives up £5,000 plus a job he loves.
—ENTRY IN HAROLD NICOLSON'S DIARY ON OCTOBER 1, 1938

T HE MUNICH PACT of 1938 still rings an ominous bell for
many Westerners born in the first half of the twentieth century. It evokes a sense of betrayal; as the historian Doris
Kearns Goodwin has said, "The Munich analogy may be
deeply rooted in political thought, but it is also rooted in the
American psyche."

For many, Munich symbolizes the folly of appeasement or
negotiating with tyrants. It has permeated the consciousness of
our own leaders. Henry Kissinger told me he remembers the
Munich event from when he was fifteen. It also resonates from
time to time among the public. Last March a letter writer to our
paper in Worcester alluded to "Neville Chamberlain, the man
who famously brought the world 'peace in our times' in 1938, on
returning from his negotiations with Hitler at Munich."

It is hard for people to remember how relatively popular
Adolf Hitler was on both sides of the Atlantic when he first rose

to power in the 1930s. American corporations appreciated the efficiency he seemed to bring with him, and Joseph Kennedy, as American ambassador to London, advocated cooperation with him. For Europeans, the ambivalence about Hitler and the fear of war were profound and understandable. Half of all French males between the ages of twenty and thirty-two had been killed in the war of 1914; the yearning for peace was deep and irresistible. In his *History of the Modern World,* R. R. Palmer wrote: "Taunted by enemies, the Western democracies behaved like Ferdinand the Bull," who "would not fight and be fierce whatever they did."

Like most people, Duff was caught up in his own feelings of ambivalence. But, like Churchill, and a few other war veterans, Duff had known death firsthand. He perhaps intuitively recognized the dark implications of the hypnotic, ego-driven ravings of a man others preferred to dismiss. These veterans, including Harold Nicolson and Harold Macmillan, were a minority and Churchill himself was out of office.

In the summer of 1933 Duff and Diana had taken advantage of "a motoring tour through Germany to stay with friends" to gain a close-up view of the dictator in Germany and to see the Nazis in uniform. Looking for "a small country inn by a stream," they eventually found one less than thirty kilometers from Berneck. They were "by now accustomed to finding every man fit to bear arms in uniform," so they were not overly surprised to find it looking like an armed camp. The owner of the inn, having learned from his passport that Duff was a member of Parliament, wondered whether he might like to meet the Führer, who was spending the night there at very short notice.

Duff accepted the offer, and though Hitler later "excused himself on the grounds of fatigue," he presented the Coopers with tickets to his speech the next day at a rally in Nuremberg. It was in Nuremberg that Duff and Diana were witness to the mob mentality Hitler inspired.

Diana records in her memoirs the visceral impression Hitler created as he moved toward the podium:

> He passed, alone, and slowly, two feet away from me. I watched him closely as he approached, as he passed, as he retreated, compelling my eyes and memory to register and retain. I found him unusually repellent and should have done so, I am quite sure, had he been a harmless little man. He was in khaki uniform with a leather belt buckled tightly over a quite protuberant paunch, and his figure generally was unknit and flabby. His dark complexion had a fungoid quality, and the famous hypnotic eyes that met mine seemed glazed and without life—dead colorless eyes. The silly meche of hair I was prepared for. The smallness of his occiput was unexpected. His physique on the whole was ignoble.

Duff later wrote, "The tedium of it was such that we insisted, to the shocked horror of the audience, on leaving before the end of the speech."

But returning home they found that their feelings of repugnance were far from universally shared. All through the 1930s pervasive weakness and disunity reigned among Western democracies, which were largely swayed by profound pacifism. Neutrality legislation and isolation sentiments in the United States tied President Roosevelt's hands. In England British students signed the "Oxford oath," whereby they pledged that they would never take up arms for their country under any condition. The French banked on the Maginot Line, which they had naïvely built on their eastern frontier, facing Germany. Meanwhile, dictatorships were spreading across Europe, with Benito Mussolini in Italy, General Francisco Franco in Spain, and Joseph Stalin in Russia.

Hitler perceived and capitalized on this situation. In 1933 he took Germany out of the League of Nations. In 1935 he broke the terms of the Versailles Treaty and began to build up his army and navy without concealment. In 1936 he reoccupied the Rhineland, which was supposed to be a demilitarized zone. In March 1938 German forces took over Austria. In each of these instances the European countries protested but took no action.

As secretary of state for war between 1935 and 1937 and the First Lord of the Admiralty in 1938 (the civilian head of the British navy), Duff was at the forefront of government decision making. Historians have speculated that Chamberlain gave him the admiralty job mainly to keep him from asking embarrassing questions from the Conservative backbenches. He ended up being even more of a nuisance than Chamberlain could have imagined.

The position of First Lord was more than he had hoped for, and there were many perks. "I like being in Admiralty House, I love the yacht *Enchantress*," he wrote. Diana was even less bashful about enjoying the trappings of the position. She started by redoing Admiralty House, including her bedroom, where she mounted new blue curtains lined with white satin, and a wreath of gilded dolphins and crowns on the twenty-foot ceiling. At the center of the room she placed a huge bed with two life-size dolphins at its corners. The rest of the mansion featured various busts and portraits of Admiral Lord Nelson and paintings of Captain Cook's voyages to the South Seas.

No cabinet job held such romantic appeal as the civilian head of Great Britain's powerful shield against the world since the days of Elizabeth I and the defeat of the Spanish Armada four centuries earlier. Every British schoolboy knew the tales of the British sea captains, like Sir Francis Drake and Sir Walter Raleigh, who had taunted the Spanish in the name of England. It was a post that Churchill had adored and, as fate would have it, one that he would soon resume himself.

The events leading up to the Munich Pact in the fall of 1938 have been examined in exhaustive detail by historians. While

Duff Cooper at his desk, circa 1950

arguments continue to this day about the origins of the First World War, there is less debate over what started the Second World War. The only real question is whether Hitler could have been stopped in time.

Most historians agree today that despite its relative lack of military preparedness, if the British government had stood up to the Nazis with unwavering determination to fight, Hitler might well have lost his momentum. There was an important group among the top German military who were at that time looking for an opportunity to get rid of the Führer. But his prestige in Germany was being fueled by the passivity of the other European nations.

Chamberlain was committed to confronting Hitler through diplomatic channels. Duff perceived Chamberlain's parochialism as the root of his misjudgments in foreign affairs: "Chamberlain had many good qualities but he lacked experience of the world . . . He had been a successful Lord Mayor of Birmingham, and for him the Dictators of Germany and of Italy were like the Mayors of Liverpool and Manchester, who might belong to different parties and have different interests, but who must desire the welfare of humanity, and be fundamentally reasonable, decent men like himself."

Czechoslovakia was strategically the keystone to Europe. By 1938 it had a well-trained army and strong fortifications against Germany. However, those fortifications were located in precisely the border area where the majority of its population was German. After Hitler annexed Austria, he enclosed Czechoslovakia in a vice, and in May 1938 German troops almost invaded. Hitler held back in the face of Czechoslovak mobilization, clear warnings from Russia and France, and what Duff believed to be "above all the very firm opposition of his own General Staff." All of this suggested that if he were resolutely opposed, Hitler might be stopped.

Duff observed that most of the public that spring, including Churchill, reacted under the misimpression that Hitler had been checked "entirely due to the firmness of the British Government . . . There is no word of truth in it." Nor was Duff encouraged by the six new members of the cabinet who had joined since Chamberlain became prime minister. Churchill had been out of power, and Anthony Eden, the foreign secretary, had recently resigned. Though Eden and Duff had their differences about Italy, Duff believed he "was a good Foreign Secretary." According to Duff, "he knew Europe."

Ironically, on August 28, 1938, Duff and Diana were on the HMS *Enchantress,* touring the Baltic ports when they were informed of an emergency cabinet meeting at 10 Downing Street the following Tuesday. They steamed through the Kiel Canal at night and two days later awoke "in an autumn mist" at anchor on the Thames. It was to be Duff's last trip on the *Enchantress.*

In the last chapter of *The Light of Common Day,* the second volume of her memoirs, Lady Diana paints a picture of standing on the edge of war that September. She describes the mood in Admiralty House: "Where was Winston? Why, stamping to and fro amongst the Admiralty's dolphin furniture, flaming his soul out with his impotence to flout the aggressor in his own way. Duff was the hard core of the bold . . . He kept a firm lid on his boiling indignation, but I could hear it singing and spitting. It gave him sleepless nights."

Duff kept a personal diary during these years. Though it was edited for national security reasons, those sections that remain paint a remarkably calm portrait of a man at odds with his boss. For the first three weeks of September he jockeyed back and forth trying to support the government in public—and getting into fights with Churchill—while privately trying to convince Chamberlain and the cabinet of the danger of appeasement.

As the crisis heated up, on the fourteenth of September Chamberlain took the initiative to visit Hitler. Chamberlain reported his meeting at Berchtesgarden at the cabinet meeting on the seventeenth, and "the curious thing seems to me that he recounted his experiences with some satisfaction . . . From beginning to end Hitler had not shown the signs of yielding on a single point," Duff recorded. There were subsequent meetings about the issue that Hitler was claiming the principle of "self-determination" for those Germans living in the Sudeten part of Czechoslovakia and offering a possible pledge to protect the remainder of the country.

On the twentieth Duff wrote: "Every morning one wakes with a feeling of sickening anxiety, which gradually gives way to the excitements of the day." And at times, such as on the evening of September 28, after Hitler agreed to a second meeting with Chamberlain, Duff still believed war might be avoided.

He had been pressing Chamberlain to allow him to mobilize the fleet since September 13. At times his boss seemed to agree, but then he would change his mind. It was not until the twenty-seventh that Chamberlain allowed Duff to "run home across the Horse Guards Parade" and order the mobilization of the British fleet. That, and other clear messages to Hitler, came too late.

The night of September 28 Duff did not sleep well. The following day, the whole cabinet turned up to see Chamberlain depart for Munich for his second meeting with Hitler. On the morning of September 30 Duff read the specific terms of the Munich agreement in the newspapers: "The German troops are to march in tomorrow and the Czechs are to leave all their installations intact. This means that they will have to hand over all their fortifications, guns etc. upon which they have spent millions, and they will receive no compensation for them."

During those sleepless nights Duff had sensed that he had one last chance to make his stand, and this was it. In his diary for that day, he wrote: "While I was dressing this morning I decided I must resign." This was his understated style. Duff's resignation was a rare event in political life. It was a gesture perhaps only dimly grasped by Americans, for whom a resignation from a status job denotes either a hidden agenda or failure. For Duff, it was an expression of his core values.

The tradition of British politics allowed Duff to make an exit statement. Though the House of Commons was waiting impatiently to hear Chamberlain describe his triumph in Munich, on the afternoon of October 3 Duff stood up and explained his decision to resign. As Harold Nicolson, who witnessed the speech, recorded in his diary, "He does it perfectly." Duff emphasized:

> We were fighting then, as we should have been fighting last week, in order that one great Power should not be allowed, in disregard of treaty obligations, of the laws of nations and the decrees of morality, to dominate by brutal force the Continent of Europe. For that principle we fought against Napoleon Bonaparte, and against Louis XIV of France and Phillip II of Spain. For that principle we must ever be prepared to fight, for on the day that we are not prepared to fight for it we must forfeit our Empire, our liberties, our independence.

As he ended his speech he lowered his tone of voice:

> The Prime Minister may be right . . . I hope and pray that he is right, but I cannot believe what he believes. I wish I could. Therefore, I can be of no assistance to him . . . I have forfeited a great deal. I have given up an office that I loved . . . I have ruined, perhaps, my

political career. But that is of little matter; I have retained something which is to me of greater value—I can still walk about the world with my head erect.

Duff spoke calmly and clearly. When he sat down, Churchill slipped him a note, which read, "Your speech was one of the finest parliamentary performances I have ever heard." Though the *London Times,* a staunch supporter of the appeasement policies, refused to publish the speech, the young *Times* correspondent who covered the House of Commons resigned as a result. Other members of Chamberlain's cabinet came very close to resigning, but Duff was in fact the only one to do so.

Chamberlain was, of course, the hero of the hour. The world rejoiced at his famous announcement of "peace in our times." Lady Diana described the noise of "millions of joy-mad people, swarming up the lampposts and railings, singing and crying with relief . . . Duff and I sat on my bed holding hands and staring at the monstrous-faced radio." She recorded that after Duff announced his decision, she "telephoned the news to Winston, whose voice broke with emotion. I could hear him crying."

Duff tried to analyze why he was so alone. He later wrote in his memoirs: "It is a curious fact that the British, who fight with the most glorious courage and the toughest tenacity, have such a horror of war that they will never support a policy which entails the slightest risk of it. Nor have we yet learnt that reluctance to take such risks is not the way to acquire security."

Duff's stance at Munich angered Hitler enough so that as late as 1942 the Führer kept confusing Duff Cooper in his public speeches with Churchill: "Or—one moment—that was not, no, that was not Churchill; that was Duff Cooper [who said that]. But as I said, each one of these is a bigger swashbuckler than the other, and you are constantly getting them mixed up."

Yet, though Duff was roundly attacked in the press, snubbed in public, and insulted in private, there was a mounting disquiet in the country with Chamberlain's appeasement policies. Of the more than four thousand messages Duff received, over 90 percent were congratulatory. Josiah Wedgwood, "the grand old veteran of the Left," wrote: "Love and admiration more than you have dreamt of will I hope compensate for loss of office and salary. Anyway this old colleague from better days is proud of you. Also I think it is a good spot on a bad page of English history."

When the British were forced to declare war against Germany the following summer, Lady Diana, who never presented herself as courageous, said she was sure that the first German bomb would land on Duff. In some ways her claims to cowardice only served to reinforce the perception of her husband's courage, and on some level her attitude was probably calculated.

Lady Diana recorded in her memoirs an evening in 1939 when the blackout had started in London and she and Duff dined with Winston Churchill and others at the Savoy Grill. Duff mentions in his diary that Winston confided to Diana that he had been asked to join the war cabinet. After dinner they were offered a lift home by the Duke of Westminster in his "outsize car," though in Duff's account of the incident in his memoirs he omits the man's name. According to Lady Diana:

> It was an uncomfortable salvation. He started by abusing the Jews, a red-tag subject where Duff was concerned—he plunged on . . . into praise of the Germans, rejoicing that we are not yet at war, and when he added that Hitler knew after all that we were his best friends, he set off the powder magazine. I hope, Duff said, that by tomorrow he will know that we are his most implacable and remorseless enemies . . . Next day, the Duke, telephoning a friend, said that if there were a war it would be entirely due to the Jews and Duff Cooper.

Munich permeated my upbringing in mostly mysterious, unconscious ways. My decision to write my senior thesis in college on Truman's secretary of state, Dean Acheson, is, in retrospect, a classic example. Acheson, a WASP Anglophile with a razor-sharp mind, was perhaps as close to Duff as I could get on this side of the Atlantic without knowing it. Duff had hosted Acheson in France after the war and had been impressed by his intelligence.*

Despite his stand against negotiating with Hitler in 1938, Duff was not a typical warmonger. Duff surprised some people in the 1920s by serving on the executive committee of the League of Nations. "It may be badly managed, it may be inefficient, but nonetheless if I could help it I would certainly do so. I disapprove also of war. I know of no mechanism that exists for preventing it other than the League of Nations," he argued at the time.

During World War II Churchill appointed Duff to several positions: minister of information, special envoy to the Far East, and finally as the British representative to the Free French in Algiers, with the prospect of being ambassador to Paris after the war. Perhaps because he believed "one cannot do propaganda well unless one believes it to be of the highest importance," because he did not get the support from Churchill he felt he needed, and probably because of his own impatience with bureaucracy, Duff's stint at the first post was short-lived. Arriving in Singapore in 1941, he was too late to change the situation. The Japanese landed in Malaya that December.

Fortunately, in January 1944 Churchill and Eden saw the value of sending Duff to represent Britain in Algiers. There

---

* No one appropriated the legend of Munich with more gusto than my stepfather. Joe brandished it over the head of five American administrations with unquenched passion. By the time the Vietnam debacle arrived, Joe had become almost hysterical on the need to have the necessary "balls" to confront the enemy.

General Charles de Gaulle headed up the newly formed French Committee of National Liberation. Duff was a good choice to help negotiate the relationship between the two headstrong leaders, who neither liked nor trusted each other. He knew Churchill intimately, spoke French, and de Gaulle respected him for his stand at Munich. Duff was also enough of a figure in his own right not to be browbeaten by either man.

Although Diana later described it as "De Gaulle and Winston . . . playing battledore with Duff as the shuttlecock," Duff seemed able to stay detached from the petty tirades that the two huge egos launched at each other as they worked out how to negotiate the final days of the war. The more de Gaulle tried to consolidate his power, the less Churchill trusted him; and the more Duff tried to explain de Gaulle's motives, the more Churchill accused Duff of disloyalty. The Coopers' shorthand nickname for these new giants of the Western world spoke for themselves: de Gaulle was "Wormwood," and Churchill was "Dumpling." Quite often Wormwood would be "doing the mule" while Dumpling would do "the mad baby." On June 7 Duff observed in his diary: "Wormwood seems to like me. Nobody can understand it. I least of all."

At one point Duff concluded about de Gaulle, after endless negotiations over the protocol of his return to France, "There was a quality in his superb intransigence that compelled my unwilling admiration." No wonder Wormwood liked him. Nor were the Coopers overwhelmed by coping with Churchill, Diana being one of the few women in the world who was not intimidated by him.

My favorite image of the Coopers managing Churchill comes from the recollections of his doctor, Charles McMoran Wilson, or Lord Moran. Having gone on a picnic in the Atlas Mountains together, Churchill felt compelled to explore a steep ravine. He got stuck at the bottom, and to get him out Diana tied a bed sheet around his waist. She then pulled him up while his bodyguard pushed the great man up from behind. Duff, who apparently shared my terror of heights, had insisted on getting out of the car as it ascended the mountain road, so he happily avoided the whole ravine business.

At the end of the war Duff had played a critical and interesting role. His old friend Harold Macmillan noted in his diaries after visiting the Coopers in Algiers that Duff "is really a charming friend and is doing awfully well as ambassador." Duff was rewarded for his work when in September 1944 he and Diana flew to their last formal home, the British embassy in Paris, "accompanied by an imposing escort of forty-eight Spitfires."

The magnificent embassy residence on the Rue du Faubourg Saint-Honoré had a brilliant pedigree. Built for the Duke de Charost in the eighteenth century, it was later acquired by Napoleon's younger sister Pauline Borghese—"the Little Pagan" as he called her—in 1803. After defeating Napoleon, the Duke of Wellington took over the house and the British line was established. Much of the great French furniture remained, however, including Pauline's famous state bed, which is still in the embassy today. Lady Gladwyn Jebb, wife of a British ambassador in the 1950s, wrote in her history of the embassy that Diana's "goddess-like beauty . . . rivaled memories of Pauline."

When the Coopers arrived, the handsome house was filled with what Lady Diana said were the "chattels and junk of diplomats, families and exiled Parisian residents." Duff was more optimistic, describing the embassy as a "perfect example of what a rich man's house should be. Neither palatial nor imposing, but commodious and convenient, central and quiet."

Duff was not caught up in the idea of ownership; he was more of a bohemian than an aristocrat, and in a sense he was more otherworldly than most of his peers. Perhaps his favorite possessions were books, and he had a library built in the embassy to

British Embassy in Paris, Rue St. Honore, Paris, France

accommodate his personal collection. The frieze around it dedicates it "to the silent friendship of books." People like his old friend and war veteran Bob Boothby, who gave the eulogy at his funeral, liked to say that Duff belonged to another, more civilized age.

What is a civilized age? I am not totally sure anyone knows. But the idea of an era when the pursuit of honor and beauty justifies a happy life sounds good. Like much of Duff's life, the ideals still sound almost unreal, but the practical reality somehow lands on its feet. What was Duff really thinking as he was getting dressed the morning he decided to resign?

Like Churchill, Duff had a rich inner life, one empowered by ideals of chivalry that had been sown into his imagination before and during his schoolboy days at Eton. The rigid British class system and its codes only reinforced these ideals. Duff assimilated them partly through his biographies of larger-than-life men, whether phenomenal diplomats like Talleyrand or extraordinary leaders like the Hebrew king David. He was constantly replenishing his creative imagination with the historical research that went into these literary endeavors, drawn in by the values they exemplified and that were closest to his heart.

As he walked home with Diana in the London rain after his career was over, Duff noticed his wife sobbing. To his surprise he realized that she was mourning the grand houses, almost palaces, where they had lived in splendor when he was First Lord of the Admiralty or ambassador to France. He felt sorry for her, but admitted in his diary that despite his many personal faults and his love of clothes and aristocratic rituals, the grandeur of these places had meant little to him. He had always thought that living in such places was like living in a hotel.

Upon Duff's death in 1954, a "Cassandra" writing in the January 5 issue of the *Daily Mirror* reflected:

> Lord Norwich died suddenly last Friday. The world knew him as Duff Cooper. I met him only once.
>
> His politics were not my politics.
>
> His upbringing, his background and indeed much of his domestic life was cast in the mold of rich inheritance, to which I am opposed.

But he was a great man.

In the wretched, scrubby disheveled years which led to Munich, Duff Cooper resigned at the supreme moment when he was being suborned to give in. It was a Very light of courage in those dark days and at the time in which he was despised and humiliated and condemned for his action.

But it was one of those great hammer-blows of disinterestedness and faith, struck at the decisive moment when the dripping climate of appeasement was tarnishing the reputation of Great Britain. Duff Cooper was splendidly right . . .

How they toss their little berries of belladonna upon his grave. The man was bold and gay and right when it was important to be bold and gay and right—and he was wrong when it didn't matter a damn to be wrong.

Duff Cooper and Susan Mary Patten, Volpi Ball, Venice, 1951

eight

Keeping
the Fire Lit

Susan Mary told me rather solemnly today that she is
going to have a baby and that it will probably arrive at the
beginning of July. She has been married nine years but this
is her first. She was very sweet this evening.

—ENTRY IN DUFF COOPER'S DIARY, FEBRUARY 8, 1948 (PARIS)

M Y MOTHER LEFT New York for Paris on Easter Sunday,
1945. She was on her way to rejoin her husband. Her first letter
home was written "in a deck chair tucked in the protection of a
three-inch gun to escape the wind, wearing a smart costume
consisting of gray flannel slacks, sweater, and a life jacket. I adore
it and so far wouldn't trade this ship for the Queen Mary or anything else." She was part of one of the last convoys headed across
the Atlantic.

The ship docked in Southampton at eight in the morning on
April 12. My mother was twenty-six and still had the big brown
eyes of the little girl she'd been on the *Pan America*. She was
strikingly thin. Though she had worked sporadically as a *Vogue*
model in New York, her real interests were political and literary.

In another letter to her mother, Susan Mary wrote: "It was a
warm and sunny day, and the lilacs, apple blossoms, etc. . . . were

out everywhere. Every ugly little house had a garden full of quinces and on the ground daffodils and primroses, everywhere that wonderful fresh English green. Waterloo Station had lots of efficient old porters."

England was a natural first stop on my mother's way to her new life in Paris. With her sharp eye for chivalry and distinction, she quickly encountered a "charming brigadier, just back from Italy . . . wish I knew his name, I think he is wearing the Victoria Cross." Soon she was dining at Duff's favorite haunt, the Carlton Grill, and spending the weekend with friends watching "six squadrons of Flying Fortresses pass overhead on their way out."

She arrived at the Gare du Nord in Paris at 6 A.M. on April 18. This earnest, attentive, and self-effacing young woman was well equipped for the unsettled scene she found in the city. With a husband "whose charm makes it easy to entertain," as she put it, she had all the aplomb needed to take on the war-frayed salons of the Noailleses and Rougemonts and Rothschilds—the "best" of the old French nobility.

My mother settled into a house on the Square du Bois de Boulogne just off the Avenue Foch in the sixteenth arrondissement, already supplied with a cook, "Elisa Vallet, smiling and cheerful." The house was rented to them by my "kind and generous first cousins." My mother explained: "For the derisory sum of two hundred dollars a month we found ourselves in this happy house which I knew well from girlhood vacations at Aunt Harriet's. Even her linen was on our bed, and despite four years of German occupation the two lovely drawing rooms retained their Louis XV walnut paneling, the Guardis hung on the wall, and the dinning room gave onto a sun-filled garden."

Europe in postwar turmoil was a feast of rescue opportunities—especially here in the city, where, as Duff's granddaughter Artemis Cooper has noted, "Foreigners who fall under the spell of Paris tend to suffer a masochistic thrill." As her friend the

English writer Nancy Mitford observed a few years later, my mother was less concerned with socializing than with saving "the future of mankind."

For Susan Mary the call for self-sacrifice was irresistible but unsettling. In June 1945, she wrote her mother that she was experiencing "blue moments." She quoted Isaiah Berlin, who described Paris as "empty and hollow and dead. Like an exquisite corpse; the metaphor is vile and commonplace, but I can think of nothing else." Susan Mary wrote that Paris was "like looking at a Canova death mask." She saw the challenge of blowing life into this drained capital much as she was dedicating her life to energizing her asthmatic husband.

Privilege and equity were constant tensions in my mother's life. After a dinner "at the overheated house of the Windsors," she wrote of her "deep embarrassment" when a well-meaning American general noticed a chilblain on one of her fingers and ordered that "a working party of German prisoners of war unload a truck of coal" for her the next day. My mother was always cold, as I remember, whether in a car or standing on the sidelines of one of my rugby matches.

These were critical years for Europe. Americans were waking up to the brutality of Stalin's regime and its global ambitions. The Second World War was barely over, but a third world war seemed imminent. At dinner an American senator shouted to the French foreign minister, "Say, Monsieur Bidault, we want to know what you're going to do when we drop our first atomic egg on Moscow!"

The French leaders were trying desperately to restore order in the country and keep the French Communists from building enough popular support to derail the Marshall Plan and overthrow the government. In October of her first year in Paris Susan Mary wrote to her mother, "[T]he wolves are at the door and Europe is possibly about to collapse into barbary." In December

Bill Patten and Joe Alsop, St. Firmin, November
1947

she wrote, "[A]t last letters are coming home; the postmen are
going back to work protected by the police."

Indeed, the safety of the postmen was crucial for my mother,
who could barely pass a day without writing several letters or
postcards. In an anxious world, letters were her lifebuoys. Married to a man with limited career prospects, Susan Mary faced a
replay of the dispiriting experience that her mother had had
when her husband, Peter Jay, resigned prematurely from the
diplomatic corps in 1926. She could tell early on that her own
husband now lacked the ambition to make a great financial or
political success.

After college Bill had worked in a brokerage firm while sharing an apartment with his college friend Joe Alsop. Three years later he moved to Marsh & McLennan, an insurance company with offices in New York and Boston. He left that company because of ill health in the spring of 1939 and in the fall married my mother. From 1940 to 1942 he worked for the civil defense in Boston and joined the Foreign Service as a reserve officer. In August 1944 he was appointed to the American embassy in Paris.

He started in Paris as an economic analyst, and then in 1949 became an assistant to the minister of the embassy, Charles E. Bohlen, another college classmate from Harvard, who was at that time in charge of the Military Assistance Program for France.

"For 8 years more," my mother wrote in 1947, "we always felt like Eliza on the ice flows [*sic*] in *Uncle Tom's Cabin,* one jump ahead of the authorities, but ambassador after ambassador stood up for Bill and insisted on his indispensability." Bill finally left the embassy in 1955 and joined the Paris branch of the World Bank, where he stayed until 1958.

Bill Patten and Ben Bradlee in the press office at the U.S. Embassy in Paris after "Election results: Eisenhower victory," November 5, 1952

Bill never had the standing in the world of power that my mother aspired to, but nonetheless she adored him. Encouraging me to make the most of my senior thesis at Harvard in 1970, she wrote: "I prefer that you did well because you like it. I didn't ever go in much for ambition, if I had I wouldn't have married your father, whose career was all too clear before we were married, and who was the best and bravest man I know."

My mother clearly felt mixed admiration for Bill Patten and occasionally vented her frustration with his limited career prospects. On November 1, 1948, she wrote to her mother: "Bill is suddenly being allowed to do such interesting work that it is pathetic to see his eagerness and pleasure, also the asthma is 100% better."

My mother couched all of her letters to her mother and family friends in a cheerleader's rehearsed enthusiasm, especially when she saw a chance to exalt noble behavior. Watching the French return from prison camps during the summer of 1945, she wrote home, "There is no question in anyone's mind about their courage," noting, particularly of the French, that "one impressive thing is the lack of bitterness towards the Germans." It's not clear to me how much she believed what she wrote, but it was her role to keep the flags flying high for "the future of mankind."

Amid this struggling atmosphere, there were few couples as appealing—and as formidable—as "Les Duffs," the affectionate name by which the new British ambassador and Lady Diana were known in French society. They were a force unto themselves, embodying all the eccentricities and charms the French expect of high nobility. The fact that Lady Diana was known for abetting Duff's affairs enhanced their reputations even further.

Les Duffs brought to the dejected capital an aura of stardom, which was deeply welcomed by the French, particularly by the sophisticated upper class. He was an aging war hero, a confidante of Churchill's, and a patron of the arts. She was a leg-

Left to right: Teddy Phillips, Duff Cooper, Duncan Sandys, Winston Churchill, Odette Pol Roger (in background), Randolph Churchill, St. Firmin, May 11, 1947

endary beauty who had graced the cover of *Time* in 1926. They were at the center of Parisian society, standing like Olympians amid the rubble of a devastated country.

Diana had established a salon at the famous embassy on Rue St. Honoré. Known as *"la bande"* or the *"salon vert"* after a sitting room in the embassy, the salon featured writers Jean Cocteau and Louise de Vilmorin and other leading lights of the French artistic community. English writer friends Nancy Mitford and Evelyn Waugh were frequent visitors. The latter wrote the former that the Coopers lived so much in their own self-created world that he doubted they had ever bothered to visit the Louvre.

Our family friend Marina, the wife of *New York Times* foreign correspondent Cyrus Sulzberger, described a visit to the Coopers' country house in Chantilly, in which she gave an insightful close-up of Lady Diana in the fifties. Marina—or

Mumbo, as we children called her—wrote to my mother: "She [Diana] was as sweet as can be. Little by little I am beginning to understand why her friends love her so. If she recognizes one at all she loves one. And she has a strange way of making one feel utterly comfortable and cozy, when the last time one thought she did not even know one. Strange disturbing and enchanting woman. And so beautiful I felt a thousand years old next to her."

Most of my parents' friends and acquaintances belonged to a generation and class accustomed to elaborate posturing and rules of etiquette. My mother was well suited to this environment. She had the habit of focusing on one or two people in a crowded room; she would sit them down, look straight into their eyes, and engage in an intimate conversation loaded with flattery.

The art of conversation was essential to the game. In Susan Mary's estimation, the ultimate conversationalist was Lord David Cecil, the chair of English literature at Oxford and the author of two books on William Lamb, Lord Melbourne, that my mother particularly admired. His understated erudition and easy wit led my mother to write in her memoirs, "He is one of the best talkers of our time," after a weekend visiting him at Hatfield House, an ancient Cecil seat.

For my mother, good conversation became interesting when it was serious. Topics were usually political, rarely commercial, and never financial. In the fall of 1948 my mother wrote: "My only real excitement is having had another fifteen minutes with General Marshall, which would have thrilled me had not Charlie de Bestegui [a famous party figure of the period] made himself the third in the group which made the conversation a nightmare."

Whether it was shaking Ho Chi Minh's hand (more "spine-tingling" than President Franklin Roosevelt's, she noted) or chatting with the American secretary of state, General George Marshall ("he exudes greatness and one's spine tingles"), my mother's attraction to power and politics inspired her journalistic proclivities. Writing to Marietta Tree in New York about one of the great Venetian balls she had recently attended, the socialite Pamela Berry, Lady Hartwell, whose house Duff found "the most amusing in London," observed that Marietta had probably already received a more vivid account of the party from Susan Mary. And, of course, she had.

My mother's skill at being what an English friend called "such an asset in society" became well known. She once transported an antique porcelain bidet across the channel. Liliane de Rothschild had given it to her to bring to Isaiah and Aline Berlin in Oxford to help smooth out a reception being held for their

Left to right: Unknown, Pam Berry, Peter Ustinov, Duff Cooper, St. Firmin, 1951

wealthy American friends the Jock Whitneys. In a letter to her friend Gladwyn Jebb she made a funny story out of being questioned at length by a French customs official about its usage:

"Do you plan to leave it in England, Madam?"
"Heavens no, I always travel with one!"
"Even when you are only over for a weekend?"
"Always!"
"Thank you, Madam, you may go."

As a little boy I noticed my mother's executive finesse from the backseat of the Jaguar she sometimes drove. When I was about nine she was pulled over for speeding by an angry French motorcycle cop. He approached the car, yelling at her in denigrating language. She responded with a deferential smile and thanked him in a syrupy tone for his good manners. Deflated, the cop sheepishly walked back to his BMW motorbike, trying to mask his bewilderment as best he could.

Duff Cooper, however, was a far more daunting challenge than the French motorcycle cop. The fifty-five-year-old ambassador disguised his natural shyness behind a reserved exterior. His intense eyes presided over a jowly face. Louise de Vilmorin's biographer, Jean Bothorel, noted how Duff projected "audacity and good fortune, was graceful in spirit as well as in manners, had a heart full of fantasy . . . his long and fine hands, the haughty demeanor, and a slightly offset gaze marked by a mysterious charm." After he fell for Louise, her friend, the writer Jean Cocteau observed: "It is exploding in his eyes. He looks like a fisherman who has caught a mermaid but who is still fishing with all his attention focused on the fishing, the ocean, the sale of the fish etc."

Duff with "Willow" at St. Firmin, 1952

Duff's diaries from the forties reveal that his roguish "habit of a lifetime" was in full force. Soon after arriving in Paris, he was rekindling old flames and starting new ones. He noted, "Marlene Dietrich, whom I hadn't seen much since Hollywood at the beginning of 1940, hasn't changed much."

Lady Diana's biographer, Philip Ziegler, gives a plausible account of Duff's early romance with my mother. Although he may overemphasize the extent to which Diana calculatingly recruited my mother, Zielger's account of the origins of the affair aligns well with what my mother told me after her revelations about Duff's being my biological father. Mother said it started in the fall of 1945 when Diana assigned her a seat next to Duff at an embassy dinner party, an unusual honor for a twenty-seven-year-old diplomat's wife. It was Susan Mary's habit to give credit to others, and, typically, she ascribes it here to Lady Diana.

In a carefully edited letter to my grandmother, my mother described her first encounter with the fifty-five-year-old ambassador:

> After dinner to my horror I was forced to play bridge with the Ambassador [Duff] against the Swedes. This took place in a great cold drawing room [of the British embassy] untouched since the days of the Duke of Wellington, lit by candles. I had hopeless cards and played very badly when I did have them, and although Duff Cooper was very kind to me I longed to be back in Washington cozily singing the Eton Boating Song with Lord Halifax. Shortly after this debacle we left, I as always cheered by Lady Diana.

Ziegler suggests that my mother was specifically chosen by Diana, who was concerned about Duff's health. By 1946 he found himself "trembling so violently" he could not reach his newspaper and had "a kind of rigor" with a high fever and later "terrible gouty rheumatic pains in my right foot." His doctor told him that his "liver and kidneys were in a bad state." Diana saw my mother as "a tranquil business, a refuge between the emotional storms of Louise [de Vilmorin] and the tempestuous orgies of the Whore of Babylon [Daisy Fellowes]."

The "Whore of Babylon" was an old English friend—the Singer sewing machine heiress, who, as Ziegler says, was "no nonsense" when it came to sex—and an old flame of Duff's from the 1920s who did not appeal to Diana. Louise de Vilmorin, on the other hand, was more of a social fixture in Paris and appealed to Diana even though she was demanding.

When Duff told Loulou (as Louise was known) in May 1945 that Daisy had arrived in Paris, Loulou "was genuinely alarmed . . . it is remarkable how other women fear Daisy even now when she is 55." Loulou was the kind of woman who, according to my mother, "threw her butter ball to the ceiling of the British Embassy dining room one day when she was not the center of attention."

As it turned out, Loulou suffered more from observing Duff's infatuation the next year with Gloria Rubio y Alatorre. Gloria was the daughter of Raphael Rubio y Alatorre, and had been married first to Count Egon von Furstenberg, then to Prince Ahmed Fakhri in 1946. The day after a party to which Duff escorted Loulou on April 12, 1946, he bedded Gloria at "the very well named Auberge du Fruit Defendu." The next day he wrote, "I have never loved anybody physically so much or been so supremely satisfied. We drove home by moonlight." The hotheaded Gloria was exactly the kind of woman who would appeal to the hunting instinct in Duff. After a tryst with her on the twenty-sixth, he wrote, "I never heard the nightingales sing so loudly as those in the trees under her window, and was never happier."

Ziegler notes that Louise had become overly possessive. Moreover, she was both anti-Semitic and anti-American, which repulsed Duff. After she lashed out at him at her country house, which as Duff says in his diary "should have hurt me but it didn't," he told Loulou plainly the next month that he "did not intend to give up seeing Gloria." He notes in his diary that it would be "much better if Loulou should go to America with her brother."

Loulou also had reason to be jealous of my mother, who, since the bridge game at the embassy, had slipped unobtrusively but effectively into the Cooper household. It was after a subsequent game of bridge, recorded by Duff in February 1947, that he "kissed Susan Mary for the first time." "I find her most attractive," he concluded. My mother had enlisted Diana's help early in the summer of 1946 with a big charity ball at Pré Catalan, "that romantic restaurant in the Bois de Boulogne." Wearing a dress that she said Balenciaga had made for her for fifty dollars, she sat between the French writer Jean Cocteau and Duff Cooper. My mother credited Diana with making the event oversold and a "huge success."

Duff's diaries reveal candidly just how emotionally one-sided his relationship with my mother was. While repeatedly referring to Susan Mary as "sweet" and noting that he "would do anything for her," after receiving four letters from her, Duff warily observes in the following May that she is "sick" with passion for him and that he is not "in love" with her.

Duff may have detected a sacrificial quality in her devotion, which he describes in his diary as "a strange imaginative affair—very flattering to me but a little disturbing. She is a sweet and charming girl whom I find most attractive, but it would be dishonest to pretend that I am madly in love with her." He responded to her gushing letter by thanking her but warned her not to get too carried away by the glamour of his position. She immediately replied, blandly dismissing his concerns.

Duff also wrote in his diary, "Nor have I the desire to cloud the happiness of what has seemed to me to be a perfect *ménage.*" My mother kept stressing to him Bill's "unfailing kindness to her," so the whole affair must have puzzled Duff. Her expressions of loyalty to her husband and her excessive modesty must have puzzled him as well. Most of his mistresses were either passionate women like Gloria or egocentric ones like Loulou, hardly the types to be overcome with ambiguous feelings of guilt.

Neither Duff nor Diana seemed bothered, however, by Loulou's jealousy of my mother, and in his July 9, 1947, diary entry Duff wrote: "I worked all afternoon, and when I returned went into the *salon vert* where there was the usual collection. Susan Mary was there and she came into the library with me for a few minutes. When we went back I had it seems the marks of powder on my shoulder which Diana brushed off laughing—but Louise took a less light-hearted view."

Duff spent part of the next six months dodging the ever-present Loulou. On January 27, 1948, Loulou came to pick him up with a car before a luncheon date he had with my mother. So Duff had the car drop him off at the Traveler's Club on the Champs-Elysées before slipping off to meet my mother at the popular Chez Larue restaurant, near the Place de La Madeleine. "We had a highly successful lunch and Susan Mary was extremely sweet. I am very fond of her."

Meanwhile, as he traveled to Europe often and had an ear for gossip, Joe Alsop in Washington had probably heard of my mother's budding affair with Duff. He had, for example, attended the ball my mother organized in 1946 where she was seated next to Duff. In late April 1947 Joe wrote my mother a telling letter about the imminent marital dissolution of their friends Marietta and Desmond FitzGerald: "I fear the worst, and think they had better get it over with. I am also of the opinion that everything would be better now if Marietta had just gone to bed with a few of the types who mooned around her all through the war. This business of being loved really for your bosom, but ostensibly for your high ideals, is on the whole deluding."

It is impossible to know how my mother read these opinions, but she did not go to bed with Duff with the alacrity that her husband's best friend seemed to be promoting. Ziegler mentions that it took awhile for Duff to get my mother to sleep with him. Though they may well have slept together during the summer of 1947, the first documented tryst was not until October—around the time of my creation.

Joe Alsop at Versailles with Ronald and Marietta
Tree, November 1947

Working back from my birth on July 4, 1948, it seems likely
that the fateful event occurred during an October weekend in
1947 at Ditchley Park, the country house of Marietta and
Ronald Tree. The handsome Oxfordshire estate had been the
designated refuge for Churchill during the war, when it was
judged best for him to be out of London—or *When the Moon
Was High*, as Ronald Tree titled his memoirs of this period.

As Joe had anticipated, Marietta had finally left her American
husband, Desmond, and by October 1947 she was in residence as
the hostess of Ditchley. Lady Diana was conveniently traveling.

Recalling Ditchley that fall, Duff wrote: "The house was looking more beautiful than ever and the new hostess, Marietta, is worthy of it. I found her beautiful, not the kind of beauty I admire most—blonde, serene like a goddess of the ancient world, serious-minded but with plenty of sense of humour . . . The arrangement of the rooms was admirable. Susan Mary and I, in the pink and blue bedrooms respectively, had practically the flat to ourselves. Bill is in a nursing home [being treated for asthma] in London."

People have asked me about my mother's motivations for her affair with Duff. The most compelling forces in my mother's life evolved from a powerful brew of ambition and duty. She needed to be in control but was instinctively drawn to men in power.

At the same time she felt a profound sense of obligation to help her country and had what Joe Alsop called a "Florence Nightingale" complex, which compelled her to try to rescue others. On the most unconscious level, she also was working to live out the unfulfilled dream of her parents: to assume the role of a major ambassadress. The fact that Duff was the *ailing* hero of Munich, ambassador of one of our country's staunchest allies, and had a beautiful wife who endorsed the affair, was a combination that was hard to resist. It was as if the manager, Diana, was sending her into the game in the ninth inning as a pinch hitter—my mother's role was to keep the game going at all costs.

Mother was helping Diana take care of Duff and at the same time gaining the confidence of an important man. By the spring of 1947 Duff was bedridden with fever and was clearly not in good health. My mother inundated him with cheerful letters, even as she told him that she knew he was also corresponding with other women at the same time.

I never saw signs that sex was a driving force in my mother's life. She was not an earthy person. I never saw her get excited by a delicious plate of food. (It was always Bill and, later, my step-father, Joe, who met with the cook and worked on menus in our households.) I never saw her dig her hands into the ground to plant something, and never saw her stroke a person's cheek or give anyone—child or adult—a really warm or lingering hug. In conversation she referred to sex with a kind of clinical detachment often couched in wry humor.

My mother was not a woman who was easy to genuinely please. I felt this from as early on as I can remember. Perhaps the best gift I gave her—probably self-interested, as I had just got my driver's permit—was a new red Camaro in the 1960s that had a powerful engine. It was the only present she ever thanked me for more than twice. She wrote me: "I never enjoyed myself more, having forgotten the joys of rapid acceleration . . . On Route 301 from the Bay Bridge to Mrs. Wisner's, nowadays a dual 4 lane highway, I couldn't resist asking Joe how fast he thought we were going, 'Too fast!' he said."

The power that Duff embodied, however, was the kind of tested self-confidence of someone who was used to high position and noblesse oblige but who still offered the chance to be near what Nancy Mitford called "history on the boil." As Mitford acutely noticed, my mother belonged to the "Henry James type of expatriate . . . A bit of the serious side perhaps, but at least they don't jabber on about art and dollars."

By the time they had gone to bed together, my mother no doubt felt guilty about cheating on her husband. But she was re-assured knowing that the sex for Duff was a passing ritual with no strings attached—or so she naïvely assumed. As she wrote Duff in the spring of 1947, "You like women, you have immense charm, and in your world it is normal."

Susan Mary holding Billy, 1948, *Vogue* magazine

A good clue as to how out of touch my mother was with her body was that during the first five months of her pregnancy she assumed she had a "liver problem." She blamed this on French doctors' obsession with the liver, but says she only noticed it herself when she became aware "how tight my clothes were becoming." Given her long history of anorexia, it was easier for her to ignore the disruptions in her menstrual cycle than it would have been for most women. Whether it was denial or ignorance, she was clearly not looking forward to getting pregnant. However, according to Marina Sulzberger's daughter, Marinette Berry, after learning of my mother's pregnancy, Marina persuaded Mother to keep the baby, arguing that it would give Bill Patten much pleasure.

My birth in July 1948 did not interrupt the affair—at least on one level. That October, almost exactly a year after their Ditchley tryst, Duff and my mother met again in a private room at the Café de Paris. Responding to my mother's insistence that "We mustn't do anything so dangerous again," Duff reported cavalierly, "It now seems that last spring Bill made her a great scene of jealousy about it. I had no idea."

There is no other record of this "scene of jealousy," but perhaps Bill discovered that he was not the one who had caused my mother's pregnancy. The letters from my mother to Duff's biographer, Charmley, apparently gave him reason to assert that Bill knew about her affair. His old friend Charles F. Adams, who used to visit the Pattens in Paris and go for walks with Bill, told me in 1997 that he didn't think Bill knew about my parentage. However, I wouldn't be surprised if Bill suspected the truth but chose not to investigate it further.

Cecil Beaton painting, St. Firmin, 1949

Even though my mother was aware that back in England he was already engaged in other illicit relationships, Charmley mentions that my mother's affair with Duff continued longer than Bill realized. My mother accepted the double standard of her involvement with Duff, fully recognizing that he had more glamorous mistresses, like Lady Ann Rothemere. My mother said she understood her secondary role and was more than willing to be accepted like "a Rangoon minister's wife" by comparison. She frequently insisted in her letters that she was dull and ordinary.

Meanwhile, my mother had become so entwined with the Coopers that her sharp-tongued Paris friend Nancy Mitford could not resist satirizing her in *Don't Tell Alfred*, published in 1960. The plot centers on a famous ambassadress—Lady Leone— who refuses to leave the Paris embassy, "having held a glittering court there, reminiscent of the great embassies of olden days" even after her government has recalled her husband. My mother is portrayed as a sycophantic and enabling American, Mildred Jungfleisch, who smuggles food into the embassy for the ambassadress.

Noticing my mother's executive strengths, Nancy character- ized her as "camp commandant you might say." When Mildred was asked what "she liked best in the world," she answered, "En- glish top policy-makers."

My mother's attraction to "top policy-makers" was more pressing than any social aspirations. She did not share Duff's thrill in socializing with royalty. What Duff and my mother shared was a love of history, literature, and foreign affairs. They both wrote historical biographies and cultivated friendships with celebrated historians like David Cecil and Isaiah Berlin.

My mother told me more than once after her disclosure at St. Mary's what a great "conversationalist" Duff had been. It was this intellectual dialogue, my mother in the role of avid student, that sustained their connection after Duff left France. And on some level she loved him, even from a distance, as the father she never had.

My mother wrote to Nancy Mitford to let her know that she was not angry about the parody of her, and in fact sent the book to friends, such as American diplomat David Bruce, to show that she had risen above it. After receiving the accomodating letter from my mother, Nancy replied that "when I saw I had a letter from you, I was so nervous I had to make Debo [her sister, the duchess of Devonshire] open it. I think you are angelic. The fact is, of course, Mrs. Jungfleisch is partly you." It was, I suspect, still hurtful to my mother, and a couple of times when we were alone I picked up her feelings of ambivalence about the novelist. Evelyn Waugh noticed my mother's resilience, writing in a letter to Nancy that my mother was "a tough, appreciative little guest" when she once spent an overnight with his family in England.

In the 1970s, nearly two decades after the men in her life had died or she had left them, my mother took her turn at writing for

Evelyn Waugh, St. Firmin, April 1953

publication. In her own indirect style she replayed her romance with Duff in her lively account of social life during the 1815 Congress of Vienna, *The Congress Dances,* published in 1984.

My mother must have identified with Talleyrand's beautiful young niece Madame de Perigord, who loyally served as the French envoy's hostess in Vienna during the conference. I never confirmed this with my mother, but the parallels between her youthful worship of Duff and Madame de Perigord's unquestioning dedication to Talleyrand are undeniable. Although my mother would not have known this, French historians now believe that the relationship between Talleyrand and his niece was platonic.

Though the affair with my mother may have been a quiet interlude for Duff, it was a transforming experience for her. She, along with some of Duff's other mistresses, helped plan a secret farewell party for Diana before the Coopers left the embassy in December 1947, though there is no record of whether she joined her fellow mistresses in performing a unicorn ballet that was created for Diana. It is hard to know whose departure my mother mourned most, Duff's or Diana's.

Some twenty years after her affair with Duff, while I was in college, my mother wrote to me, saying: "London is gay as a cat & I was wined & dined & spoiled, but also spent the last week with Diana who hasn't any servants poor love, so I was scrubbing & cleaning & carrying trays up four flights." For someone I never saw wash a bathtub and who was used to having breakfast in bed by herself for all of her adult life, this devotion reveals the profound admiration and love she had for Diana. Nancy Mitford had visualized this scene of devotion a decade earlier in *Don't Tell Alfred,* in which Mildred is seen carrying a picnic basket of food into the embassy "like a raven" to nourish the famous Pauline, Lady Leone. When someone comments admiringly on this effort, we are informed that in fact "Food means nothing to Pauline."

Bill Patten, Beaulieu-sur-Mer, summer 1951

nine

The Sad Brave Smile

Everyone I passed will, I feel sure, benefit from the
sad brave smile I bestowed on them & resolve to lead
better, cleaner & more honorable lives.

— FROM A LETTER OF BILL PATTEN'S DESCRIBING BOARDING

A FRENCH LINER ON HIS WAY TO THE UNITED STATES

THE SUMMER BEFORE HIS DEATH

In the spring of 1960 the door opened quietly, and there, standing in the back of our classroom, we saw Froggy, our headmaster. Mr. Sprawson had deep lines in his face. He never raised his voice, and seemed to drift around the school as if in a trance. None of us at Beachborough School had ever before seen him interrupt another teacher's class.

Froggy was an ex-RAF night bomber pilot and had been the captain of one of the old Lancaster bombers that flew into Germany at night. He spoke little, and never about the war. He had appeared a few years after I arrived at Beachborough, and reminded me of a nondescript actor in one of the black-and-white war movies we were allowed to watch once a week in the library on an old linen screen.

"Billy," he said quietly, "please come with me." I froze inside.

Marina Sulzberger and Duff Cooper, St. Firmin, March 1953

Teachers, especially the headmaster, always called us by our last names.

I followed him down the main hallway toward the head-master's wing and into the private lounge that he and his wife used for themselves. It was a surprisingly pleasant room, looking out as it did on the front terrace of the school where we did our morning exercises. It felt like a cozy sitting room, something you would see in a real home, not in an institution. There, sitting on a couch, were my mother and Marina Sulzberger. Mrs. Sprawson was there too, I think, standing. I knew instantly why my mother was there.

I had grown up with my father's wheezing, as he had the bedroom next to mine. It was a muffled sound that I assumed would last forever. But when I saw my mother on that couch in the headmaster's office, I knew in an instant that my life was going to somersault.

Bill Patten, my father, had died on March 26, 1960, in Paris.

The details of Mr. Sprawson's face have stayed with me more clearly than those of my father. I was ten when I met Mr. Sprawson and knew him for only two years before my father died, but his face and quiet catlike walk remain etched in my mind.

Over Easter my mother took my sister and me on a vacation to visit friends in Genoa. On a table in the living room of their villa I saw a book titled *My Brother's Death,* written by Marina's husband, Cyrus, a journalist. I started flipping through it, fascinated by the gruesome descriptions of Roman emperors using humans to experiment with agonies on the threshold of death. As I closed the book, I noticed it was dedicated to my father. Sulzberger wrote in the dedication that Bill Patten "understood the problem."

What problem? I hadn't seen a problem. What kind of dirty secret had been kept from me? I kept thinking of the horrible torture scenes in the book, like there was something tucked away in my reptilian brain that I should have known about but that had been obscured from view.

One of the difficulties of working on this book has been trying to find ways to bring my father Bill Patten to life. Unlike the other three main characters, there is almost no written material about him, and my own memories are very sketchy. After four years of trying to resurrect him, I have been forced to realize how much his life was hidden from me as a child, how much his memory is wrapped in family myth, and, finally, how different I am from him.

I can understand how Bill might have chosen to look the other way after he learned of his wife's affair with Duff Cooper, but it is difficult for me to reconcile the coziness of their relationship, particularly considering the high-handed way Duff seemed to treat my father in Paris. Their friendship—and there seems no better word for it—can be seen through Bill's letters to my mother, which I doubt were untruthful.

If, as I believe, Bill had suspicions about my birth, it's strange to me how quickly he seems to put them aside. Throughout my mother's affair Bill was actively socializing with Duff. Although my mother had told Duff in May 1947 that her husband was a Puritan who would never forgive her if she were unfaithful to him, it appears that Bill not only forgave my mother but also got along famously with Duff. Six months after my birth, Bill writes to my mother, who is in America, about an "unusually pleasant" visit to the Coopers' country house with his dog Charlus. At lunch, he writes, "Duff got into one of his veiners over the Times with Frank Giles," and he ends by saying, "Billy and I miss you frightfully." These "veiners" were well-known signs of Duff's temper, when the veins on his face would stand out.

Later that same month, amid a busy social schedule, Bill mentions that Duff Cooper "forgets" a dinner date at his house, which did not seem to annoy my father but left an uncomfortable social mix. Bill seems to have smoothed things over and accepted that the date might have slipped from the ambassador's mind, and rather amazingly he displays no signs of irritation about having been stood up. This apparent lack of bitterness is one of the mysteries I face in rediscovering my father.

All through the late forties and early fifties Duff and Bill regularly appear in photos together either in the little courtyard of our house on the Rue Weber or standing together outside a church in Venice. Lady Veronica Maclean, the wife of diplomat and World War II spy Sir Fitzroy Maclean, compiled a cookbook of "Diplomatic Dishes" from her worldly friends in Paris and London. In addition to the recipes, there are two or three pages showing the exact seating arrangement at several dinner parties. In January 1950, the month my sister was born, we see the seating chart for a dinner at the American embassy. The host, ambassador David Bruce, was a Southern patrician who had first married a woman from the wealthy Mellon family and then a younger woman he had met during the war. What caught my eye was the seat of the *New Yorker* correspondent Janet Flanner: seated on her right was Duff, and on her left was Bill. Both my mother and Lady Diana were absent.

Beyond the fact that they lived in the same social circles, I expect Duff liked Bill, as everyone seemed to, and, as mentioned before, was not entirely comfortable cuckolding him. Still, I feel a messy swell of emotions when I think about Bill's response. Sometimes I feel contempt, sometimes admiration. There is no clear or easy answer in my mind as to how Bill "should" have reacted to my mother's affair with Duff. And no one alive today has all the facts about the situation.

Bill also has been illusive to me partly because he was always one of the popular guys and I wasn't. As one of the last to be picked in stickball games at Groton, I feel a vague kind of cultural barrier between my father and me—the same feeling I had when I arrived at Groton and was teased mercilessly for my English accent. It is as if Bill belonged to some kind of club into which—even though his old friends try to be nice to me—I will never really be accepted.

In adulthood, my best friends—many of them Cubans, African Americans, and hippies—have tended to identify as outsiders, as I do. I still feel a kind of unconscious irreverence, which erupts when I find myself surrounded by the New England WASP world in which the father with my name grew up. It's as if I set myself up to make a blatant faux pas in these situations. Despite the huge changes in my life over the past decades, I have never completely reconciled myself to Bill Patten's Boston Brahmin world.

In September 2007 my second wife, Sydney, and I attended the funeral of my Harvard classmate George Peabody Gardner, known to most of us as "Peabo," at Harvard Memorial Church. The historic church was packed with WASPs, and I found myself sitting next to an impeccably dressed and youthful-looking Tony Zane, the retired headmaster of St. George's School, whom I had not seen in more than thirty years. I realized then that I was possibly the only man in the church wearing a light-colored suit.

More profoundly, when Peabo's son, Gus, spoke about his father's life, how Peabo had never accomplished huge feats but did small things with love and grace, how he worked hard for Harvard but how the family always came first, and when Reverend Peter Gomes, who had worked with Peabo at Harvard, called him "one of the good guys," I began to feel my father's presence. Walking out of the church at the end of the service, I felt a hand tap me on my shoulder from behind. I would not have been surprised to find myself looking at Bill Patten.

In addition to feeling out of place in Bill's own WASP backyard, as I look back at my early childhood in Paris, I see that in those days Bill was largely hidden from me by intermediaries. Most of the hands-on child rearing was done by my governess, Mademoiselle Oger, whom we called Mazelle. She supervised my daily routine until I left for boarding school at the age of nine.

Mazelle replaced the English nanny, Miss Clark, when I was about three years old and we still lived on the Rue Weber. My sister, Anne, and I lived on the top floor. I remember the day Mazelle arrived; she walked into the bathroom, where my sister and I were taking a bath together, supervised by Miss Clark.

Growing up, Anne and I attended French private schools near the Avenue Victor Hugo, and I found them mostly dark and terrifying. I was perhaps three or four the first time I was sent to one of these places. These early schools inhabited grim buildings that were tucked behind courtyards and down bleak alleys and run by exasperated teachers. There was no connection

Nurse Clark with Billy at Christmas, 1950

between these noisy hostile environments and the high ceilings and quiet formality of our home life. In 1956 we moved from our house on the Rue Weber to an elegant apartment on the Avenue d'Iéna overlooking, rather appropriately, La Place des États-Unis.

Life at home revolved mostly around Edmond, the butler; Jeannine, the tight-lipped maid; and Nicholas, the gentle white-haired Russian cook, whose faces I remember as distinctly as my father's. Edmond had a bump on his forehead and generally carried the world on his shoulders. I have no recollection of Miss Clark, the English nanny who took care of us the first four years of my life.

From the beginning my mother's letters to her mother reveal dubious feelings about my existence: From Biarritz two months

Le Cours Berge, Paris, author top row, fifth from left, 1955

after my birth, she wrote her mother that taking care of me was "becoming much more complicated a game. His favorite nurse's day out game is to simulate a violent colic attack, turn purple, howl like mad, legs drawn up on his chest & fists clenched, body rigid. When I pick him up he gives me a seraphic smile and goes heavily to sleep, but of course if I put him down the pain starts again."

My mother continued to see more streaks of Duff's veiners in me. In November 1949 she writes her mother from the French town of Senlis: "I bought Billy a biggish truck to push about but it was badly made and he broke it at once by sitting on it, I suppose thinking to drive it. He is very destructive and violent—his first idea is to throw anything new as hard as possible on the floor to see what happens, preferably on marble as it makes more noise. However, he is as sweet-natured as ever."

My development as a baby seemed to perplex her. Her letters to her mother in the summer of 1951 refer to my "strange" fascination with trains. I was taken to a bridge near the Gare du Nord, where, according to my mother, I spent a rapturous hour hanging over the sooty tracks looking at every sort of train that came by. "He has lost his fear of their noise," she reported.

Occasionally, having a toddler around seemed to bring some pleasure into her fragile sense of family life. Shortly before Christmas of 1950 she wrote to her mother about coping with "the usual nightmare of intra-American entertaining and getting together with people one doesn't want to see. However, I am enjoying Billy's enthusiasm, he knows something is up and calls it Kissmas—he has gotten the idea that it has something to do with kissing."

By the time I was eight, in her letters to friends my mother had turned me into a little political pundit. She wrote my godmother, Marietta Tree, in 1956, that "I found Billy hotly political." She continued: "Billy lectured me fiercely on Suez. He feels very gunboaty and is extremely worried lest this be another Munich." Of course, I had never heard of Suez, let alone Munich.

My mother was sometimes aware of the blocked communication between us even when I was eleven. After a weekend in the fall of 1959 at the Berrys' when she dropped in to see me at Beachborough, she wrote Marietta that for once I seemed "a touch homesick," and she confesses that "it was torture to have him cling tightly to my hand & not be able to find out what had gone wrong, he will always be too brave and too pent up."

Whereas I have clear images of our butler and nannies, my father Bill remains a fuzzy but touchable memory. I remember sitting on his lap; I could feel the unshaved bristles on his face, and he smelled of Old Spice. He sat next to me in the rowboat on the Lac du Bois de Boulogne and was patient in teaching me to feather the oars. One day, as I was lying lazily in the bath before being sent to bed, he reminded me to wash well.

Bill and Billy Patten, Senlis, 1957

My father had a big dimple above his chin, and dimples appeared on his cheeks when he smiled. He used a wooden walking cane with a burled handle. He usually wore English-made custom suits with a waistcoat and a gold watch chain. He would ask me to blow on the side of the gold watch to make it open.

My cousin and ex-mother-in-law, Kitty Jay Bacon, who lives on a beautiful farm in Vermont, told me recently that when she was a little girl, my father evoked a "sense of safety" when he visited her family's compound in Westbury, Long Island. I was interested that she used that phrase, raised as she was in the athletic, foxhunting world on their great estate. No great athlete himself, Bill somehow conveyed a sense of comfort to people in far better physical condition.

Billy and Anne Patten, Paris, 1952

Perhaps the key to Bill's projection of safety was time; I remember that he climbed stairs slowly, moved slowly, drove slowly, and lived slowly enough to absorb the moment. This could be felt easily next to my mother's brittle impatience. Bill had no choice but just to be, which gave him time to listen well to people and make them feel heard.

In contrast to my mother's air of detachment and coolness, the photos in our albums show Bill lifting my sister and me with the natural ease of a confident parent. A childhood friend from Paris, Vicky Mortimer, whom I had not spoken to in more than forty years, said recently that the memory of Bill brought back to her "that wonderful character with a delightful laugh, who loved children and mesmerized them with his way of peeling an apple."

Billy and Anne Patten between David and Marinette Sulzberger, St. Firmin, 1953

Last winter, in an old hatbox in our attic in the Pyrenees, I found another batch of letters I had never seen from my father to my mother in the forties and fifties. What emerges is how central the lives of his children were to him. He describes in detail his visits to my English boarding school, going to see the children's movie *Sinbad the Sailor* with my sister, and sailing back to the States with my sister and our French maid, Jeannine. His anecdotes are detailed and vivid. He reports to my mother in February 1949: "Billy has completely recovered & is learning to use his vocal cords more & more each day. The house rings with his gurgling & shrieks of mirth."

After visiting me at Beachborough in the spring of 1959, my father wrote my grandmother about watching me score a few runs at cricket, and how my face was assuming "its more mature form & expression. His nose is distinctly forming & a bit prominent. His mouth will not be large & his jaw firm. SM [Susan Mary] says these are all the characteristics of Mr. Jay."

He writes of how one Easter weekend he is apparently alone with the children at St. Firmin, the Coopers' country house outside Paris, and while we are outside egg hunting he notices that it has started to rain. He mentions this to Lady Diana, who scoffs it off, saying that it will do the children good to get wet. He then castigates himself in the letter for not standing up to her and refers to himself as a "milktoast." But apparently the rain soon stops and he describes his relief. This self-deprecating anecdote resonates in my mind, especially when I think of how much Bill tolerated Duff's presence in our household.

The "milktoast" image he refers to here emerges in Bill's letters when he seems to be dancing around the issue of my mother's loyalty to him. In one letter addressed to her in Grosvernor Square, London, and written from "Your mother's" in Maine, where he was staying with the children the summer of 1959, he says he had previously written "a dull letter" to remind her that "you are married." He makes light of it, but it appears that he crossed out "*were* married" and replaced it with "*are* married."

From the French liner *Flandre*, which he took with Anne and Jeannine in the summer of 1959, Bill writes a letter to my mother, revealing the sense of powerlessness he felt at times, almost a kind of embarrassment at all the extra trouble he was causing with being ill. Although I never saw him in a wheelchair, he describes the special reception he is given when their Paris train reached the maritime station with perhaps a small note of sarcasm:

> We formed a convoy or Flying Wedge led by Nurse then self "roulant" orderly furnishing the front with Anne & Jeannine & porters & various passengers were scattered to right and left, mail trucks moved & the baggage left was allowed to be only half filled in order not to crowd the gallant buffoon. Up we went to [the] appropriate level, across a pleasantly draughty covered shed toward a ramp

leading to the open quai on which passengers were going up—naturally we skirted the queue[,] at the head of which I took the salute of the French Line Officials, local gendarmes, customs men and representatives of the 2eme Bureau. Out to the open quai and up the gang plank to the waiting lift [and from] there down to our state-rooms. Everyone I passed will, I feel sure, benefit from the sad brave smile I bestowed on them & resolve to lead better, cleaner & more honorable lives.

Writing from Mount Desert Island in Maine that July, he starts by saying: "Anne really is a treasure, not that the other one isn't too. She has behaved so well & has been such a good companion, really ideal." Trying to update my mother on current U.S. politics, later in the letter he writes: "I have faded from the World Picture to an incredible extent & feel I shall remain in the shadows until you get here."

Bill's letters to my mother tell the story of a man whose world centered on his wife and who felt comfortable in the social world she had created for them in Paris. Life is "hellish" in her absence; he misses her with an uncomplaining but totally unfeigned passion. His energy is divided between being stoic on the one hand and lighthearted on the other, often making himself the butt of his own jokes. He writes again that summer: "I have found nobody of either intellectual or sexual interest to arouse me from the state of lethargy I always feel when we are separated."

As my mother sets off to the United States in September 1955 on the liner *Isle de France,* Bill gently teases her. A lovely twenty-five-year-old just-divorced American girl is living in an empty apartment nearby, about whom he writes:

> She was perhaps not quite of Our World—she uses both a spoon and fork on melons cut in half—but she is so pretty that it would be

Bill and Susan Mary Patten, Senlis, June 1947

enormous fun to do a Pygmalion with her & she is lonely (I think) &
so am I (I know). But you will soon be back & unless the weather
breaks cool and clear have no fears for my fidelity—I cannot be romantic and wheeze at the same time as you know, furthermore my
progress in that direction could not be termed rapid by any stretch of
the imagination.

He ends the letter telling my mother: "I worship you!"

Despite this affection, my parents' bedrooms were distinctly
set apart from each other in our large Paris apartment. My
mother's bedroom was in the middle of the apartment facing the
interior courtyard. My father's bedroom was in the front facing
the Avenue d'Iéna. He had a big walnut dresser on the top of
which he would empty the contents of his pockets. My room was
next to his, somewhat larger. It had tall ceilings, a marble fireplace,
large John Leach hunting prints on the walls, a huge chandelier,
and a balcony. It also served as a guest room when I was away at
school. My father and I shared the bathroom between our rooms.

My sister lived at the back end of the apartment next to Mazelle's room, while I played alone with my toy soldiers in a room on the front side, facing the park. A long, narrow servant hallway connected the front and the back of the apartment.

One day I walked into my father's bedroom without knocking. The curtains were closed, but I could still see the two massive steel oxygen tanks that stood near the head of his bed attached to a ghoulish-looking rubber mask. My mother was sitting in an armchair next to his bed reading to him. The book was called *The Ship That Died of Shame*, the tale of an unemployed postwar captain who feels forced to sell his honor—and that of his ship—to a sordid smuggling scheme. I was upset at the time that my mother would be reading him a story that resonated so much with the theme of shame.

There was a dark cloud in his bedroom that Bill and my mother tried energetically to shield us from, but the gallantry of their public performance did not quite have the same inspiring effect on me as it did on their friends. It was not the prospect of death that cast the gloom so much as the hushed efforts to cover up something.

Looking back, I imagine Bill was as trapped as we were by my mother's benevolent cover-up schemes. She herself recollected in her first book: "My chief problem during those years was how much I should share my desperate concern about Bill's health with the children." She added: "It was hard for them to understand how their gay, fun-loving father could change overnight into a gasping, suffering figure, smiling heroically through an oxygen mask. Anne bore the brunt of the strain, for Billy soon went off to boarding school."

One day, out of the blue, my father asked me if I could do anything I wanted for one whole day, what I would like to do. I must have been about nine or ten. Given the highly scripted routine I was used to in a home life—planned by my mother but im-

Bill and Billy Patten, Versailles, October 1950

plemented by Mazelle—this invitation felt almost subversive. I am not sure what I answered, but I will never forget the question.

That may have been the day we went to see a movie together, *Moby Dick,* with Gregory Peck as Captain Ahab. Nor do I know for sure whether his question also rang a little alarm bell: the fleeting idea that my days needed to be infused with a little joy or even that these days were numbered. Or perhaps it was the excitement of imagining that a real world existed beyond the reaches of the "high command," which was what my mother's authority felt like.

I know it really happened because of a striking event on the way home in the taxi. I must have given my father an indication that I knew we were nearing the Avenue d'Iéna, because he asked me how I knew we were getting close to home. I told him, feeling quite clever, that I could tell because the driver turned on his radio to see about answering another call.

I have such desperately few memories of Paris that I have studied in detail the elegant family scenes captured in my

Bill Patten and Duff Cooper, Venice, September 1951

mother's beautiful photo albums. She created these albums on her own, writing the captions in her large elongated scrawl. In close to a dozen of these leather-bound albums, some with our initials on them and some with the years, my mother has recorded an extraordinary documentary set in the finest houses in Europe, revolving around the Pattens and the Coopers. I compare this with the fact that in neither Duff's nor Diana's memoirs is there a single mention of a family called "Patten." The pictures are real, but did this elegant tableau she created with a camera exist in real life?

Duff showed an instinctive distaste for the camera. In Venice, for example, Bill is in a white blazer with navy slacks; next to him is Duff in a light gray jacket and white shoes. Bill looks quite comfortable in front of the camera, but Duff projects a faintly tormented aura. Bill is smiling and reminds me of my sister, Anne; Duff's eyebrows are furrowed and he looks away from the camera.

Bill's graceful appearance apparently made a mark on the writer Evelyn Waugh, who wrote in the 1950s to Nancy Mitford that he had recently run across a "well-dressed Yank." He then made elaborate efforts to conjure up the correct spelling of the name "Patten" as if it belonged to an obscure Native American tribe.

These photographs make me think of us a little as well-dressed puppets, all dancing to my mother's tune as she saw fit. Fortunately, by sheer good luck I recently received some private letters that offer some more intimate insights behind this manicured portrait of our home life.

In the fall of 2007 I received a package from England from a Lord Swynnerton, the son-in-law and literary executor of Sir Gladwyn Jebb. Gladwyn was a man I dimly remember who was ten years younger than Duff but who held the same job in Paris as British ambassador between 1954 and 1960, the year my father Bill died. He had requested on the package that it be delivered to my mother unopened in the event of his death. The package contained her love letters to Gladwyn during the last years of my father's life. He had kept them with the intention of returning them to my mother but died before Lord Swynnerton could deliver them to her.

I had heard vague rumors of a liaison between Gladwyn and my mother but nothing more than that. These forty or so letters furnished an unexpected glimpse into her private thoughts, largely addressing her anguish over my father and his failing health during the last years of his life. They undoubtedly refer far more to my father than her letters to Duff did a decade earlier when Bill's death was not so imminent.

While it was certainly a romantic affair, with the titillations of a covert relationship, it also had the flavor of tradition and equanimity that always appealed to my basically risk-averse mother. In May 1960, after Bill's death, my mother wrote Gladwyn that his wife "Cynthia lunched here yesterday. I was so pleased, as I thought she seemed without dislike or jealousy of me. I overheard Joe whining to her that I was out with a different man for every meal (untrue) and I thought Cynthia looked relieved and happy."

According to these letters to Gladwyn, a Boston doctor had told my mother in the summer of 1959 that Bill had only a short time to live, and this death sentence was repeated by our French doctor in November. He warned her to expect to walk into Bill's bedroom one morning and find that his heart had stopped. "As it stands today, the doctor gives him about three months," my mother wrote to Gladwyn. She then asked Gladwyn whether she should warn me, explaining, "he is a self-controlled little boy but a worrier underneath." Presumably he advised her not to.

Bill and Billy Patten, Maine, summer 1952

My mother's flow of private letters from our summer home in Maine to Gladwyn during my father's final summer are gallant, entertaining, and a bit disingenuous. "Maine is always exhausting, I think family life in American family resorts always is," she starts off on August 3, in the absence of our governess.

> We are very group minded in Northeast Harbor, yes indeed. We have sailing groups and rowing groups and mountain climbing groups and tennis groups, divided into different age groups. After two days here I awoke to the sound of pouring rain, the music of archangels couldn't have sounded sweeter to me, but the pursuit of pleasure is inexorable, it appeared that on rainy days group activities continue indoors, one learns to tie knots and so on. Anne is made for this life, a natural conformer she has dozens of friends, poor Billy said to me, in humble admiration, "Isn't it wonderful how quickly Anne has learned to get on with the Americans?" Now, four days later, he is all right too, and is acquiring nearly as good a nasal accent as Anne.

She also portrays her role as smoothing out tensions between her mother and Bill: "Both spend most of the day lying about on the beautiful terrace of this house just on the verge of having a frightful row, but not quite having it, which would perhaps clear the air." My mother had a habit of projecting her own inner angst onto people like her mother and husband.

Sometimes the letters provide refreshingly honest glimpses into our home life, free of my mother's usual contrived cheerfulness. Writing from Northeast Harbor four days later, she tells Gladwyn: "Tonight the harbor has two yachts in it full of Bill's oldest Boston friends, Charles Adamses and Crockers and Cabots who have all gone far out of their way to see him, so we are off to a gay evening. I wish to God he was well enough to enjoy this sort of thing, but I am concerned about his fatigue. He turns the most awful blue gray color if he is long away from his oxygen tank in his room."

On September 1 she wrote Gladwyn, thanking him for his most recent description of staying with the chancellor of the exchequer in Scotland. She then reveals how much she relies on his letters:

> I take your letters up the mountain to read, close held in a pocket of my shorts, then I choose a sunny corner with a splendid view over the bays then I send the children off to look for some little known bird's nest, like the blue heron, and while the two poor little things hunt hopelessly I sink happily back against my warm rock and open the dear, longed for grey envelope and have my holiday . . .
>
> It's been a baddish ten days, Bill is weaker and discouraged. I think of Queen Victoria all the time—do you remember a vivid letter, I suppose to Crown Prince Frederick—in which she says that Prince Albert is so brave but that he complains ceaselessly of being tired—and begs her make the doctors find some answer for this—it's Bill's one complaint—again and again, "I'm so tired, so tired."

Susan Mary Patten, Lake Garda, August 1951

Toward the end of this six-page letter she adds: "It is hard to muster vitality, sometimes I don't think I can face going into Bill's room and I pause weakly, supinely at the door, I think of you and strength flows back and I turn the knob with ease. You are strong. I can't talk to my friends any longer about Bill, it's too pitiable, and I am told that I am considered hard boiled because I am so damned cheerful, but I can't talk, except to you."

Sir Gladwyn was at our family's side when Bill died the following spring in Paris. He was not only at the funeral at the American Cathedral on the Avenue George V but also, at my mother's coaxing, wrote letters of condolence to my sister and me. In his supportive letter to my mother, he noted that at the funeral: "I saw Anne firmly take hold of her grandmother and conduct her from the church! Billy was a little overwhelmed, perhaps, but he will soon recover." All I remember from the day of the funeral was being promised a ride on a Vespa by a young American at the reception at our apartment after the service and, to my immense disappointment, his not following through on his offer.

Writing from the village of Le Castellet in France's Var region on our spring vacation the month after Bill's death, my "exhausted" mother confides in Gladwyn: "Sad I am—not for Bill's dying but for his living so unhappily these last years. I tried, and failed, to make him share the fear and loneliness I saw so often in his eyes. The frustrating pain will never leave me—closeness is all & a cleverer, more tactful woman could have helped him." Gladwyn replied: "In a word, you succeeded in making a success of a life that practically nobody else could have made a success of; you added to the sum total of happiness when anybody else would have reduced it by quite a lot; and all that without getting sour & bitter, but always remaining kind & good."

My mother's anguish is a reminder of how easy it was to look at Bill as "a well-dressed Yank" without seeing the struggle behind the finely cut tweeds. In a perceptive letter of April 6 to the *London Times* after my father died, Lord Salisbury, head of the Cecil family, and former undersecretary of foreign affairs, noted that people should not forget the physical torture that lay behind my father's laughter: "Only by an occasional twisted smile could one know how much he was suffering."

I have reread the letters of condolence my mother received after Bill's death. Perhaps the most reflective one came from my parents' old friend Isaiah Berlin. He starts his letter by admitting his problems with believing in God. His observations about Bill paint the portrait of a man who lived with a firm New England sense of belief in the existence and goodness of a higher power:

> Did Bill die a Christian? Somehow I feel that he did: He possessed splendid roots in the firm tradition in which he grew, and so very solid and authentic, & dry skepticism and cautious agnosticism was no part of the stuff from which he was made—goodness me how I

admired his moral qualities, his uprightness, integrity, simplicity and goodness of character. I admire this and love it more than other qualities. I don't mind about charm or cleverness (of which he possessed more than enough)—the whole edifice which you built was so very handsome & fine & generous, & above all at all times, in all ways, young, fresh, unworn out, full of feeling & human.

It took a man of great feeling and humanness, I think, to perceive this "edifice" so clearly. I knew Isaiah a little from my weekends at his house in Oxford when I was in boarding school with his stepson, Peter Halban. Their house offered a kind of sanctuary from the school. Isaiah's wife, Aline, projected the same kind of warmth and gentleness.

Sometimes, however, I feel disappointed that Bill tolerated my mother's affairs so nobly—even for the sake of the handsome edifice, which people like Berlin seemed to admire so much. I get tired of hearing what an "attractive" guy he was, and sometimes long to discover some nasty little traits that would make him more human to me. So it was refreshing when in 1973 an old friend of Bill's broke through the halo my mother and others had planted over his head.

I had moved from Stanford Business School back to Massachusetts to find out more about Bill, arriving in Boston without a job. Bill's old friends rallied around, and one of them, Ephron Catlin, whom I did not know, hired me at the First National Bank of Boston. During my interview in his office I remember the shock of hearing Catlin say that my father had been "a lousy businessman." I appreciated the touch of reality he added not only to the picture I had of my father, but also to my image of the world of writers and diplomats I had grown up with, who mostly disdained the realities of business.

Still, Catlin admired Bill and would have agreed that his classmate's courage was the non-triumphant kind, the courage to play through the daily pain, not the kind of heroic action that gets recorded in history books. The fact that I was hired so quickly reflected my father's ability to establish and maintain the kind of human relationships that often outlast great political or financial feats.

After his death, some of Bill's best friends, Joe Alsop, Cy Sulzberger, and Charlie Adams, organized a scholarship at Harvard in his name to help students "who are traveling the hard road of self-development against odds." It has helped an extraordinary range of young people—from blind boys from the Bronx to Native American mothers—gain a decent college education.

But as hard as I have tried to disentangle Bill from the myths, it is perhaps in that world of legends where he belongs. He lingers in a warm and sunny haze, leaning on his cane, whistling *Pop Goes the Weasel!* He remains the smiling clubman, the laughing mixer of martinis, the "well-dressed Yank." At the same time, he is more than ever my father, the man I love.

I may not understand Bill Patten any better now than I did when I started writing this book, but I feel our kinship more strongly in mysterious little ways. Rather to my surprise, for example, I found this past year when I went to the Groton School campus to do some research on him, as I walked across the windy playing fields and into the dreaded basement of the schoolhouse, for the first time in my life I did not feel like an intruder or an alien.

Evidently my father lived on in that world of happy legends for my mother. She held him equal to Duff and her other friends from that period. In one of her most intimate letters to Sir Gladwyn, written to him the month after Bill died, she says she went to her desk and, as if by chance, found a letter from Duff that he had told her not to open for some time. Duff had died six years earlier. She tells Gladwyn that Duff's letter was "written shortly before he died for me to read now." She continues: "It could

Billy Patten, Corsica, 1960

easily have been from you, you write very much alike. He is cheerful, says that he won't live long but hasn't wanted to spoil the fun by telling me so, that he wants me to remember that Billy might go to Eton, which is arranged, but that this is my business . . . That there is however an argument for Eton."

Then she reports that Duff

naturally imagines that Bill dies soon after he did, and that I have been married for the last five or six years to a man who is either to become British ambassador to China, or the Secretary of State of the Russo-Atlantic Alliance, which was to have its capital in Berne but I have moved it to Paris because M. Balmain can't bear Switzerland . . . I cannot help feeling, just having put down this letter, that Duff and Bill and you might walk into this flat tonight, the three of you laughing having just come from the club.

Joe Alsop and Susan Mary Alsop, 1961

ten

Nabbing
My Mother

Live all you can; it's a mistake not to.

—FROM HENRY JAMES'S *THE AMBASSADORS*, QUOTED IN A LETTER

TO MY MOTHER FROM ARTHUR SCHLESINGER JR. IN 1960

JOSEPH WRIGHT ALSOP V came thundering into my life in the spring of 1961. He arrived at Beachborough within a year after my father Bill died. I was twelve and had already been away at boarding school for three years.

Eighty boys, the entire student body, were waiting in line in the main hallway to have our hands inspected by the prefects before going into the dining room for lunch. I heard a commotion coming from the headmaster's reception room. I could not make out the face, but I noticed a bald man in an olive-green suit marching down the line examining the face of each boy, almost as if it were a police lineup. Then, to my astonishment, I recognized my mother standing farther back with Froggy, our headmaster. The inquisitor was my godfather Joe Alsop. He was utterly out of context, or so I thought.

I was plucked from the line and invited to join him and my mother for lunch at the King's Arms, a local pub in Banbury, the

Beachborough School, Westbury, Northamptonshire, England

main town serving North Oxfordshire. I knew Joe a bit from his periodic visits to Paris, and I called him "uncle" not because I knew him well but because my mother expected me to. He was a tightly wound, physically compressed figure, and today he was elegantly dressed wearing his usual lively bow tie. What I remember most about the lunch was that after tasting his meal, he indignantly sent most of it back to the kitchen. It surprised me at the time, but even more so when I think that pub food is, after all, pub food. What was he expecting? I had seen my father return some food once in Paris, but he had done so almost invisibly, with a smile. Joe seemed genuinely outraged.

Joe Alsop was a nationally syndicated columnist who had worked in Washington most of his life. For thirty years his column, "Matter of Fact," appeared in nearly three hundred papers around the country. His work spanned the surrender of Japan in 1945 to the fall of Saigon in 1975. He partnered with his younger brother Stewart for the first twelve years of his journalistic career.

During this initial period Stewart tolerated his older brother's bossy style, no doubt because of their joint success. Reviewing a biography of the two brothers by Robert Merry titled *Taking On the World,* Stanford historian David Kennedy wrote, "To a degree equaled by few of their peers, and rarely exceeded in the history of their craft, Joseph and Stewart Alsop reigned in their time as the very highest panjandrums of American journalism."

Crusaders, Scoundrels, Journalists, an anthology of America's three hundred most intriguing newspeople from Thomas Paine and Mark Twain to Oprah Winfrey and Ted Turner, includes the Alsop brothers in the category "Political Animals." Their quote is taken from congressional loyalty hearings in 1948 and reads in part: "Does it really matter in America whether a man's . . . ancestors landed decorously on Plymouth Rock? There have been countless instances when, during loyalty hearings, individuals have been asked where their parents and grandparents were born. An entirely American response would be that it is none of the loyalty board's damn business."

That sounds like Joe. He used to castigate people who talked openly about an "American aristocracy." His reaction made me think of Shakespeare's line "The lady doth protest too much, methinks." Joe was obsessed with people's pedigrees. What made him squirm was when people talked about it openly.

The Alsops were a family of Connecticut merchants and gentlemen farmers. Joseph II accumulated a respectable fortune through shipping, but lost much of it in the economic panic of 1873. He still managed to leave his son, Joseph III, enough to live a comfortable life in Middletown until a cousin walked off with most of his assets. That left Joe's father, Joseph IV, with little choice but to make his own way when he graduated from Groton. Rather than pursue a career in New York or Boston, cities in which he had many connections, he bought a farm in

Theodore Roosevelt and Douglas Robinson

1902 near Avon, Connecticut. There he grew tobacco and raised dairy cattle. Three years later he met his future wife, Corinne Robinson, the niece of president Theodore Roosevelt.

I remember Corinne vividly. She wrote me a congratulatory letter after I was accepted by Harvard in 1966: "You met a difficult challenge and in my opinion have won an outstanding victory and though I am only a 'kind of grandmother' I am just as delighted by what you have done as though you were my very own."

Corinne was a lively and irrepressibly inquisitive woman who would interrogate the girlfriends I brought down from Harvard for country weekends on the farm. She would innocuously say, "Come here and sit by me, dearie," and then drill away at them with incisive questions. There was always the risk that Grandmother might be lying in wait when we came down for

Corinne Robinson Alsop Cole, Avon, Connecticut, 1960s

breakfast in the morning from the little second-floor bedrooms. I eventually devised a system of convoys that made it more difficult for Corinne to single out one of my friends as they headed across the dining room.

Joe inherited his curiosity from his mother; he had a similar ferocious appetite for engaging other people, but without her feminine charm. In answer to a question in 1966 about whether I should accept Harvard's offer to start with sophomore standing, Joe's good friend McGeorge Bundy, who as a dean there had been one of the architects of the program, wrote to me, urging me to collect more advice: "And who has a better right than Joe Alsop's step-son to ask questions of anyone—and on any subject? You do not have to ask them with Joe's inimitable snarl—but it is better to snarl a question than to smirk in the silent pretense of knowledge."

Joe adored Corinne, something I sensed when he became horrified the few times I was openly angry with my own mother. His maternal heritage fascinated him. He kept a photo of Henderson House, a stone castle in upstate New York built by his thrice-great-aunt, Harriett Douglas, in 1832. Corinne's grandfather inherited the house forty years later. His son, Corinne's father, Douglas Robinson, married Corinne Roosevelt, Theodore's bright and vivacious older sister.

Much has been written about the Roosevelt women. What stands out most vividly to me is the closeness, nearing on incestuous, of the family in which the future president grew up. The older sisters were passionately attached to their little brother "Teedie," so much so that Theodore had to persuade Corinne to marry Douglas Robinson. Although the marriage had some early challenges—separating from the Roosevelts was no easy charge—it was ultimately a long and successful one.

According to Joe's biographer, Robert Merry: "Corinne came closest to the Rooseveltian ideal [which] meant making people love you even as you dominated them. It meant walking into a room filled with people and conquering it. It meant converting Teddy Roosevelt's force of personality to female uses." That description of Corinne Roosevelt reminds me very much of Joe and his mother. The Roosevelt DNA is strong stuff.

Joe's mother and father, Corinne Robinson and Joseph Alsop IV, married in 1909 in a small ceremony that was subdued by a recent family tragedy. Not long before the wedding, drunk and quoting lines from Tolstoy's *War and Peace*, Corinne's brother, Stewart Robinson, had climbed out on a window ledge of Harvard's Hampden Hall and fallen to his death.

Joe kept the triumphs and tragic missteps of his extended family well in mind. He regularly preached to family members about how imperative it was for "our tribe to keep our noses above water." He got some morbid joy telling and retelling the

Nurse Agnes Guthrie "Aggie" with John, Stewart, Corinne, and Joe Alsop, Woodford Farm, Avon, circa 1917

story about Stewart Robinson, but he also reveled in the successes of his family, especially those of his nephews and nieces.

When it came to personality, Joe surely got his mother's genes. This was evident early on. Robert Merry writes that "little Joseph displayed a strong will, furious temper, and rare intellect." Even though he grew up on a farm, Joe had little interest in physical activity and essentially no interest in—or talent for—sports of any kind. He spent as much time as he could immersed in books, becoming something of a young bibliophile.

Although Joe could trace his lineage with authority, he was something of a country boy at Groton. In addition to being very fat, Joe was self-conscious about the faint tinge of manure on his boots. Even in my day at Groton a social chasm existed between those students who came from rural places and those who were from elegant suburbs on the North Shore of Boston or from private schools on the East Side of Manhattan. It was not until Joe

Joe Alsop, circa 1932

arrived at Harvard in 1928 that he was able to trump this nasty social division.

As so many young readers do, Joe naturally turned toward writing. He would have been delighted that historian David Kennedy described his work as a "craft" rather than a "profession." Joe considered himself a craftsman, one who preferred simple and direct language to ornate prose. According to his memoirs, President Nixon's White House counsel John Dean was so offended when Joe described him as a "bottom-dwelling slug" after the Watergate scandal that he went to his dictionary to find out exactly what a "slug" was. Having grown up on a farm, Joe certainly knew the definition, as did, I suspect, most of the reading public.

Joe acknowledged that his family had pushed him into journalism to keep him away from academia, where they feared he would become a full-fledged alcoholic like some of his forebears. Having spent years in the news business, I can say firsthand that this is "out of the frying pan into the fire" thinking, but journalism certainly suited Joe well. It also gave Joe some ammunition in the late 1960s to inveigh against the fashionable advice to "follow your bliss." He was naturally drawn to the academy and kept sneaking back into it through his erudite writings on art collecting and archeology.

No doubt, Joe gave his parents ample reason to worry about his drinking. In 1937, at the age of twenty-seven, he wrote one of his early books, *Drink, Eat and Be Thin: The Full Story of the Martini Drinker's Diet.* An early practitioner of the have-it-both-ways path to a trim figure, Joe advocated a low-carbohydrate diet that combined sirloin steak, hollandaise sauce (if real), maître d'hôtel butter, and a half bottle of claret.

A doctor's stern warning about his limited life expectancy if he didn't bring his weight under control jolted Joe into action in 1937. He went through the newly created Johns Hopkins diet program in Baltimore and lost sixty-five pounds in three or four months. The rest of his life, as his semi-serious book about the martini diet suggests, was a constant battle to maintain what became an impressively well-controlled physique while still indulging in the epicurean delights that are duly celebrated in his memoirs.

Though he lost the physical weight, Joe never quite lost the portentousness of a fat man, including the solo-induced bellows of raucous laughter. Even in his early career, his blimplike profile proved irresistible to artful writers like A. J. Liebling, who described Joe as "orbiting the earth like the moon, descending for a day or two now and then to lecture an Arabian King or a Bessarabian prelate on his duties."

Having chosen journalism, Joe never hesitated to capitalize on his family connections to both the Oyster Bay branch of the

Roosevelts and their Hudson River cousins. As a cub reporter for the *Herald Tribune* in the 1930s he dined with his close cousin Eleanor and his more distant cousin Franklin Delano Roosevelt at regular family dinners, which they held on Sunday evenings at the White House. Although he complained about the poor quality of the cooking, Joe took full advantage of his privileged vantage point by writing *The 168 Days* with Turner Catledge, a book about FDR's unsuccessful attempt to enlarge the Supreme Court, which became a best seller in 1938. He later wrote another book about FDR's administration titled *The Men around the President.*

Joe's personal relationship with FDR helped him secure a position in the Far East during the war, in which he served as a key aide and promoter of General Claire Chennault, the founder of the Flying Tigers. This field experience had a profound impact on Joe. He devoted nearly a third of his memoirs to his four years in Southeast Asia, a region that would consume his attention two decades later.

The war forced Joe to leave the sidelines and experience the action firsthand. At Groton, at Harvard, and then as a young reporter, Joe had positioned himself as an observer, an owl perched comfortably above the fray. In the war there were no safe perches. As he later wrote, "My years in China . . . were the only ones of my professional life in which I ceased to be a commentator from the sidelines and became a minor actor in the historical process itself."

Joe describes his "ridiculous" departure for the Far East the summer of 1941 in a Pan American clipper. He wore his "ceremonial naval finery" and carried a borrowed sword and "a huge Colt .45 pistol, terrifying to look at and a full 8 pounds in weight." Joe slipped while getting off the plane in San Francisco, "causing extensive traces," he noted, "on my formerly crisp dress-white trousers."

Despite all sorts of colorful adventures, such as smoking opium and expeditions across the countryside in wicker chairs carried by four men, during this time in China Joe confronted serious physical challenges, which he had carefully avoided through most of his life. After Hong Kong fell to the Japanese on Christmas Day 1941, and Joe's last chance of escape on a flight was foiled by his seat being taken by "Mme. H. H. Kung's very large, well-fed dog," he took the advice of the American military office in charge and changed back into civilian clothes. He had "a fair number of second-rate sapphires" sown into the collar of his tweed jacket in preparation for his internment.

Never missing a chance to illustrate the idiocy of passivism, Joe describes moving into the living quarters the Japanese had chosen for them on the Stanley Peninsula. There, in an "enchanting small villa above the rocks," they found the severed head of a "famous Chinese aesthete-intellectual and aggressive pacifist" who had paid dearly for his attitude of "be nice to the men from the north." Instead of worrying about the corpse, Joe scavenged through the dead man's library "and took as many books as I thought would fit into the bag I had brought out to Stanley expressly for the purpose." This included the *Analects of Confucius*, which he read during his time in camp with the help of "a wonderful American professor, Dr. Charlotte Gower."

After his liberation and return to the States, with the help of Roosevelt's aide Harry Hopkins, Joe returned to China as a civilian lend-lease administrator. There he became deeply involved in the politics that eventually led to General Joseph Stilwell's recall. The stiff and acerbic "Vinegar Joe," as he was known to his troops, was detested by the Chinese leader Chiang Kai-shek and his followers. But it was a long struggle devoted mainly to lobbying for the man he admired, the charismatic General Chennault. Despite General Marshall's objections, in February 1944 President Roosevelt gave Joe a commission on Chennault's staff,

General Chennault awarding Joe Alsop the Legion of Merit award, July 1945

where he worked "seven days a week, often twelve to fourteen hour days." He stayed in China until August 1945.

Joe emerged from the war with a newfound physical self-confidence to complement his abundant intellectual confidence. The war theater also gave him a direct opportunity to see powerful egos operating at full force and, quite often, at cross-purposes. Joe was accustomed to being in the presence of powerful men, but not as an adversary. The animal spirits unleashed in China and Southeast Asia were a very different beast. He had a remarkable vantage point to see close up the political machinations of extremely ambitious men.

During this period Joe met Duff Cooper. Traveling with General Chennault in Burma in December 1941 just before Pearl Harbor, Joe escorted Chennault to a meeting at Toungoo Station. There Chennault met with Duff, whom Churchill had recently appointed as special minister for Far Eastern affairs. The most memorable aspect of this meeting for Joe was walking into Lady Diana's compartment and finding that "she slept with the pupils of her eyes rolled up into her head so that what was left of her glorious eyes, still open, looked like a pair of white marbles." "Later," Joe wrote, "Lady Diana would become a dear friend, and I ceased to be disturbed by the memory of those white marbles . . . Diana went on being the most beautiful woman in the world until she was sixty."

The war galvanized Joe's view that America's proper role in the world was as an activist keeper of the peace, a promoter of freedom willing to use a Rooseveltian "big stick" as necessary. He recognized that the Communists were an emerging threat, and he believed that America should use its power to

Joe Alsop in Korea, 1950

promote global stability. He believed that America was the natural inheritor of Great Britain's role in the world. When it came to political philosophy or gentleman's clubs, Oxbridge or Savile Row, the Foreign Office or landed estates, Joe was a deep Anglophile.

Joe's self-confidence and willingness to stand up to powerful figures was tested during the McCarthy era. In what TV newsman David Brinkley would later call Joe's "greatest moment," Joe—and his brother Stewart—defended Robert Oppenheimer against the demagogue senator Joseph McCarthy. Shortly after Joe's death, Brinkley recalled on National Public Radio McCarthy "terrorizing this city, the town caved in, the press caved in . . . except Joe Alsop and his brother, who attacked him relentlessly in their column day in day out."

Of course, I was unaware of all this. Joe swept into my life with little warning. His disruptive arrival at Beachborough with my mother is my first real memory of him. The previous winter, during a walk in Chantilly over a vacation break from school, Mother had told me she was planning to marry him. I remember pushing my bicycle ahead on the path so she would not see my tears.

My mother must have been aware of my consternation, because I recently came across a letter to her from Duff's son, John Julius Norwich (Duff had been created Lord Norwich in 1952). Calculating as ever, my mother had asked John Julius—the Byzantine scholar who I would learn decades later was my half brother—to talk to me about the benefits of this marriage. I have absolutely no recollection of this conversation, but my English half brother told my mother I had already processed the whole thing and that any persuading on his part would have been superfluous: "Billy has an interest in other people and in things

totally outside his own experience which seems to me very remarkable in a boy of his age. Your influence and Bill's have
had a marvelous effect—the admixture of Joe's should make him
a paragon."

Though my mother probably wrote to me about it, I was unaware at the time that she and Joe were married in a quiet ceremony in Chevy Chase, Maryland, while Anne and I were still at
school in Europe. I suppose the reality landed on me in Paris
during my winter vacation from school. I was barely even aware
that Joe was visiting. I had been allowed as a special vacation
treat to go out to see a play, so I came home later than usual. Before going to bed, I knocked on my mother's door to say good
night, and walked in to find her sitting up in her single bed with
this man sitting up next to her. My mother and Joe were in their
dressing gowns both with books in their laps, looking like two
china dolls in a shop window.

It felt illicit. I never imagined anyone sharing my mother's
bed—least of all my godfather, Joseph Alsop, who I'd assumed
never took off his suit. He had always looked so formal to me. As
far as I knew, my mother always slept alone in her own single
bed, usually smothered in face cream—it never occurred to me
that she would allow anyone near her in bed.

As a twelve-year-old, I was at a loss trying to process this se-
date tableau. I recall thinking, "Who is kidding whom here?" but
that's all I remember. I have no idea if they welcomed me into
the room or shooed me away. Joe would have been naturally welcoming, while my mother would have resented the intrusion.
But I have no idea how they responded to me as a pair.

What I did know was that my European childhood was
coming to an end. That summer we left Europe and returned to
live in the Unites States. We fell, like Alice in Wonderland, into
the dizzying world of Joe Alsop.

I have in recent years pieced together what I can of the courtship between my mother and Joe, which set the stage for our future life in Washington. Joe's improbable campaign to nab my mother began with his condolence letter over Bill's—his "best friend's"—death. Apologizing for sounding "ghoulish," Joe suggested that from what he had seen of Bill in the recent months, there seemed to be a lassitude on Bill's part that would have made life not really worth living for him. Joe's letter was a preface to increasingly frequent correspondence—some highly personal, others very pragmatic—that he sent my mother over the next year.

Despite her outward social success in Paris, my mother was more vulnerable and isolated than many realized. She had financial flexibility, but no platform from which to exercise her higher ambitions. Joe saw the opening and moved quickly. Within a month of Bill Patten's death, he was writing regularly. He spent two weeks in France in May 1960 with my mother, ostensibly chasing my sister Anne's godmother, the magnetic Odette Pol-Roger, who had befriended Winston Churchill after the war. It was the beginning of a nine-month campaign, which he pursued no less avidly than his friend Jack Kennedy did the White House.

Joe had first met congressman Jack Kennedy in 1947 in a Georgetown apartment where Kennedy was living with a band of female relations, whom Joe remembered as being stunningly beautiful. Joe was soon admiringly characterizing Kennedy as "a Stevenson with balls." His brother Stewart had already publicly labeled Adlai Stevenson an "egg-head," borrowing the expression from his younger brother, John. Joe took the spherical metaphor a tad closer to where it counted. By 1958 Joe was presciently writing to his friend Evangeline Bruce, wife of the American ambassador to West Germany, that Jack would be a "perfect candidate" for the presidency.

Joe had been already been grooming Jacqueline Bouvier Kennedy for the role she would need to play when Jack started his presidential campaign, reassuring her that gaining the presidency was the "only game worth the candle." Detailed as always, Joe even advised her on where to buy maternity dresses— perhaps Bloomingdale's would be politically savvier than Givenchy. Jackie was well aware of her husband's infidelities, but Joe and others explained that she owed it to the nation to stand by him.

The timing of Joe's decision to get married during the year of Kennedy's presidential election does not seem coincidental to me. Bill Patten died in the spring of 1960, Kennedy was elected that fall, and Joe married my mother the following spring. Just as Jackie provided her husband with a degree of cover, my mother gave Joe legitimacy as a family man, someone who would seem above reproach as a confidant to the president.

Indeed, Joe used all of his connections to help the Kennedy campaign. His brother Stewart had been in the Office of Strategic Services (OSS), as was his close friend and classmate Richard Bissell, who would later be charged with trying to remove Cuban president Fidel Castro. Bissell, like Joe, was not shy about blurring professional boundaries. During the presidential campaign, Bissell secretly briefed Jack Kennedy about covert plans to overthrow Castro. This allowed Kennedy to corner Nixon during the debates by pontificating about the need to be tough with Castro, while Nixon was forced to disavow invasion threats because he did not want to tip the administration's hand. Given the parties involved, it was very likely that Joe knew all about the plan to trap Nixon.

Joe's close relations with the intelligence community in Washington were partly motivated by his need to conceal his homosexuality. In addition to having deep personal contacts within the agency, Joe's anti-Communist credentials were impeccable. On separate occasions he threw British diplomats out of his house for disparaging the United States. It was later revealed that two of these diplomats, Donald Maclean and Guy Burgess, were Soviet spies. That fact was unknown to Joe at the time, but this sort of story would have resonated positively with the Kennedy men.

As Kennedy gained momentum through the summer and fall of 1960, so did the deluge of letters from Joe to my mother. Ostensibly reporting on the campaign, Joe's subliminal message must have been immensely alluring to my mother: he would have great access in a Kennedy White House. If my mother was susceptible to any aphrodisiac, it was political power. Joe had managed to create a hospitable and lively home with the help of a Filipino couple, Maria and José. But merging with my mother would propel him into a grander league, armed with French cooks and French maids, whom Joe was more than ready to introduce to the best food and wine merchants in Georgetown. While appreciating my mother's braininess, Joe doubtless figured that such a gifted hostess would provide effective bachelor cover and, more important, would add luster and appeal to his household.

My mother's late-night letters to Gladwyn Jebb from Hossegor, France, through the summer of 1960 are spiced with colorful anecdotes that she had just received from Joe and others about Kennedy's presidential campaign, as well as accounts of Joe's desperate attempts to gain her hand: "I tell him that much as I enjoy his letters I really don't want to marry him."

These letters suggest that she had positioned Gladwyn Jebb as a kind of avuncular adviser, a junior Duff-like figure with broad international experience, as he had served at the United Nations before coming to Paris. In one letter to Gladwyn she shares her concerns, particularly about Anne, who she says has "fallen to pieces" and looks "like a waif from a Felleni film." Then out of fear that "I'll bore you with this whining," she reminisces about the evening she and Gladwyn spent together two years before, when their own affair started. Later she mentions casually:

> Now I must write brief lines to three men who have asked me to
> marry them, of all things. I suppose this happens all the time to all
> divorcées and widows but I'm rather inexperienced and find it em-
> barrassing. All three proposals were by letter from America some
> weeks ago, and I wrote at once saying no go . . . Two are girlhood ad-
> mirers who I think would run a mile if I accepted and they had to
> face the consequences, which include divorcing nice if dull wives.

She admits about one of them, "I fear you will think [he] is
just the thing for me, the next best hope to the legendary American Senator you are always conjuring up."

At one point, figuring that Susan Mary will probably fall in
love with someone else, Joe makes a rather pathetic offer of a
temporary marriage—maybe two years—until she finds the
love of her life. After refusing the offer, my mother tells Gladwyn that Joe speculated she might already be in love with
someone else.

But Joe Alsop offered more to my mother than his powerful
position in the American capital and his close rapport with
an appealing young presidential candidate. As an expatriate
widow with two young children, she must have been attracted by
the clannish familiarity of everything he represented—the
shared childhood, Groton and Harvard friends, and the extended East Coast social network of friends and relations they
had both grown up with. Joe offered a seamless extension of the
life she had shared with Bill Patten.

She knew that Joe was gay, but told me many times that she
had married him assuming she could "cure" him of his homosexuality. Joe had squarely admitted to her he was gay in a marriage
proposal that he had typed on an airplane. His candor may have
reinforced her sense that this was just a minor impediment that
could be dealt with in due time, especially since physical love-
making was not a high priority for her.

Joe's comprehensive and meticulously planned campaign to win over my mother continued. Writing from Cape Cod, Joe's good friend Arthur Schlesinger Jr. told her that he hoped she would "continue to support our beloved friend," quoting from Henry James's *The Ambassadors,* "Live all you can; it's a mistake not to. It doesn't so much matter what you do in particular, so long as you have your life. If you haven't had that what *have* you had?" His use of the itinerant James, with his well-documented and cultured transatlantic perspectives, was a shrewd source to draw from for a woman with both a zest for travel and love of fine literature.

That fall my mother's close friend and British counterpart, Pam Berry, wrote that Joe had managed to get her "on Lyndon Johnson's Whistle Stop tour of the South . . . We are flying to Miami where we meet the Vice Presidential Plane, to join the motorcade . . . I am so looking forward to it." The fact that a sophisticated European was so enamored by the thrill of an American presidential race would have intrigued my mother all the more.

With Kennedy's victory now a reality, and facing the ghastly specter of another "holiday" season without a husband, my mother's defenses against Joe seem to have finally crumbled. Apparently, Joe had come to Paris for another week in November, presumably with intimate details of the successful presidential campaign and exciting plans for their future. My mother wrote Marietta Tree that "Joe of the letters—a very shy, complicated, brave and fine man—really does exist & what is more I find this new Joe very attractive." She goes on to say, "[T]he extraordinary thing is that I've fallen in love with him." She asks Marietta not to tell her husband, Ronnie, yet, because she still has to tell her own mother.

Writing Marietta again in December 1960—in a letter omitted from her book *To Marietta from Paris, 1945–1960*—my

Joe in pool with his nephew, 1950s

mother devotes most of her news to her visit to a Paris clinic where my sister Anne's appendix has just been removed. She writes triumphantly: "[T]his may well explain her nervousness and apparent unhappiness—school had been going badly & I was just about to start psychiatry." My sister, who had been going to private French schools and mainly living with my parents when my father died, felt the loss of him dramatically.

Almost as an afterthought, writing, she says, "in Anne's room" at the clinic, my mother then casually discloses, "I do hope you will be pleased to hear that I have decided to marry Joe Alsop." She tells her old friend that "as the correspondence continued I began to know a new Joe that I didn't know existed and I began to think, oh, well, it would be a good idea for the children etc. and being a hopeless romantic couldn't make up my mind."

My mother was anything but a "hopeless romantic," but indecision was intolerable for her. Already familiar with the clanlike warmth of the Alsop family and their social milieu, stimulated by the prospects of the new administration in Washington, and

Joe and Susan Mary Alsop marriage, All Saints Protestant Episcopal Church, Chevy Chase, Maryland, February 16, 1961

recognizing the child-rearing support Joe was offering, there were more pluses to offset whatever lingering doubts she may have had about Joe. It's also possible that Gladwyn Jebb endorsed the idea.

Joe quickly got the green light to write a characteristically direct letter to my grandmother. He confessed, "I've loved Susan Mary for a long time, and during most of that time I've had to keep the feelings to myself, for reasons which are only too evident." Acknowledging the hastiness of their decision and the raw memory of his classmate Bill's death, Joe observes, "I don't myself care very greatly about the conventions of mourning, but I suppose it's an advantage to observe them."

My mother sent the announcement of their engagement to me at Beachborough. It had appeared in the January 11 issue of

Avis Bohlen, Blueberry Ledge, Northeast Harbor,
Maine, 1970s

the *Herald Tribune* in Paris. What surprised me at the time was
that the article referred to my mother as a "wealthy widow." I
had no idea that we were a wealthy family. The following month
my mother and Joe were married at All Saints Episcopal
Church in Chevy Chase, Maryland, less than one year after Bill
Patten's death, while Anne and I were still in Europe. The reception was held at my grandmother's house on Twenty-ninth
Street in Georgetown.

The moment word was out, my mother began to receive a
cascade of letters from close friends on both sides of the Atlantic. Cy Sulzberger championed Joe's "deep, warm affection
for children and the remarkable ability he has to communicate
with them and secure their trust and love." Joe's neighbor in
Georgetown, Avis Bohlen, wife of his old friend and confidante

Ambassador Charles Bohlen, wrote in December: "Joe came bouncing in last evening[;] burbling is the only way I can describe his speech. Such happiness glowing in every direction—and of course I was reduced to tears. Why is it tears come when you contemplate so much happiness?"

All of these letters were congratulatory, but some included gentle warnings. Joe's brother Stewart cautioned, "You must be prepared to stand up for your rights, but you can be dead sure that you won't be bored." Perhaps the most comforting letter my mother received was from a Harvard classmate of Joe's, Charles "Swig" Stockton, who had been a witness to her marriage to Bill Patten. He wrote, "I know I needn't tell you that behind the protective mask he affects, Joe is the warmest and tenderest person imaginable."

Phil Graham, publisher of the *Washington Post*, wrote a funny note and enclosed a copy of the toast he had made to Joe on his fiftieth birthday: "Joe is a paradox. He is a recitative-doom singer and he is one of the optimists of our age. He is a raspish geyser of bad temper and he is a gentle fountain of friendship. He is constantly on the brink of falling to monasticism and he is inexorably drawn to involvement in the noisy world. He is cuttingly cynical and he is splendidly and sentimentally naïve. He is the most impossibl[y] possible man alive."

One of the more prescient letters came from Marietta Tree's daughter, Frankie FitzGerald, who was my mother's goddaughter. In what strikes me as only partial jest, she ventures: "One thing disturbs me—and that is that it may not be a practical arrangement. Can you cook? Your chefs will be so enraged when they hear about each other that they will either resign or feed you nothing but soufflés in violent, jealous competition."

Little as I remember of the period, I do remember some awkwardness in Paris before we left for Washington and entered Joe's all-consuming world. Perhaps because she had no one else with whom she could confide, my mother told me how unnerved she had been by Joe's rudeness toward several of her French friends at a recent dinner party. It must have been very upsetting to her, especially after her decade with Bill Patten, whose gracious forbearance was legendary.

The most insightful comment on the new marriage was passed on to my mother by Joe's mother, Corinne, who wrote a nice letter welcoming my mother to the Alsop tribe. She began, "[T]hough 2720 Dumbarton Avenue has always been Joe's house—I now consider it Yours." On the same opening page she could not resist passing on a clue about her son by quoting Joe's secretary, "Miss Puff . . . that glorious character," who had written her saying, "Mr. Alsop thinks—in fact he knows—that he invented marriage."

I was quickly enrolled in the second form, or eighth grade, at Groton School. As a veteran of boarding schools, I was not overly worried about the new sports like baseball and football that I would be facing, but instead had optimistic visions of decent food.

Joe and my mother took me to Corinne's house, Woodford Farm, as a stopover before the final drive to the school. On our last leg of the trip from Avon to Groton, Joe sat in the front seat giving instructions to Aldo, his family's handyman and occasional chauffeur. An excellent driver herself, my mother sat in the backseat with me, giving constant suggestions about alternate directions to take, when to pass, and what speed to drive. My mother's polite but pointed voice clearly irritated Joe. In fact, it probably infuriated him. But Joe couldn't drive a car, so his authority with my mother and with Aldo was circumscribed, to say the least. Joe hated feeling powerless, and my mother loved to be in control. The mutual frustration I sensed in the car that morning set the tone for most of their marriage.

Renovations at 2720 Dumbarton Avenue, circa 1961

eleven

In Camelot's Court

I had been brought up in the milieu of the English upper
class and prepared, therefore, in my education and
manners, for an England that by the time I was 20 had
simply ceased to exist. Then along came the discovery of
Dumbarton Avenue and a world where everything I had
been trained to expect existed among the flowers, the
breakfast things, the inconsequential chat.

—LETTER TO AUTHOR FROM DUDLEY FISHBURN, OCTOBER 2004

THE HOUSE AT 2720 Dumbarton Avenue looked like a converted garage on the outside. Joe's excuse was that when he
bought the lot in the 1940s he didn't have enough money to invest in both the outside and the inside of the house, so he had
focused on the inside. He had camouflaged the pale yellow cin-
der block exterior with small shrubs and trees as best he could.
And he took perverse delight in the fact that his house had
prompted the District of Columbia to pass zoning regulations to
make future houses conform to the historic red brick style of the
rest of Georgetown. It reinforced the uniqueness of the house.

Whether you were the president of the United States or a
Christmas caroler, you entered the front door of Joe's house after

Living room with view of garden, 2720 Dumbarton Avenue, Washington

ascending a circular set of stairs to a small entrance porch. Once you entered the dark green door you found yourself in a small vestibule with a black-and-white chequered floor made of some type of epoxy. In a little waist-high niche on the left Joe had placed a small marble statute of a woman holding a boy, whose head rested in her lap. If you walked straight ahead, you found yourself in the dining room, but there were two more immediate doors to the right and left.

The door on the right was usually closed and led to the kitchen. The doors to the left were bifolds and opened into a long living room. The wall on the right of this room was lined with floor-to-ceiling bookshelves, which were reflected by the mirror above the marble mantelpiece on the opposite side. The mantel was flanked by two large dark brown Japanese silk screens mounted on the walls. This main room stretched all the way back to a gold lacquer Louis XIV Boule desk, beyond which the floor-to-ceiling windows looked out on the loggia and garden at the rear of the house.

Joe added a wing to the house when he married my mother, one that neatly enclosed his ornate little garden in a rectangular horseshoe. The opposite wing housed Joe's working office, where his secretary also worked. A loggia with brick flooring connected the two wings, and Joe's framed Connecticut ancestors looked out on this scene from the walls of his dining room inside, which backed up against the kitchen.

The new wing of the house enclosed my mother's blue-and-white-wallpapered bedroom, which looked out on the garden. Above her bed hung a French drawing of my nine-year-old sister, Anne, in three ballet poses. Joe's bedroom was belowground, underneath hers, and was just big enough for his single bed and window looking out onto a tiny courtyard, but with a large bathroom and large tiled shower and huge closets to house his innumerable Savile Row suits.

Joe's favorite colors for both clothes and fabrics were dark olive greens, browns, and classic blue-and-white stripes for upholstery. The furnishings were a mixture of oriental objects made of jade and lacquer, and French Louis XIV furniture. For my wedding in 1970 he gave me an eighteenth-century French mahogany backgammon table with secret compartments.

My mother's wing looked across at Joe's office, and between them was a little fountain surrounded by a manicured patch of lawn and tightly trimmed box bushes. Two medium-size magnolia trees stood in the rear of the garden, and next to them, tucked behind my mother's wing, was a tiny black pool framed by the exterior corner walls of the house. When I had forgotten my front door key, I could shimmy up between a telephone pole and these walls and slip into the house.

Jeanne and Jeannine Saunier, 2720 Dumbarton Avenue, 1960s

My sister and I lived down below in the front part of the house, with my sister's bedroom looking out at Dumbarton Avenue. My bedroom, which doubled as the guest room, had two single beds and looked out on the same tiny courtyard as Joe's bedroom. Between my sister's room and mine was a windowless laundry, where Mimi and Jeannine watched soap operas and sewed and ironed.

Jeannine came from Normandy. My mother had brought her from Paris, where as a young girl she had started working for my parents. Mimi came from the Mediterranean; Mother had poached her from another family in the French embassy. Only Gemma, a northern Italian who came from the Turkish embassy and eventually replaced Jeannine, slept in the house.

When we first arrived in Washington my mother enrolled Anne in the Potomac School, where I heard she was very popular. In 1964 Anne was sent away to St. Timothy's in Maryland, from

Joe Alsop in Garden Room at 2720 Dumbarton Avenue, Washington, 1960s

which she was eventually kicked out. She returned to live at home and attended the National Cathedral School. Joe helped her with her homework, showing the same hands-on involvement that he would use with me at Groton.

Though Anne and I often skirmished as we had in Paris, her letters to me at Groton show her loyalty and warm heart. She confided in me about her boyfriends and was never critical of our mother or Joe. Other than the TV in the laundry room, I believe Anne had the only one in the house.

Joe was as concerned about Anne's clothes as he was about mine. One day as she was leaving the house he asked her where she thought she was going in blue jeans. "To my therapist," she replied. "But darling," said Joe, "I thought patients were supposed to be in love with their psychiatrists."

Joe supervised the details of the household with precision. Still in his dressing gown and brandishing an oversized china teacup, most mornings after breakfast he would sit down in the garden room with the cook to go over menus for the day. He drank black coffee and would open a small pill case and drop in a couple of tiny tablets, which I assumed were a sugar substitute. Home from Groton, where the food was mediocre, I was especially appreciative of Joe's attention to superb food. Indeed, he was obsessed with fine food and used to admit that he was envious of how much butter I would spread on my toast in the morning.

In the late afternoons before guests arrived, Joe would often invite his contractor, George Ankeny, a tall, thin Virginian with one lung, to join him for a scotch and soda. George, the handyman who took care of the physical needs of the house, always seemed to have a knowing smile on his face when he sat in the living room. I understood that smile, given Joe's inability to hammer a nail into the wall. We all knew how totally dependent Joe was on people like George, and how he felt the need to cozy up to them to ensure their loyalty.

It was crucial to have all aspects of the house looking spiffy and working properly, as it provided the working props for Joe and Mother's almost nonstop entertaining. Together they crafted an atmosphere that visitors tended to remember. Dudley Fishburn, an English friend of mine from Harvard, who became the editor of the *Economist* in the United States and later a member of Parliament, captured the feeling of the house in a letter he sent to me after my mother died:

> 2720 Dumbarton Avenue was one of the great adventures of my life. Each visit sticks clearly in my mind. And at the center of each memory stands your mother: always welcoming, always flattering, and epitomizing for me a world in which for many years (but not forever) I was in love. I had been brought up in the milieu of the English upper class and prepared, therefore, in my education and manners, for an England that by the time I was 20 had simply ceased to exist. Then along came the discovery of Dumbarton Avenue and a world where everything I had been trained to expect existed among the

flowers, the breakfast things, the inconsequential chat. On my first visit, your mother engaged me in conversation about Louis XI and his belligerent righteousness and that of the Johnson administration in Vietnam—turning at this point with a smile to bring into the talk the Secretary of the Army who had just popped by.

When I asked Dudley once why he didn't see my parents more often, he told me that they sometimes intimidated him. Still, hard as he could be on his peers, Joe had a soft spot for younger people. His warmth toward Anne and me—and his nephews and nieces and many of our friends—was disarming and genuine. When he let his guard down, the heavy veneer of social pomposity he had carefully built up over the years became fairly transparent—at least briefly.

Rosemary Mahoney, an assistant to the writer Lillian Hellman one summer on Martha's Vineyard, tells an anecdote about Joe that captures for me his enthusiasm for the young. The Vineyard was one of the few summer spots where Joe felt comfortable, partly because he had good friends there, including Katharine "Kay" Graham. Rosemary said:

> Joe Alsop walked into the kitchen in his bedroom slippers and said, "Good morning, my dear! How are you!" . . . Alsop rubbed his hands together, heartily preparing to take on the day. He had a cigarette holder clamped to his teeth and wore a purple robe with lilac piping. His slippers were dark leather. His hairless shins as he stood in the morning light gave off a high polish, and his heavy eyeglasses were two large tortoiseshell circles, round as coat buttons.

Joe never made me feel like I was in the way or unwelcome in his home, but I sometimes felt I was intruding with his distinguished guests. I would skip out of the garden room before politicians, diplomats, and military leaders arrived for interviews

Mrs. Longworth, Joe Alsop, and Donny Graham, 1960s

in the civilized setting where Joe used to ferret out information and shape worldviews. I remember one morning seeing the fresh-faced young congressman George H. W. Bush, later President Bush, come bounding into the garden room with a sprightly air.

My main role in the house was to mix drinks in the little bar that was tucked away under the bookshelves at one end of the living room. The large silver ice bucket was camouflaged in a dark oriental barrel. Occasionally, Joe would drag in politicians who, from my adolescent viewpoint, were totally out of place against the Louis XIV gilt furniture. One evening, for example, two friendly senators from the Midwest, Fred Harris and Walter

"Fritz" Mondale, arrived with their wives, and I could not help wondering what they were thinking as Joe laid his high Oxonian speech on them.

But despite his pomposity, I never worried that Joe would fail to entertain. He was skilled at what his friend Kay Graham noted as "giving pleasure." After his death she said that "more than almost anyone I knew, Joe gave pleasure and got pleasure." And after the initial shock of his pomposity wore off, I noticed that most people, even those like my mother-in-law Kitty Bacon, who disapproved of his Vietnam stand, warmed up to his charm when they met him in person.

During a holiday from Groton in the early sixties, I joined Joe for lunch at his home with an improbable, but representative, cast that included one of his favorite cousins, Alice Roosevelt Longworth, along with Truman Capote and Marina Sulzberger, who was visiting from Paris. I remember them laughing mischievously about how President Kennedy had gotten their friend Marella Agnelli to swim nude with him in the White House pool. The thought of the ethereal Marella—wife of Gianni Agnelli, who became the head of Fiat—cavorting with anyone shocked my schoolboy sensibilities. At my mother's behest, I had once driven this patrician-looking lady to a hairdresser near Dupont Circle. She was utterly unassuming, but I remember wishing I had something more elegant to drive than my mother's Chevy Camaro.

Joe was fascinated with the sexual activity of others and had, I suspect, a very rich fantasy life speculating about them. When he talked about sex his eyes would get round and shiny. One day after a lunch with some friends in Manhattan, Joe and I were left alone and he commandeered a cab that was already occupied. The two startled passengers were a young couple. Apologizing for his intrusion, Joe later asked me with a smirk where I thought they were headed. I had no idea. "They're headed for an afternoon in bed," he exclaimed, as if it should have been obvious.

He seemed to particularly relish keeping me up to date with the sexual escapades of his friend Lord Antony Claud Frederick Lambton. An occasional guest at Dumbarton Avenue, Lambton was forced to resign from the British cabinet for consorting with prostitutes. One night after a dinner party at home Joe told me with a grin that Tony Lambton had managed to snare a family friend as they left for the night.

Joe summarized his sexual etiquette by quoting Mrs. Patrick Campbell's remark that "it doesn't matter what you do in the bedroom as long as you don't do it in the streets and frighten the horses." I always thought of horses parading down Dumbarton Avenue whenever Joe repeated the quote, something he did often.

Except for mentioning it in a letter to my mother while he was courting her, Joe's homosexuality was never discussed between us. I grew aware of it slowly, not really assimilating the information for a long time. Later on in the seventies I remember feeling sad when my mother once told me that Joe had told her he never paid for sex, because I doubted it was true. But it highlighted the desperate loneliness he must have felt at times.

His insecurity around the topic was transparent in the way he would make caustic jokes about gay men. Joe made condescending remarks about one of my college roommates who later came out of the closet. Had Joe not been so obviously insecure about this issue, I might have lashed out at him. Indeed the 1950s was an unforgiving time to be homosexual. Rosemary Mahoney recalled an incident that took place when Joe was staying with Lillian Hellman on Martha's Vineyard. Rosemary overheard Lillian saying openly to another guest, "Joe is a fag. There's no reason for my liking him except that he was very good during the McCarthy period."

Luckily for Joe, it was only after his death that his secret life was disclosed in the public media. He must have lived with the constant threat of exposure. In 1957, when Joe was reporting from Moscow, he was entrapped by the Soviets, who engineered photographs of him cavorting in a hotel room with another man. Within days they confronted Joe with the prints and threatened to blackmail him. Never hesitating, Joe refused to cooperate and reported the incident to his Porcellian Club friend Chip Bohlen, who was then the American ambassador in Moscow. Chip helped Joe get out of Russia immediately. Joe then filed a written report of the incident and of his gay life with the CIA, which made it to FBI director J. Edgar Hoover. Though Hoover reputedly had the photos sent around town, no one in Washington took advantage of them.

Most people, like his younger brother, John, who lived in Connecticut, assumed Joe was asexual. Given his macho posturing, this was an easy impression to have of him. His brother Stewart, however, was worried that exposure would threaten their professional standing. Some years earlier, Joe had been picked up by vice police in San Francisco, and Stewart had helped cover up the incident. This time, however, the incident replete with compromising photographs raised issues of national security.

Comparing Joe's courage of standing up against the demagoguery of McCarthy with his stand against the KGB, Henry Kissinger told me once that because there were others who also saw the evil in McCarthy, it was probably more courageous for Joe to stand up alone to the Russians. Nodding his head ominously, Kissinger observed that the consequences of being exposed would have been "really bad."

The fact that a large number of people in the media, and even political enemies like Joe McCarthy, had access to this graphic evidence and did not use it against him demonstrates the strength of journalistic norms during the postwar period.

The widow of Phil Geyelin, editor of the *Washington Post*'s editorial page, told me recently that Phil simply threw the pictures of Joe in the trash. This degree of respect for privacy seems almost unimaginable today.

Looking back at Joe's intense relationship with the Kennedy family, his worship of JFK, and the amount of time he spent with the president and Jackie (the journalist Seymour Hersh says Joe was the president's favorite journalist), I wonder if the coziness between JFK and Joe wasn't reinforced by their mutual secrets around sexual issues. Knowing that Joe was gay, Kennedy is reputed to have a made a caustic remark when he heard that Joe was getting married. But for a man with his own dark side, Joe's bravura performance must have impressed the president.

Jack Kennedy, of course, came perilously close to "doing it in the streets." As we now know, his bravado was not an occasional romance but an ongoing obsession, almost a pathological dependency, that was extraordinarily risky. It was only thanks to the loyalty and discretion of those around him that his sexual obsessions were kept secret. Joe and many others honored the code of silence.

The only time I met President Kennedy was when he appointed my godmother, Marietta Tree, as ambassador to the United Nations Commission on Human Rights in 1961 and I briefly shook hands with him in the Oval Office. I met Jackie Kennedy and Jack's brother Robert several times after his death. The Kennedys, however, were omnipresent in Joe's life and, by extension, my mother's as well.

Of course, Joe and Jack Kennedy were bonded by far more than a willingness to take sexual risks. The aspiring politician and the seasoned opinion maker had complementary interests—public positioning for Jack and incomparable presidential access for Joe. Needless to say, as a columnist, Joe was a forceful advocate for

Kennedy. He notes proudly in his memoirs that Jack Kennedy, often but not always with Jackie, had more private dinners with him than with any other member of the media, and possibly more than anyone outside his own family.

One of the most notable examples of this coziness with JFK occurred on the night of Kennedy's inauguration. During the evening of January 20, 1961, with five inaugural balls under way, snow had unexpectedly begun to fall on Washington. Leaving the last ball—and with Jackie already in bed at the White House—the new president resisted the temptation to cavort with Kim Novak and Angie Dickinson, who were at one of the formal balls, and chose a safer place to relax after his historic day.

Joe had run into Averell Harriman's godson, Peter Duchin, at the last ball, and Duchin offered him a lift home before the snow got too heavy. Joe lured Peter into the house and used him as his cohost. My mother was still in Paris, and he desperately needed help, having already found two guests beating on his door when he arrived. While Joe liked to characterize the presidential visit as "impromptu," it was, of course, far more choreographed. Given the security concerns, it would have had to be carefully planned.

Although Joe himself may have feigned surprise, the other guests must have been genuinely astounded when the doorbell rang late that evening and the young president entered the small hallway of 2720 Dumbarton Avenue. "He looked as though he were still in his thirties, with snowflakes scattered about his thick, reddish hair." The president explained that Jackie was so tired, "she had simply fallen into bed in the White House." When the president sat down, everyone in the room stood and applauded. Terrapin soup and champagne were served while people continued streaming into the neighborhood until the street became congested with onlookers and U.S. Secret Service cars.

In a variety of later reports of this party, rumors have surfaced about JFK's having sex with Hollywood starlets brought along by his brother-in-law Peter Lawford. This is possible but unlikely, as the president arrived just before 2 A.M. and left one hour and twenty minutes later, and the house was logistically un-suited for a discreet liaison. Peter Duchin told me that Kennedy spent most of his time talking with Senator John Sherman Cooper and his wife, Lorraine, noting that his absence from the living room would have been conspicuous. Still, Joe would not have felt bashful about covering for Kennedy if he had slipped down into one of the bedrooms downstairs.

The following week Joe joined the president and Jackie at the White House for a cozy Sunday evening dinner of fresh caviar and bottles of Dom Perignon. It must have brought back memories for Joe of Sunday evenings with his Roosevelt cousins almost three decades earlier. The new president and his guests explored the White House, discovering, among other things, the porthole-like contraptions that the Eisenhowers had used to hide their "his and hers" televisions. The other guests that evening included artist Bill Walton, Franklin Roosevelt and his wife, and conductor Leonard Bernstein and his wife.

White House records show that Joe and my mother social-ized with the Kennedys with a degree of frequency that today would be seen for someone in the media as creating an unhealthy conflict of interest. In fact, Joe's attachment to the president struck me as filled with traits of lover's jealousy. In his journal en-try of January 10, 1963, Joe's old friend Arthur Schlesinger Jr. notes: "We dined tonight at the White House. The other guests were Joe and Susan Mary and Lee Radziwill. I thought Joe looked a little disappointed when we entered the room, but he ac-cepted the situation philosophically." This was several years be-fore Joe started to lambaste Arthur because of his opposition to the Vietnam War.

While Joe enjoyed advising Jackie on redecorating the inte-rior of the White House, his real satisfaction came from advising the president on important political decisions. He had already helped Kennedy select Texas senator Lyndon Johnson as his running mate,* and was soon advising him on prospective cabinet positions—in particular, promoting Douglas Dillon as a candidate for secretary of the treasury. Joe relished participating directly in momentous events rather than just writing about them.

Much as Joe loved being part of the action, however, he also found solace in a more academic, solitary existence. He was conflicted throughout his life by his scholarly capacity for reflection and his temperamental instinct to act. As David Halberstam later observed in *The Best and the Brightest,* Joe "wrote not to enlighten but to effect." Joe was not satisfied writing on the sidelines. The title of Robert Merry's biography of the Alsop brothers, *Taking On the World,* is an apt summary of Joe's incredibly grandiose style. For example, he had no qualms whatsoever about admitting that he had cooperated with the CIA for many years. In 1977 he told Carl Bernstein of the *Washington Post* that "the notion that a newspaperman doesn't have a duty to his country is perfect balls."

While Joe was taking on the world, my mother was forced more and more into the role of observer, a role she handled with initial resiliency. She did not seem jealous of his close relationship to women like Kay Graham or Polly Wisner (later Fritchey). In a letter to her friend Marietta in 1971, my mother described a hilarious scene after Joe left her with his then-secretary, Miss Armstrong, a good-looking young woman from Nebraska:

---

* According to Arthur Schlesinger Jr.'s journals, "improbably enough" Joe let his friend Phil Graham, the publisher of the *Washington Post,* do most of the talking when they met alone with JFK at the Beverly Hilton in July 1960. Jack said, "That is right and I mean to do it."

A huge Cadillac with Kay, Polly, and Joe and chauffeur drove off (headed for a cure at Hot Springs), with the servants and Miss Armstrong on the steps waving gaily. Hardly had it turned the corner before Gemma, the parlormaid from the Veneto, burst into tears and said she could not take one more minute, and was returning to Italy—eight years had turned her into an old woman. Miss Armstong, a cool cucumber, said, "May I invite my friend in to swim?" I said "of course, would she like lunch?" "It's a he—Mr. Clively." Mr. Clively then sprang out of his sports car—a handsome black—dashed by me—we are still in the hall—next scene he is cavorting on Joe's lawn, stark naked but for a sort of African belt with beads. Miss Armstrong, in a bikini, looked up occasionally & nervously at the house, but did not seem to mind the divots Mr. Clively's beautiful black feet were digging in Joe's newly planted turf.

This was an amusing example of my mother's detachment from the details of maintaining the house.

But while she did not worry too much about the garden issues, my mother backed Joe politically, gingerly finding ways to make herself useful. Writing a representative letter to me at Groton, my mother began by conveying Joe's concern that perhaps I was "taking one subject too many." Her focus quickly shifted to the central point, however—a recent small dinner she and Joe had attended at the White House.

She was "Delighted to find Mrs. Kennedy . . . very funny & pretty. I sat by him & the conversation was mainly general and nothing to report as it was all very frivolous & light hearted. I always feel grateful if Joe & I can make him smile & take his mind off his responsibilities for half an hour—and I like and admire him more each time I see him. Yesterday we lunched at the British Embassy for Noel Coward."

In February 1963, ten months before President Kennedy was killed, Joe and my mother enjoyed the poetic opportunity to host

Lady Diana at Camelot's court. It began with a dinner at the Dumbarton Avenue house, where Diana was introduced to Robert and Ethel Kennedy, Edward and Joan Kennedy, Teddy Roosevelt's daughter Alice Longworth, and several senators and their wives. The next day Joe took Diana to meet vice president Lyndon Johnson in his Senate office, having done the same for my sister and me a year earlier.

The climax of Diana's visit was a small Valentine's Day dinner at Joe and my mother's house, which the president and the First Lady attended. Diana's English was perfectly good, but acting as if the guest of honor were French, Joe insisted on interpreting everything she said to the president throughout the evening. Still, the evening was a memorable success. Joe's cook, Jeanne, outdid herself with her *bombe Jeanne d'Arc*, and Joe tossed financial care aside and served a Lafitte 1947 wine along with Moet & Chandon sparkling wine.

After dinner, Diana and Jackie had a chance to talk, and they hit it off. Diana thought that the First Lady was far more beautiful than she had expected, and Jackie was delighted to find that Diana was astonishingly well read. The president was impressed as well. "What a woman!" he exclaimed to Joe as he left 2720 Dumbarton Avenue. He invited Diana to a forthcoming formal dinner at the White House.

Joe and Susan Mary dined with the president and Jackie shortly before they left for Texas in the fall of the same year. My mother remembered in a 1994 interview that "the President was not happy about taking Jackie to Dallas, because she wasn't feeling strong enough—that was the year she lost the baby, Patrick. But she was determined to go." The president asked Jackie to show them the pink Schiaparelli suit she was going to wear. "Oh, Jack, it isn't much," she said. But she had the suit brought down to show them. "It was a lovely evening—a cozy dinner in the residence. We said goodbye and wished them well in Dallas."

Caroline Kennedy, 2720 Dumbarton Avenue, 1960s

John F. Kennedy's assassination was, of course, utterly devastating to Joe. He was far more emotional about the tragedy than my mother, who predictably launched into making herself useful to Jackie by helping her reply to the vast number of condolence letters. But Jackie was clearly miffed when she received my mother's comforting accolade about how nobly she was bearing up under the strain. According to Arthur Schlesinger Jr.'s journal, she asked him, "How did she expect me to behave?"

For Joe, it was not just about appropriate behavior. It was not until I saw him make his annual pilgrimages to Arlington National Cemetery over the years to come that I realized what a deeply sentimental man he was. Ten years after the president's death, he told *Time,* "Kennedy's being killed was also the beginning of the end for us."

Joe wrote a final column on Jack Kennedy, "Go, Stranger!" published in the *Washington Post* (and also syndicated). He emphasized Kennedy's courage, comparing the dead president with the Spartan soldiers who made their last stand at Thermopylae. The comparison of King Leonidas's soldiers' voluntary sacrifice with Kennedy's death seemed to me a little stretched, but it was fully consistent with Joe's view that leadership required "manly" traits and the profoundly poetic resonance of the Greek poet Simonides's famous epitaph "Tell the Spartans, passing by, / That here obedient to their laws we lie."

In his memoirs Joe recalled the "staggering emotional loss among those who had known and worked with [JFK]." He closed with the emotionally revealing observation that after the assassination, "the Washington landscape was littered with male widows." Vulgar perhaps, but he was referring to the knights of Camelot. Joe considered himself a charter member, less in the inspiring terms of the musical but more in the grimmer context of the Greek soldiers who sacrificed their lives to save the rest of their army.

His less sentimental cousin Alice Longworth, whose own father, Theodore Roosevelt, had once been shot by a madman, thought Joe was being too "boy-stood-on-the-burning-deckish" about his conspicuous grieving. But Alice observed the Washington political scene over the years with a degree of detachment her younger cousin could not share. She did not suffer from Joe's need to affect decisions on the world scene, and JFK's presidency had given Joe a degree of opportunity to do so to a degree beyond his wildest dreams.

Joe Alsop retired from journalism a decade later, and after 1963 the interior of 2720 Dumbarton Avenue never again filled with a thrill equal to the brief, memorable years of Camelot. Though Joe lived a quarter of a century after JFK's death, it was fitting that his memoirs, *I've Seen the Best of It*, should end with the assassination of his hero and friend.

Porcellian Club, Harvard College, Bill Patten seated front row far left, Joe
Alsop next to him, 1932

twelve

Making the Club

If asked to join both [clubs], the lowest possible
"low posture," as the Japanese call it, is clearly indicated.
—A LETTER FROM JOE TO ME MY FRESHMAN YEAR AT HARVARD

IN HIS MEMOIRS, Joe reverentially recalls "being taken by the PC," the Porcellian Club, and labels it "the undergraduate citadel of what I have called the WASP Ascendancy at Harvard." He devotes six pages to his Harvard club compared with half a page on life at Harvard College itself. There on the second floor of a nondescript building on Massachusetts Avenue in Cambridge, Joe had found a home among men of his own background who not only tolerated but also often delighted in his eccentricities. He had been rescued from the farm where he grew up—and from oblivion.

Bill Patten also had been in the PC, whose emblem was the pig. The two-foot brown leather pig in our library in Paris came from Bill and Joe's old club, and Bill carried a little gold pig on his watch chain. But Bill never mentioned "the Porc," so I was unaware of what it meant until my freshman year, when a couple of sophisticated-looking older classmen—Woody Brock and an

Englishman named Rudolph Erlanger—invited me to a fancy French restaurant in Cambridge. I was still pretty innocent about the implications of this invitation, though Joe certainly would not have been when he arrived at Harvard. Tragically, I had not yet received his letter advising me to assume a "low posture, as the Japanese call it," and could not imagine taking this kind of thing seriously.

Although Joe pretended to write and talk about the Porcellian Club with anthropological distance, getting elected was central to his identity, his deepest sense of self. Arriving as an oddity from Groton and a potential hick from Connecticut, Joe must have looked on the others who were part of this world in awe. Charles Devens, for instance, was a handsome man, captain of varsity baseball and football teams, and a godlike figure to the boys on the sidelines.

Joe's father, a Yankee gentleman farmer, tried to intercede with the headmaster, Reverend Peabody, when he saw his overweight and uncoordinated young son being forced to play sports upon enrollment at Groton. It was a touching show of paternal sensitivity, but it had no effect whatsoever on Groton's rigid code of athletic Christianity. This only added to Joe's sense of misery as a Groton student, where sports defined so much of one's success.

When I arrived in 1961 the school was supposedly ending the "Bloody Sunday" hazing ritual, but during my first semester there I did witness some of it. The rituals involved, among other things, having the older boys take the new boys down to the basement, known as "the great white way," and flush their heads in the toilets. One fat first-year student ended up in the infirmary after he was put in a barrel and rolled down some granite steps. (As the veteran of an English boarding school, I was easily able to anticipate and dodge the hazing.) The inexperienced and obese little Joe would have been an obvious target for this kind of brutality, especially in a less regulated age. But for as long as I

Dean and Alice Acheson, 1960s

knew him, he respected the WASP tradition of never talking about such humiliations.

When it came to hiding the legacy of a place like Groton, Joe was in good company. I once asked Dean Acheson, Truman's secretary of state, why he never referred to his years at Groton in his autobiography about his early years. Dean answered succinctly, "It was too painful. I didn't want to bore the reader." He did not elaborate.

It was only with trusted old friends like my father that Joe might let his guard down about his weight. After they had roomed together in New York in the late 1930s, Joe wrote Bill a patronizing letter about some money he still owed Bill, saying, "You will never make a business man, dunning as poor paying a debtor as myself so inefficiently." Joe goes on to mention how his own career was blossoming, "owing to a fortunate connection with the

Joe Alsop, third from left, at a men's dinner in Washington, D.C., 1941

Saturday Evening Post," and adding, "and I am rapidly becoming a fat harlot. Fat does not matter much in my end of the harlotry business, so I hope I will not grow superannuated at once."

The PC was a glorious refuge from the common herd—just outside the reach of the masses but offering the possibility of genuine comradeship. The PC also had the luster of being viewed, along with the A.D. Club (which originally stemmed from the Alpha Delta Phi fraternity), as in the top tier of Harvard undergraduate clubs. Joe had found a quirky, elitist institution that matched his own quirky personality and set his ego on a rocket trajectory.

Though Joe repeatedly claimed that there was no such thing as an American "aristocracy," he was fixated by elite society on both sides of the Atlantic. Alastair Forbes, an Englishman who knew the Boston Brahmin world well, observed that Joe was never more delighted than when Robert Cecil, Lord Salisbury, a descendant of the Cecil family from the time of Elizabeth I and a friend of my parents, told him to call him "Bobbety."

Joe certainly worked assiduously to look the part. With his round tortoise-shell glasses, bow ties, and dark-colored English suits, Joe struck me rather as an Oxford professor—an academic who moonlighted as a journalist rushing off in Diamond taxicabs during the day to scold White House aides. Maybe his intrinsic professorial bent reinforced his need to lecture colleagues on how important it was for journalists to use "shoe leather" and deride political commentator Walter Lippmann for never stirring from his office, but at all times he took care to look as well "turned out," as he put it, as possible.

For all of Joe's preaching about getting out in the world, he knew he could always come back to his perch in his own little leather throne in the library. He liked to say that book stacks were better interior decoration than any wallpaper, but he obviously reveled in the books themselves. He had been a bibliophile for years and even had a special ladder designed to reach the books on the top shelves of his living room.

Joe's encyclopedic memory—he received outstanding grades at Groton—was perhaps his most basic armor. He never needed to boast about it; it was my mother who repeated the story about Endicott Peabody, "the Rector," giving the school a holiday in honor of Joe's perfect score on his college English exam. Joe's sparkling intelligence empowered him throughout his life, whether through his ability to tell long-winded jokes or to hold his own with the Isaiah Berlins of the world.

Joe had a single-minded ability to make important friends who shared his cerebral brilliance. His immense erudition helped him cement friendships with White House power brokers like McGeorge Bundy during the Kennedy years, Walt Rostow during the Johnson years, and Henry Kissinger during the Nixon years. Each came to the executive branch from academia, and each was well equipped to appreciate Joe's unique intellect. Over the years, Joe lifted himself far beyond the range of his New England peer group.

The world of books led to another kind of club, the world of academia, to which he had originally aspired before his family, as he says, intervened to get him a job in journalism. But he never renounced this world, and in the same way that Duff wrote respected biographies while holding full-time government jobs, Joe edged into the scholarly world with *From the Silent Earth,* his carefully researched study of the Greek Bronze Age in Crete, published in 1964. The book's introduction was written by the great Oxford professor Sir Maurice Bowra.

In some ways this acknowledgment meant far more to him than any journalistic scoop. While it bothered Joe relatively little to be criticized by his media colleagues, he was far more anxious about not being taken seriously by the big names at Oxford and Harvard who were in his field. On some primal level it affirmed his need to be taken seriously in a way that journalism, which he always called a "trade," could not. On the other hand, without having to worry about earning any university tenure, he had the advantage of tackling this world of academia largely on his own terms.

In the early seventies Joe would visit my family in Boston on his way to visit art historians like Dr. Emily Vermeule or Far Eastern experts like ambassador Edwin Reischauer at Harvard. A letter Joe sent to me in 1971 reveals the extent to which scholarship trumped politics for him: "Much to my surprise, I have discovered that despite my disapproval of his politics, I like the *New York Review,* Bob Silvers, really enormously. Talking to him, in fact, is almost like talking to Sir Isaiah Berlin." Of course, Joe had a practical angle as well: "If the Silvers-Alsop friendship goes on as it started a couple of weeks ago down here, I can be pretty sure of my book being reviewed on its own merits,

Joe Alsop and Isaiah Berlin, 1950s

instead of being slashed to bits as the handiwork of a dreadful war-monger."

Joe worked tremendously hard on his scholarly endeavors. His secretary, the spirited Miss Puff, wrote to me at Groton, updating me on Joe's progress with his book on the Bronze Age:

> Joe is slowly getting his book to press but it is really like Mr. Dick's history of England. Instead of King Charles' head always getting into it and preventing completion, small items like oracle bones from China and did the Moguls in India use Persian as a court language or administrative language, are constantly causing all sorts of footnotes, changes, deletions, substitutions and harried calls to the publisher in New York . . . All his finger nails are down to the quick and no one can get a straight answer out of him because he has removed himself to 1138 BC or thereabouts. The horrors that await him when he returns to this civilization!

At my daughter Eliza's graduation from Groton several years after Joe's death, the commencement speaker, David Halberstam, told a story about Joe's first day at Groton. On hearing from Mrs. Alsop that her little boy loved to read, the headmaster, Reverend Peabody, replied sharply, "Well, we'll knock that out of him." This emphatically anti-intellectual attitude was no joke, yet I was always amazed by how much reverence my stepfather showed for Peabody when I asked about him. Books and reading remained at the very foundation of Joe's being throughout his life, but it was almost as if he could not bring himself to publicly admit that he had outfoxed the Rector.

For the most part, when it came to serious scholarship, Joe was strikingly deferential. But to those he did not value, he could be merciless. At my graduation from Harvard, I brought him over to meet professor John Finley, the charming master of Eliot House, where I had lived during my sophomore year. Finley had been unfailingly supportive with recommendations, and I felt grateful to him. To my dismay, and for some reason (probably related to Harvard politics) that Joe never bothered to explain to me, my stepfather simply turned his back on Finley.

Although Joe's efforts as a stepfather were genuine, our relationship was surprisingly formal. We shook hands in an almost ceremonial way and never hugged the way I do with my own son. Joe moved with a certain stiffness, his head usually bent forward when he was walking. He had never fallen in the mud with any joy on a soccer field, and he would never join us in a casual game of Scrabble or cards. One evening in the fall of 1970 I came home to Dumbarton Avenue probably drunk and suddenly hysterical about the crazy idea that I would be getting married in a couple of months. I remember Joe standing in the vestibule, totally paralyzed by my outburst of emotion, for once unable to do or say anything. Eventually my sister came in and hugged me.

Joe was most at ease ensconced in his leather chair next to the living room fireplace with a book in his lap, a cigarette in one hand, and a tall glass of what he claimed was a "very weak" scotch and soda on his side table. Alcohol and literature were his most faithful companions. Armed with these, he could look down on the world and deliver his wisdom. I remember him leaning forward in front of his Japanese screens with his head cradled in the palms of his hands and his elbows resting on his knees as I waited with mounting impatience for him to finish one of his long, erudite sentences.

As he got older, Joe asked me to stay with him a bit longer each evening. Occasionally, he would ask me if I thought his drinking was problematic, but he was never particularly concerned with my answer. Later, when I knew more about sobriety, I would tell him that only he knew the answer to this question about his drinking, and he would gaze balefully at the floor. It felt like a little ritual, as if by asking the question he could feel that he was still in control of the situation. He would say that he had looked at himself and knew all he wanted to know.

Our most intimate moments were when we teased each other about seemingly trivial topics. Joe enjoyed it when I teased him about the poor taste of his English-made shoes or his ornate pearl-handled silverware. He accepted these jibes with a rueful smile, as if to say, "Come on, give me a break; you know it could be a lot worse!" He would sometimes ask me why I didn't like his shoes. He warned me to stay away from suede shoes, which he associated with the softness of the art world, and badgered me to wear the "hard" shoes worn by bankers and brokers. They were a sign of gravity and seriousness, he insisted.

Although Joe paled at the sight of blood from a skinned knee, he was fascinated by war. He managed to legitimize the need for combat not because he thought it was pretty but because it was part of the essence of life. He followed the troops during the Korean War and impressed his colleagues with his physical courage and stamina. War was a merciless part of human history, as merciless as the human predicament he faced in his own life. If he could prove his courage, he could prove his manhood and on some level connect the lonely scholar to the human community, perhaps assuaging some of his loneliness.

He was excited when he found anthropological evidence for man's brutish nature. He visited Nobel Prize laureate Dr. Konrad Lorenz in Germany, and in the sixties wrote a series for the *New Yorker* about Lorenz's research with geese and his behavioral theories about man's inborn aggression. Lorenz's dismal theory that love itself comes from the same aggressive instinct as the urge to kill gave scientific evidence for Joe's strident views on the merciless nature of human history.

After his last visit with Joe in Georgetown in the late 1980s, Gore Vidal remembered:

> As always, Joe was for war anywhere any time in order to "maintain the balance of power." He had used this phrase for so long that no one had any idea what—or whose—power was to be balanced. I was for minding our own business. He sounded like his great uncle; I sounded like my grandfather. As always, we played roles for each other. I was Henry James, returning to the collapsing empire from wicked, thriving Europe, and Joe was Henry Adams, weary with absolute wisdom . . . Joe was an absolute romantic, and differed from Henry Adams in that he thought of himself as a participant on the battlefield as a brave journalist, which he was, and in the high councils of state, where he liked to bustle about backstage to the amusement of the actors.

Joe's old friend Arthur Schlesinger Jr. put it a little more simply: "To be opposed to war was uncongenial to Joe." When I

Joe Alsop wearing a "Down with the Harriman-Bundy Clique of War-Mongers" sign with Averell Harriman and McGeorge Bundy at a party in Washington D.C., 1960s

recently asked another of his old friends, Henry Kissinger, whether Joe would have supported the recent invasion of Iraq, he answered in his deep guttural voice with one word: "Passionately!"

Much like his great-uncle Teddy Roosevelt, who believed that both the nation and the man need to be tested in war, Joe was, as Vidal observed, a kind of "rough-rider" groupie. Joe had a long-standing personal affection for senior military men, particularly successful Israeli generals like Moshe Dayan and *Yitzhak* Rabin, whose lives were radically different from his own. In Joe's memoirs there are more photos of the "physically impressive" general Claire Chennault than anyone else. Joe admiringly called him a "game-cock from the wilderness."

In *A Bright Shining Lie*, the biography of the maverick soldier John Paul Vann, Neil Sheehan nicely captured Joe's worship of the military. Vann, a Vietnam War hero, was very much in the

Robert McNamara sitting in Joe's chair at 2720 Dumbarton Avenue, 1960s

Chennault tradition of the courageous and unorthodox warrior. Recounting Vann's funeral at Arlington Cemetery in 1972, Sheehan recalls how Joe "had come to have a singular affection for this Virginia cracker who so differed from him in background and personality."

Joe was not the "cruel" man James Reston once called him. I never got any sense that he enjoyed inflicting pain. In some respect, his own internal pain was so great that he could not control himself from dumping it on others, especially someone close to him like my mother, who reminded him of his vulnerabilities.

Some who only knew him from a distance could detect this pain. In his history of the *New York Herald Tribune,* Richard Kluge pinpoints the source of Joe's offensiveness: "Even those who were fond of Joe Alsop conceded that he was a mite imperious; others found him downright arrogant . . . It was as if these mannerisms were designed to distract those encountering him from his unsightly girth, to insult before being insulted, to terrorize lest it be discovered that he was the one terrified."

When he didn't feel threatened, Joe could be oddly magnanimous. My mother sent me a remarkable account of a visit to our Dumbarton Avenue home by Rod Knoop, one of my hippie roommates at Eliot House, in January 1971. After getting married in the nude on a mountaintop, Rod had dropped out of Harvard and joined a large free-love commune in the Midwest. Writing to me in Brussels, my mother described Rod's attempt to convert Joe:

> Rod & friend were bearded, very clean, having stopped off at the Y.M.C.A. to bathe, very gentle & sweet, unable to eat or drink anything except fresh orange juice, & adorable to Joe, who they had clearly come to convert. He was equally gentle, and listened speechless while they told him of their faith. The worst sins are not alcohol, tobacco etc. but argumentativeness and "ripping off" which means interrupting people. Joe became more and more like the Roman centurion before Jesus, humble & meek—they stayed two hours and moved on the next day.

My mother's interest in young people was more sharply focused than Joe's. She was scouting the next generation of leadership. After a Vietnam veteran's antiwar demonstration, she wrote me presciently, "John Kerry seems to have star quality, first of all he is very good looking, then he speaks well. I should think that he had a political future." This gravitational pull to power came up twenty years later when I was driving Mother to Maine one summer in the eighties and we were talking about my wife Kate Bacon's family. One of her brothers-in-law, Frank MacNamara, had recently run for Congress. My mother looked over at me and asked, "Is Frank important yet?"

I suspect Joe was far more fascinated by the originality of a Rod Knoop than what he may have seen as the more conventional ambition of a John Kerry. Joe had a natural curiosity about the cultural oddities of life. In contrast to my mother, he never made me feel like I had failed by taking different paths in life. He seemed to genuinely enjoy my company.

Joe used to sit next to me when I drove a car and would draw his breath in mock horror at my driving habits. The fact that he couldn't drive limited his credibility, but it didn't lessen his sense of authority. While Joe and I could talk playfully about a wide range of topics, Vietnam was a particularly sensitive subject of discussion. He never asked me directly what I thought of his columns, but he might suddenly lambaste some friend of the family for being a turncoat on Vietnam. When his friend Bob McNamara started to express doubts about the war, Joe would pronounce him a secretary of peace rather than a secretary of war. I had no strong ideological feelings and skirted the issue by telling him that his columns were getting boring and that he should probably retire and concentrate on art history. I knew he really didn't care what I thought about his columns, but the words "a bore" had a small sting to them that might make him think.

I was gentle with Joe because I also knew something about being a loner. I had walked around the same circle at Groton that he had, sat in the same pews he had, and because of my English accent had been made to feel like an outsider, though never to the same degree Joe had been. I was rescued by, among other things, being on a couple of varsity sports teams.

In his obituary of Joe for the *Independent*, the English journalist Henry Fairlie acutely observed that Joe was "something of a loner," who "probably suffered more than any of us know." Fairlie ascribed Joe's suffering to his experience as a Japanese prisoner of war, but I suspect that this physical discomfort during the war was mild compared with the five years of humiliation he suffered at Groton. He could do something about his condition as a POW, but he was mostly powerless about the vicious social codes at Groton.

Joe's fury, like Captain Ahab's in *Moby Dick*, grew out of his rage at being handicapped and powerless. Ahab had his leg taken away from him; Joe, his sense of manhood. For Joe at Groton—being an odd and cerebral guy instead of a popular athlete—the feelings of shame intensified as he matured as a closeted gay man in a deeply homophobic world. It is easy today to forget the vicious abuse so many gay men suffered in our country just a few decades ago. Joe and my mother would have been shocked to see the issue of homophobia brought out so openly as it was in the powerful and critically acclaimed 2005 movie *Brokeback Mountain*.

Fairlie, himself a hard-drinking and outspoken Englishman, understood Joe better than most, particularly Joe's hidden qualities and his compulsion to be a contrarian. This obsession for standing apart from the crowd helps explain the view that, as the former *New York Times* columnist Leslie H. Gelb wrote in 1995, "For all his contacts, Joseph Alsop may have made more dragons than he slew." As Gelb points out, "That he so early and courageously condemned Senator Joseph R. McCarthy's witch hunting makes his harangues about gaps and dominoes that much more perplexing." Gelb was right. If there were no hideous McCarthy figures in sight, Joe had to dig up or create some "really nasty piece of work." President Jimmy Carter, whom he called the worst president since James Buchanan, came fairly close to filling the bill, not so much because he was evil as because Joe saw him as so massively inept.

A number of people said Joe had mellowed after he retired, but I always thought that was because they were no longer being subjected to his columns. Even though he had stopped being a journalist, his research on the origins of art collecting and other assignments kept him fully occupied, and he seemed to me as opinionated as ever. In some ways his prejudices hardened, such as his pro-Israeli and anti-Palestinian sentiments and his vocal contempt for most "wooly-eyed" liberals and "second-raters" in general.

Around the time I came back to Massachusetts in 1973, Joe started to think about retiring near Boston. I took him one day to the Somerset Club, a private social club on Beacon Hill. It was around the middle of the day, and the club was fairly empty. Suddenly Joe spied a tall man named Ham Robb, who used to live in the club. Joe evidently recognized him and went up to him, saying, "Hello, Ham, how are you?" The man looked at Joe as if he had never laid eyes on him before.

Maybe that was just what he needed to make up his mind, and he soon decided against Boston. On some level he was still that fat eccentric who, though they voted him into the clubs, never really belonged. Compared with the many and varied worlds in Washington, Boston had a special kind of parochialism, and the fact that Joe had even considered moving there showed the pull that academic life still held on him.

Over the years, Joe's old Groton and Harvard friends had generally grown to accept him. But that's not to say they really understood him. In the late winter of 1996 I ran into Joe's old classmate Charles Devens, a stellar example of the WASP species Joe so admired. He was sitting quietly like a statue of George Washington in the morning room of the Somerset Club, overlooking Beacon Street and the Boston Common. A quintessential Brahmin and a State Street banker who in his youth had pitched for the Yankees, Charlie had lived with Joe and Bill Patten throughout their years at Groton and Harvard. He was one of my parents' oldest friends. He was also my other godfather.

Charlie thanked me politely for sending him Robert Merry's well-researched biography of the Alsop brothers, *Taking On the World,* for Christmas. He had always been punctilious about sending me twenty-five dollars at Christmas, and I thought it was about time for me to repay him. Much as I admired Charlie Devens, I had always felt awkward in his august presence and was never totally comfortable talking with him. As I was getting up to leave, he turned and said, "My God, I had never realized until I read this book that Joe was a homosexual! Is it true?"

Joe Alsop and Bill Patten at 2720 Dumbarton Avenue, circa 1964

thirteen

Launched by Joe

This letter will be a red hot poker
stuck up Walter Thayer's ass.

—JOE ALSOP TELLING OUR LAWYERS THE EFFECT OF HIS
PERSONAL LETTER TO WALTER THAYER, OF WHITNEY COMMUNI-
CATIONS, CONCERNING THEIR INTENT TO PURCHASE THE *BELFAST
REPUBLICAN JOURNAL* AND OTHER MEDIA PROPERTIES IN MAINE,

DECEMBER 1978

BEFORE A THANKSGIVING luncheon at 2720 Dumbarton Avenue in the mid-sixties, as oysters were being passed around, I stood in the far end of the living room near the garden with Joe's brother Stewart. Stew asked me if I realized that Joe was reliving his life through me. Hiding my surprise, I answered no and we moved into the dining room.

After dinners at his house, Joe would herd the men into the garden room. It was a funny little room that had a big skylight; a black-and-white tiled floor; two bronze birdcages, each with doves; and an eclectic mixture of art on the walls, including a painting of a woman's head by Picasso. Joe liked to remind us that a female family member had reputedly chopped off the signature to make it fit into the frame.

We would sit around the glass table while the brandy, maraschinos, and cigars were passed around. Joe would turn to the great men of the world and say, "Tell me, ahum, ahum, ahum . . . what, ahum, ahum, ahum . . . is your ahum, ahum, ahum . . . definition of success?"

It was an entirely rhetorical question, as most of the veteran diplomats or cabinet officers knew well. We would sit politely through Joe's endless "ahums," each uttered with his head down resting on the palms of his hands, and with a half-inch cigarette ash destined for the marble floor dangled from his fingers. Only newcomers, the uninitiated, would be foolish enough to hazard an answer.

If there was an educator in the room—an "important" man like Yale president Kingman Brewster, former Harvard dean McGeorge Bundy, or eminent Oxford don Isaiah Berlin—Joe would needle him a little, trying to seduce him into the game. Even they, wise men that they were, tended to demur. Joe would then grace us with his own answer. "Two things," he would begin, "climbing the top of your tree, whatever tree you pick, and becoming part of the larger world." There was little dissent from his worldly audience, most of whom were perched at the top of their very tall trees.

While he was not usually trying to make his guests adopt his opinions, the case with me was quite different. Over a twenty-year period, Joe delivered a constant flow of advice on everything from clothes, to school, to my romantic life and career decisions, in the sincere belief that I would benefit from implementing his plans. He wrote many letters to me beginning when I left for Groton, most of which focused on building my self-confidence. He consoled me about my average grades while actively scheming about how to boost them. His letters were personally typed and hand-signed, "All my love, Joe."

As I progressed through Groton, Joe's interventions became increasingly evident. He regularly conferred with my math teacher, hired a law school student to tutor me in German, and conspired with Harvard officials about the best strategy for getting me admitted. By the time I got to Harvard, Joe felt he could be quite explicit in his advice. He always took care to add an "Esq." to my full name on the envelope, and in his letters Joe began to be very specific. A letter he sent to me during my freshman year included the following directives:

A. Because of Mr. Bundy, be sure to get your hair cut before dining with the Lothrops.

B. Be sure to send a polite acceptance of the Aldrich anniversary invitation, and put this down as a *must* in your engagement book.

C. Let me know further about the car. I tried to make the accident sound as unworrying as possible to Mummy, but I must say I am a little bit worried about it. So be very very careful when the car is restored to service.

D. Observe parietal rules!!!

Joe made the remark about parietal rules because of an incident involving a girl in the shower in my dorm, Wigglesworth. I had a female visitor, as we freshmen often did. When the janitor came in to clean up the bathroom, he flushed the toilet, reducing the cold water coming out of the showerhead and prompting my girlfriend to squeal and jump out of the shower into his arms. For this I was brought before the senior tutor and reprimanded. My parents never mentioned it.

Sometimes Joe's instructions arrived in the form of yellow Western Union cables. Shortly before Thanksgiving of 1969, I received in my dingy off-campus apartment a telegram that read; "YOU ARE DINING BRITISH EMBASSY WEDNESDAY PLEASE BRING DINNER JACKET AND ARRIVE IN TIME. JOE."

Since Joe had paid for my English-made dinner jacket, I naturally felt beholden and no doubt arrived on time, though I have no memory of that evening at the British embassy.

Joe and Susan Mary Alsop, Anne Patten and Bill Patten at Bill's Groton School graduation, 1966

After eight years in boarding schools, I was taking full advantage of my freedom, far less conscious of Joe's concerns for me than I had been at Groton. But his directions kept coming with regularity. He frequently congratulated me on what he saw as my great courage, often contriving to find excuses for my mishaps. After my second serious car accident in two years, sending my friend Sam Blagden through the front windshield of my Saab outside Eliot House in January 1968, Joe wrote me that he hadn't known until my sister told him that I was color-blind. He added that he'd realized my Jay grandfather had "some sort of defect of vision which affected his judgment of distances, and in consequence, since he was also as fearless as you are, he was constantly cannoning into other riders or trees or God knows what. A horse, at any rate, has some distance judgment of its own. A car does not."

I was touched by his concern, but much of this advice felt pretty irrelevant coming from someone who didn't even have a driver's permit. On the other hand, I also neglected to pay attention to one area where his expertise was almost unmatched: social clubs. Thus, when Joe wrote me my freshman year about Harvard clubs, it went right over my head. He wrote:

> If you are asked to join the AD or PC (and be sure to reply in the most formal manner and immediately, as to a very grand invitation from a respected older person) I shall be very happy indeed, as will Mummy and Granny. It puts a kind of gloss on one's college time, which may not be important later, but is important at the time. I beg you, remember Daddy's and my classmate Bill Gay, to whom nothing ever good happened except joining the PC. If asked to join both, the lowest possible "low posture," as the Japanese call it, is clearly indicated.

Joe's letter perplexed me: was it really important or not? Either way, I was having too good a time to worry much about it. I promptly antagonized a Californian from the Porcellian Club and soon offended a member of the A.D. I had worn bell-bottoms to one event and was not sufficiently deferential at another, so despite being solicited by both clubs at various drunken weekend outings, I was blackballed by one and not invited by the second.

When Joe heard of my failure, he wrote immediately, assuring me "it doesn't matter a damn." Then he flew up to Boston and took my friend David Sulzberger and me to dinner at the posh Boston restaurant Locke-Ober. The next day he bought me a new dinner jacket and ordered two new suits for me from his tailor on Savile Row in London. He later wrote to me extolling "the blue pin stripe and the rather dashing hounds' tooth tweed." I began to get an inkling of just how much the Harvard clubs—especially the Porcellian—meant to Joe.

My classmate Alberto Raurell, a dashing Cuban who had gone to Phillips Academy, convinced me to join the Spee Club, of which he was the president. It was a far more eclectic group, ranging from scions of wealth like Willy Hearst to brilliant writers and members of the *Harvard Lampoon* like Doug Kenny, but I never spent much time there.

Though he did not intend it, the harder Joe worked to train me, the less chance I had to gauge my own merits. I watched my childhood friends get into and through Harvard fine without any coaching from their fathers. The more Joe reinforced my chances with the help of his famous friends, the more powerless I felt. I think that perhaps he understood this feeling, but he could not resist offering his direct interference.

Joe told me once that my goal in life should be to live in the style to which I had become accustomed. That said more than he may have realized. Instead of encouraging me to pursue any specific interest, he was really telling me to hedge my bets and work on feathering my own nest. It was the opposite of what he preached in the garden room, and the clear message was that I would do better to stay out of anything really competitive, let alone aspire to being the best at anything.

Thus Joe's intense supervision effectively helped undermine my own sense of career ambition. It now seems unsurprising that in my early life I focused mostly on short-term emotional needs like security, autonomy, and a home of my own. It was clear to me that I could not compete in the realm of giants that used to sit around Joe's garden room smoking cigars after dinner, and that I needed to find a different playing field. I never even felt as intelligent as most of my Harvard peers, and not nearly as narrowly focused and driven as my Stanford Business School classmates.

On the other hand, I felt I had a more varied and interesting mix of friends than most of my classmates. Joe was also keeping a closer eye on this aspect of my life than I realized at the time. Writing to me that freshman fall, he says:

> I was a little bit worried by your seeming-frame of mind the other evening. To be specific, you struck me (and Joe, too) [his nephew, Stewart's oldest son] as more blue than I had seen you in a long time. As I hate to see people *I* care for greatly blue, I keep wanting to do something about it, without knowing precisely what to do . . . Grandmother Cole as psychoanalyst is Joe's advice, but if something is really on your mind I hope you will talk to me about it.

He ended the letter with his particular attention to details: "Also, is Mrs. [Arthur] Marion Schlesinger correct in her contention that you had lost Mrs. [Kitty] Bacon's gloves by the

Kitty Jay Bacon holding Sam Patten, 2720 Dumbarton Avenue, July 1971

time you left her party? P.S. Mrs. Schlesinger was also full of compliments on your 'beauty.' I am not sure I know what to make of this."

Kitty Bacon, the youngest daughter of my great-uncle, De-Lancey Jay, had recently left her husband and moved her brood of six children to a house on Francis Avenue, where I sometimes went for tea. My most vivid memory of that house is being drawn to the well-stocked refrigerator in the pantry. Kitty told me years later that she always knew when I had left the house, because she would hear me slamming the refrigerator door shut on my way out.

Although the late sixties at Harvard and elsewhere were famously rebellious, it never occurred to me that even in that radical context I was perceived as pushing the limits. In my own mind, I was simply going with the prevailing flow. In retrospect, after eight years of boarding school incarceration, I was acting out, drunk with the incredible freedom of college, which was intensified by the chaotic ethos of the late sixties.

For my senior thesis I picked a topic that would ensure the minimum amount of time doing library research. I knew that Dean Acheson was a friend of Joe's and that I could probably get to interview him. So even though my major was European history, I decided to focus on Acheson's decision-making style. The topic was approved. Since most of his advisers were also family friends—Dean Rusk, Chip Bohlen, George Kennan, Luke Battle, and Paul Nitze—I was able to interview them all quite effortlessly with my tape recorder. That was the easy part. Less fun was having Joe make me rent a dreary room in a boardinghouse where I could get away from my friends and party life and concentrate on my thesis. I doubt I would have earned my honors without Joe compelling me to hibernate alone the way I did for a few weeks.

During the spring of my junior year and through the summer, I dated an artistic and rather shy girl named Kate Paley, the daughter of CBS founder William Paley. Eager to see me settle down, and delighted by the wealth and pedigree of her parents, Joe made overt, even embarrassing, efforts to convert this relationship into marriage. Kate and I had lived together over the summer, which gave Joe high hopes for our future together. When I told Joe that things between Kate and me were shaky, he quickly produced airline tickets and invited us to join him on a business trip to visit S. I. Hayakawa, president of the University of California. He also funded dinners for us at Lafayette, his favorite French restaurant in Manhattan. Much to Joe's disappointment, however, Kate fell in love with someone else.

Then, as fate would have it, my senior year I had the good luck of meeting Kitty Bacon's eldest daughter—another Kate. She had arrived in Cambridge on a bus from Cape Cod, carrying a guitar and sporting a head of thick, curly brown hair. I felt embraced by the warmth of the Bacon family, my generous-hearted cousin Kitty and her six lovely children. Kate had a well-earned reputation for rebelliousness, which added to her appeal.

The summer of our junior year I had been the best man at the wedding of my roommate Alberto Raurell and a handsome red-haired girl from Philadelphia named Lydia Apple. One evening the following fall, as the two of us were crossing Harvard Square with our bicycles, a truck almost hit us. No doubt influenced by Alberto's decision to marry, I felt that I must seize the moment, and by the time we reached Kitty's house, which was now on Brattle Street, I decided to ask Kate if she wanted to get married. She accepted.

Later that month I met Joe and my mother at the Lafayette restaurant and announced our plans to get married. The two of them were on their way to Vietnam. My mother blanched at the

Joe Alsop with Bill and Kate Patten at their wedding, Cambridge, Massachusetts, December 1970

news, because, I think, the very concept of marriage seemed unnerving to her. It is possible that her increasing difficulties living with Joe were part of the reason. In fact, although I was unaware of it at the time, she was already thinking of leaving him.

Although Joe later wrote me a thoughtful letter about the dangers of falling in love "on the rebound," he heartily supported my decision to marry Kate Bacon. He bought her some lovely jewels, invited her to meet his grand Washington friends, and sang her praises to everyone. He arranged my bachelor's dinner at the Metropolitan Club in Washington and ordered the outfits for my ushers, picking their shirts from Sulka's in New York City. As I was headed for an internship in Brussels, he sent out a barrage of letters on my behalf to his old friends, including Jean Monnet, founder of the European Economic Community.

Kate and Sam Patten, Los Altos, California, 1972

Kate and I were married in Cambridge in December 1970. The *Boston Globe* published a photo of Joe at our reception on Brattle Street talking with Mrs. Charles F. Adams. The caption next to it read: "Girls discuss the servant problems." I have always assumed it was a typographical error.

After six months working for the European Common Market in Brussels, Kate and I returned to Washington, where our son, Sam, was born. I had applied to Stanford Business School but was on the waiting list, so our immediate future was in limbo.

I had applied to business school largely to please Joe, but also because I had no clear idea what to do with my life. Joe had preached to me for years that business was "a central part of the

American experience," so when he learned that I was on the waiting list at Stanford, he rolled out two of his big guns—Robert McNamara and David Packard—to get my application the attention he thought it deserved. Once again I was ushered into an elite school partly through the unsolicited assistance of Joe.

Kate and I moved to Palo Alto, California, with our baby son in September 1971. I was taken aback the first day at the business school when the dean, Arjay Miller, welcomed my class warmly and then projected what our future earnings would be. *What do salaries have to do with education?* I wondered. I had no idea what a mortgage was, and the idea of getting a "good deal" was still a pretty nebulous concept, certainly nothing I had ever heard discussed at our family's dinner table.

To make matters worse, I had little aptitude for linear programming and systems analysis, disciplines for which Stanford was justly famous. Fortunately, a number of my classmates were older men, former navy pilots or nuclear submarine officers, who were willing to coach me. Dollar-focused as many of my classmates were, the commercial culture at Stanford was remarkably benign. I was able to sneak off to take classes in American art and European history. My art professor told me that my paper on Edward Hopper was one of the most original and well-written papers he had read at Stanford, but leaving the business school to pursue art history didn't seem like an option. I had bought too heavily into Joe's agenda for me.

Meantime, my mother was a harsh Eastern foil to my Stanford classmates. During the spring of my first year there, she and I had a confrontation that became known in the family as "The Yosemite Incident." Looking back thirty-some years later, I am not surprised that the great explosion happened during a period of my life when I felt the most intellectually disoriented.

I had invited my mother to join me on a tour of Yosemite National Park. As we traveled through the majestic forest, she made some polite remarks about the trees, but overall the experience seemed to leave her cold. We stayed at the famous Yosemite Lodge, a rustic gem whose Western charms seemed lost on her. After a few drinks, she made some condescending remarks about my sister's marital problems, and her familiar sarcastic tone made me absolutely furious.

Since I had also had a few drinks, my recollection of the conversation is imprecise. I don't believe I ever raised my voice, but I remember saying—in clichéd terms—that we lived on "completely different planets." I wanted her to know how far apart we were, how totally disconnected I felt from her.

If my intent was to hurt her, her subsequent letter confirms that I succeeded. It was only rereading her thank-you note three decades later that I realized she had actually absorbed the conversation. Although I obviously received the note years earlier, my recollection had been that she glossed everything over in a ritualistic "thank you for a glorious visit."

Written on a yellow legal pad, her Yosemite letter stands out against the usual elegant stationery of some embassy or grand house in Barbados. My mother wrote with what I think of as uncharacteristic honesty:

> Your sermon, as you call it, at the hotel however threw me badly off base. I should probably have helped you most by bursting into tears, throwing the candlestick at you, and walking out. That way you would have known that you had got through to me. My icy calm was probably to you, most inhuman. In fact, I was in trauma—for every word got through to me and I was furiously angry, as well as bewildered by you. It was as if an old, old friend with whom I had had good times & sad times for 24 years had suddenly turned on me . . . I thought that I was facing a stranger—and that if I could just take it, in the morning the nightmare would have disappeared. That was a mistake.

Susan Mary Alsop, circa 1960

> You and Anne feel alike about me in many ways, I have not been a
> particularly good mother as you see it, and you are probably right.
> But I don't feel in the least bit guilty, because I have tried my hardest
> and if I have failed you at least I have done my best, not from a sense
> of duty but from pleasure.

It was a brave response. The first part was surely true. If my
mother had cried or thrown a candlestick at me, it would have
been the sort of human connection I had been looking for all my
life. Although trapped in her iron cage of good manners, she apparently realized deep inside that her "icy calm" was inhuman. I
failed to see that then, but I am glad to know it now.

The two years in California passed quickly. It never really occurred to Kate or me to stay on the West Coast. There was something about the rarified air of Palo Alto that unnerved me, and the idea of returning to Bill Patten's home turf felt comforting. So I turned down job offers in San Francisco and Chicago and decided to head back to New England. After graduation, I drove our U-Haul back to Boston. Even though I had no immediate prospects, I felt like I had arrived home.

Kate and I found a magnificent old brick house in the shadow of Bunker Hill in Charlestown, just across the Charles River from Boston. Charlestown was a remarkably tight-knit community in those days. People looked out for one another in a wonderful way that I had never experienced in Paris or Washington, D.C. The ever-expanding Duffy family lived across the street from us, and the Duffy daughters were wonderful babysitters for Sam. Mr. Duffy worked in the post office, and Mrs. Duffy spent most of her days sitting with her cousins in deck chairs on Monument Court and keeping an eye on our house. One spring day, Mrs. Duffy was sitting there in one of her plastic beach chairs and looked up to see Sam standing by a third-floor window in a Superman costume. She immediately called Kate, who rushed upstairs to grab Sam before he was able to test his magical powers.

For me, these were Maurice Sendak years. The inside of our three-story townhouse was *In the Night Kitchen,* and Sam was the little naked boy falling into the milk bottle. And because Boston was undergoing severe racial tensions at that time, outside of our house, where racial fights took place, was *Where the Wild Things Are.* Although we took Sam to a private school on Beacon Hill, we empathized with the Duffys, who were enraged by the school busing that roiled the city.

Boston is a city not known for its warmth, and I was surprised by the welcome given to us by my father's old Groton and

Harvard classmates. I had known some of these men—including Charles Francis Adams, chairman of Raytheon, and my godfather, Charlie Devens—as distant figures when I was growing up in Europe. Their interest in me, of course, had everything to do with their loyalty to Bill. Remarkably, even the most august of them were tolerant that we chose to live in an Irish enclave of the city, which had once been a navy base and was now famous for its bars and tough "townies."

Soon after returning to Boston, my godfather invited me to join him for dinner at a big round table in the men's dining room of the Somerset Club. So here was the legend in person, all six trim feet of him, wearing a British blue pinstriped suit. Devens was gracious, considerate, and avuncular. But as I struggled to find the right words and the right tone, part of me wondered, *What am I doing here? What have I done to deserve this?*

I was touched when Charlie Adams gamely came to our house for dinner. In those days, Charlestown was an unfashionable neighborhood, but one that was well known to Adams. During World War II he had commanded the USS *Fogg*, which periodically visited the Charlestown naval base. As he parked his Rolls-Royce on our street, the thought must have crossed his mind that these tough Irish townies had ruled the place for generations. As a naval officer, he may have been welcome, but as a Yankee who belonged on Beacon Hill, he could not be sure.

On the whole, I was still following Joe's script. I wore my Anderson & Sheppard custom-tailored suits to the First National Bank of Boston, where I worked in the commercial lending department. I joined the Somerset Club on Beacon Street. And I was touched but a little unnerved when Joe and my mother sent me their investment portfolios. They must have thought that carrying a briefcase and wearing well-polished lace-up shoes made me a knowledgeable adviser. In fact, I was totally inexperienced about investments, but too embarrassed to tell them.

My best friend at the bank, a football player from Detroit named David Ormes, reminded me over martinis at Pete's on Broad Street that we did not belong at the First National Bank of Boston. David, an ambitious African American, was busy closing aggressive letter-of-credit deals with Japanese clients and had made enough waves to be transferred to New York. I knew the time was coming to make my own exit.

That same year, I bumped into my Harvard classmate Ira Jackson, who was working for mayor Kevin White. He asked me what I was doing. When I told him I was a banker, he exclaimed, "Oh, you old fascist!" I was taken aback, but not offended. I liked Ira. He told me proudly that the mayor had kept Richard Hill, the chairman of our bank, waiting for half an hour before seeing him. After living in Charlestown for a few years, I was hardly surprised by the deep schism between the Irish and the Brahmins.

After a year, I resigned from the bank and joined a real estate partnership in the South End, a fragmented city neighborhood with some promise. My first projects involved renovating Victorian apartment buildings on a seedy street next to Bay Village. At the age of twenty-five, I finally was learning about the meaning of money. Collecting rent, evicting tenants, and paying off city inspectors, I was plunged into the rough-and-tumble stuff that my Stanford professors had never addressed in their elegant theorizing.

Although Kate and I enjoyed living in Charlestown, the city itself was becoming uglier by the day. Busing children across Boston to achieve racial balance was a noble experiment, but it ravaged neighborhoods, including our own, which became a flashpoint for some of the ugliest violence. As the protests became rampages, and the tension in the streets escalated, it became clear to Kate and me that we needed to move.

We now had two children; our second, Eliza, had been born on April 11, 1974. We wanted them to grow up in a safer

Sam, Eliza, and Kate Patten and Susan Mary Alsop, Charlestown, Massachusetts,1975

environment, where we could more easily share in their lives. What had at first drawn me to Boston, the ghost of Bill Patten and his cozy WASP world, now felt like it was hemming me in. Kate and I explored places like Salem without success. We were not interested in living on the North Shore or in Cambridge, overly familiar haunts, so we decided to look beyond Boston.

Our stepping-stone to Maine was another real estate venture. After leaving the bank, I had been renovating an old farmhouse on a spectacular 150-acre property called Eastholm on the island of Vinalhaven in Penobscot Bay, about two hours east of Portland. To do this I had formed a partnership with a bachelor named Guido Goldman. Although Guido was unfamiliar with Maine, he seemed to like our family and enjoyed the fun parties we had in the large house. He lived in one wing, we lived in the other, and guest rooms were in the middle.

In the process, I became close to the islanders. I cleared the fields with an old tractor, bought the old garage in town, and joined the local Lions Club, which held its happy hour in the garage. Some lobstermen took me deer hunting on neighboring islands for a couple of days, which involved night hunting and cooking parts of the deer for breakfast. We spent the winter of 1977 on the island, Kate walking Sam down our mile-long driveway each morning to catch the school bus.

My transition from Maine visitor to Maine newspaper publisher might not have happened if our caretaker had not told me that he had caught a neighbor pilfering rocks from one of our beaches. I met the offending party, a friendly lawyer named Hoddy Hildreth, returning to Rockland on the ferry. He apologized and invited me to have lunch in Portland with his cousin Rusty Brace, who ran newspapers and lived in Camden.

Following this lunch, Brace invited me to his office in Camden, and there in his big office overlooking the harbor, he offered to sell me the *Belfast Republican Journal,* the paper that his father had owned and run. I called a cousin of mine, Jay Iselin, who ran a TV station in New York, and asked for help in making the deal. Jay gave me the names of several potential investors. "Maine," he said optimistically from his Manhattan office, "is no longer a jumping-off place to nowhere." It was a wonderful phrase that I wanted to believe.

Jay suggested I contact his friend Dick Saltonstall, as Dick had written a book on Maine and was yearning to live there. At the time, Dick was living in Virginia. He was forty-one years old, married with four children, and working as a freelance writer. I called Dick, and he came over to Eastholm from his summer place in North Haven in a small boat with an outboard engine. Dick was buoyant about the idea of moving to Maine, and we hit it off. Later that afternoon, we agreed to become partners and celebrated by smoking cigars as we gazed across the

Richard Saltonstall Jr., Maine, circa 1974

Fox Island Thoroughfare, which separates Vinalhaven and North Haven. Dick, it turned out, was as eager to leave Virginia as I was to leave Boston. Both of us were looking forward to forging a home in Maine.

As a journalist, Joe took a special interest in our plan to buy the *Republican Journal*. I didn't realize it at the time, but Dick's uncle Leverett Saltonstall, a governor and U.S. senator from Massachusetts, had met Joe at a Porcellian Club dinner soon after Joe's admission to the club. Given the value Joe attributed to tribal connections, this enhanced his enthusiasm for my prospective partnership.

Kate and I and our two children left Boston and bought a home in Camden, Maine, during the summer of 1978. Kate was pregnant with our third child, Sybil, who was born on October 26.

We settled into mid-coast life easily, but as the fall progressed, Rusty Brace kept postponing the closing on the sale of the newspaper. Kate and I started to get worried. After probing around, I discovered that Brace was secretly trying to sell his paper to someone else. The much wealthier buyer turned out to be a New York media conglomerate, Whitney Communications, founded by Jock Whitney. Fortunately for us, but unbeknownst to Rusty Brace, the Whitneys were old family friends of both the Pattens and the Alsops.

Dick and I were in a strong but not unassailable position, because I had a written offer and acceptance from Brace. Our lawyers filed suit against Rusty Brace for specific performance, warning us that we might not win in court, but kept the suit private from the media. After tactfully getting the nod from Jock Whitney's brother-in-law Bill Paley, Joe drafted a letter to Walter Thayer, the president of Whitney Communications, threatening an ugly social brouhaha if his company did not back down. Joe mentioned in passing that his friend Bill Paley, the chairman of CBS, had recommended the lawsuit.

Joe's hand-delivered letter to Thayer began ominously: "I went to Bill Paley with the information that the little paper had in fact been offered to Bill and Dick . . . who were planning their futures around it." Joe took obvious relish in calling Thayer on the carpet on social and moral terms by using the biblical metaphor of Naboth's vineyard—and the divine retribution that fell on King Ahab and his wife, Jezebel, after they destroyed Naboth and his family for a vineyard. "You may not realize it," he wrote, "but you have placed me in the most difficult personal position. Unless I am mistaken, my father went to both Groton and Yale with Jock's father."

Joe reinforced all of this with a detailed accounting of the cozy relationships that the Patten, Alsop, and Saltonstall families had enjoyed with the Whitneys over many years, stressing his own warm feelings for Betsey Whitney and her two sisters, Babe (Paley) and Minnie, who he referred to as "my own cherished friends more years than I care to count."

Joe rightly guessed that his letter would be passed on to Jock Whitney, who would not want to see his company entangled in an unpleasant social imbroglio, especially when the stakes were so modest. Thayer's reply to Joe was prompt and chilly. He said that at his request the seller had come to New York to show him firsthand our correspondence. Seeing my signed letter of acceptance for the first time, Thayer immediately authorized Whitney Communications to withdraw from the purchase.

Throughout our meetings with the lawyers, Joe had described his letter to all of us as "a red hot poker stuck up Walter Thayer's ass." As it turned out, Thayer had been condescending to Joe in the early sixties when he was president of the *New York Herald Tribune*, which was owned by Jock Whitney. This was Joe's chance to get back at him. The subtext of Joe's letter to Thayer was that even though he ran a media conglomerate, he was still the Whitneys' footman. And in some circles these things still mattered. The old WASP tribe had *not* lost its ability to sting, and that gave Joe immense satisfaction.

It was important to Joe that his "red hot poker" had a moral edge to it and was not just petty revenge. Thayer and Brace were violating the basic trust of gentlemen—a code embodied, as far as Joe was concerned, in his own Porcellian Club at Harvard and Jock's Scroll and Key club at Yale. The fact that connections mattered more than money was at the core of his code of honor.

The potentially messy experience and threats of lawsuits affirmed Joe's feeling that business was basically a form of combat. I remember him telling me in a morose tone that he would not like to meet Kay Graham's business adviser, Warren Buffet, alone in a dark alley at night.

My family's move to Maine had certainly not been part of Joe's grand plan for me, but it is unlikely that Dick and I would have made it off the launching pad without Joe's help. His intervention had tipped the balance in our favor, in what our lawyers agreed was a dicey legal claim. He had taken personal initiatives and risks on my behalf, which were consistent with his sense of tribal loyalty.

Susan Mary Alsop, 1971

fourteen

Mother
Breaks Away

Goodness, it's depressing to know so many ambassadors!
—LETTER WRITTEN TO ME IN THE LATE 1960s FROM MY MOTHER

M Y MOTHER AND Joe's marriage had never been free of tension. I had witnessed storm clouds even before we left Paris that winter of 1960–1961. My mother told me that Joe had been incredibly rude to some French friends of hers at a dinner party. He later had apologized, but compared with Bill Patten's gentle good manners this must have been a brutal awakening. Once we arrived in the States, Joe's ritual of outbursts followed by profuse apologies seemed to me the likely scenario for the whole marriage—an ugly pattern that my mother would eventually get used to. If Joe had gotten away with abusing waiters and contractors all his life without retribution, it seemed, he could probably do the same with his wife.

My mother began writing to me about her problems with Joe when I was a graduate student at Stanford in the early seventies. Meanwhile, Joe would talk with me, over his very weak scotch and soda, about his problems with her. He would say rather mournfully, "I just don't know what I have done, but you know I can't help it—I seem to bore your mother." I would sit and listen, knowing in some vague way that the problem had nothing to do with his boring her. But I got used to these litanies, figuring they would go on and on just as their marriage would go on and on.

At the same time as she sent me requests for advice about Joe, however, my mother wrote me letters about how "marvelous" he had just been, describing the smoothly running household. What seemed to still bother her most were the public scenes Joe would make, usually after he was fairly drunk.

I had become accustomed to the tension in the house in the sixties, when I would come home from Groton for vacations. Joe's anger at my mother came in the form of tight lips, menacing frowns, and a compressed fury that seemed to be shaking his end of the dining room table. What hung over the scene were less Joe's nasty words than the intense exasperation that seemed to be broiling inside him. Partly because part of me could identify with his anger, partly because I knew my mother was basically tougher than Joe, I observed these scenes embarrassed but fairly unmoved.

My Groton classmate David Bruce remembers Joe verbally demeaning my mother in front of other people. I think this behavior was more shocking for David to witness, coming from his own subdued family, than it was for me. My mother's only response was to look at the floor in a martyrlike pose, which I knew only enraged Joe more. Still, as Joe's biographer, Robert Merry, points out, by the late sixties her "reputation as a witty dinner companion during the Paris days now counted for little, and she frequently just clammed up when guests came to Dumbarton."

This need to shut up and just listen in Joe's house was dramatized in my mother's report of a gruesome incident in the sixties. One day the police came by to ask why nobody in the house had reported the screams of a woman being assaulted right outside the previous evening. The victim had even been banging desperately on Anne's window. My mother told me that Joe's friend the Duc de Ventura had been singing to entertain Lorraine Cooper, who was dining with them. But she told the police that Joe's laugh "drowns out everything." The police officer reportedly replied, "Must be fun to live with—how do you get a word in edgewise?"

The feeling I sometimes got from Joe was that my mother had somehow betrayed him or was plotting some kind of hideous insurrection. It was as if he were waking up to the fact that she had just planted one of his cherished pearl-handled knives in his back and was smiling about it. One ongoing issue between them was whether my mother could invite her friends to visit. Joe distrusted those friends, like Marietta Tree, whom he saw as co-conspirators. He needed absolute control of the household.

Body language provided some of the few clues I picked up about what was really happening in my mother's home. One day in the late sixties I was asked to drive Marietta to the airport after one of her visits to Georgetown. I knew that Marietta and Joe viewed each other skeptically at best. Though Marietta said nothing about my mother or Joe, as we drove down the parkway I realized from the uncharacteristic grimness in her voice that she must have witnessed something that had shaken her up. This was my first clue that something was seriously wrong.

In retrospect, it seems my mother had been edging out of the marriage for some years before she actually moved out. She was probably not conscious of this, but in the late sixties she exhibited a brazen level of independence by taking overseas trips without Joe, revisiting old haunts and exploring new parts of the world. There was probably not one single defining moment in this process, but there was one particularly emblematic trip that I remember even made Joe slightly uncomfortable.

In March 1969 my mother decided to join her brother-in-law Stewart Alsop on a trip to the Middle East. He was traveling with his old OSS buddy Tom Braden. Joe grumbled to me about the appearances of his wife traveling with his brother, but he seemed resigned to it. My mother had traveled far and wide before with female friends, but setting off with such an attractive-looking man as Uncle Stew struck me as something of a threshold event, especially given how youthful he seemed next to Joe. Describing a farewell party for the McGeorge Bundys a few years earlier, my mother had written me, saying, "there is still life in the middle age Washingtonian," since she had seen Stew "dancing the Watusi at three A.M."

Although Stewart was every bit as attuned to social subtleties as his brother Joe, he was more restrained and less patronizing. Though I felt a certain aloofness in his approach to young people, he had taken me bird hunting a few times and I respected him. It would have been hard for me to imagine my mother and him as lovers, but Stewart was certainly a far more athletic and good-looking man than his older brother.

Until this trip my mother had mostly stayed in Joe's shadow. When traveling in Europe with Joe in the sixties, she would write to me describing her visits to old friends and museums while saying, "Joe is seeing the Prime Minister Lord Home and Harold Wilson the all but future Prime Minister." Or if she went alone, she would take a friend along, like Dottie Kidder, an old classmate who had a lovely apartment in Paris. But now she was traveling alone with two men who were her peers, and the agenda included bona fide political crises: a general strike planned in Paris and rumors of war in Cairo.

After living in Paris as a Patten, my mother now bore the name Alsop and was a veteran of "The Center," Stewart's term for the power fulcrum of Washington, D.C. No longer the young wife of a junior diplomat, she had dined privately with presidents in the White House and had hosted intimate dinners for the leaders of the free world.

One of the first nights in London my mother dined at Frank and Lady Kitty Giles's house. Frank had been editor of the British *Sunday Times*, and they had been close friends of our family in Paris. My mother was seated that night next to the queen's private secretary, Michael Adeane, and as she later wrote her mother, he was

> just what you would expect—highly informed but tells one about his cats, meanwhile drawing one out like no one has drawn me out since President Kennedy—just the same brilliant gift of asking questions. He must be good at his job. My other neighbor was the Permanent Secretary of the Foreign Office. I had just heard that Sammy Hood was retiring without so much as a pat on the back . . . so burning with rage I turned to the perfect, faceless present head of the Foreign Office and gently mentioned Sammy, murmuring facelessness is deception. He flattened me completely by saying, "Bachelor ambassadors don't do in the big embassies. Such a pity he didn't marry you." This took my breath away.

My mother continued, "Of course Sammy had never asked me to marry him and I told Sir Dennis so, coldly. He said, 'Forgive me for being indiscreet, but he would have—Joe Alsop didn't let the grass grow under his feet, did he?' I said, 'Can you prove that?' 'Yes, but I'd rather not.' Very odd. I changed the subject to Madame Pompidou—a rich vein and the hottest scandal in years."

Viscount Hood, known as Sammy Hood, was one of those tall, thin, impeccably dressed figures standing discreetly in the background in photos of house parties at Chantilly after the war. He was a counselor at the embassy in Paris from 1948 to 1951 after the Coopers had left, and was a frequent figure in my mother's photo albums.

Not only did these ultrathin British diplomats adorn her photo albums, but they accrued in Washington as well. She had written to me earlier about the British ambassador to the United States, David Ormsby-Gore, Lord Harlech, and his wife, saying they were "the most distinguished representatives of their country to be sent here for years." She continued with an unconvincing sigh, "Goodness, it's depressing to know so many ambassadors!" and then, with barely masked regret, recalled, "when Daddy and I were young we had so many bright young diplomatic friends, merry youths they were—now every last one is an ambassador."

On an earlier trip to London she wrote about trying to cheer up the former ambassador Lord Harlech, who had recently lost his wife in a car accident. They had been old friends from the Kennedy years. Mother wrote that she had let him drive her around the city in "his horrible car—a super racing model worth 8,000 pounds." Returning to the American embassy to discover it was locked up for the night—and not being willing to "climb the embassy wall" at the residence—she returned to Lord Harlech's apartment:

> I went in his ghastly car to David's flat—poor man such a dreary little place—I fell into bed (luckily there were two—in different rooms). The next morning dawned the Glorious Fourth, your dear birthday[,] and we drove back to the Embassy[,] where since antiwar riots were expected police were every two feet & on the doorstep was no less than the superintendent of Scotland Yard, who said, "Good morning Lord Harlech," not a muscle twitching, me still in full evening dress, flaking make up & diamond earrings.

This letter about David Ormsby-Gore came in the summer of 1968 just after my birthday, when I was working an oilrig in Texas and my sister was preparing to marry George Crile, an event largely orchestrated by Joe. Mother had the same skeptical feelings about this marriage as she did about mine two years later, referring to Anne and George as "wandering around in a happy daze, poor things."

But on this trip a year later with Stewart, my mother still made an effort to placate Joe. Writing several days later from Paris, a city seething with anti–de Gaulle sentiment, my mother consoled Joe that he was not missing out on anything "serious." In order to make her case, she described a pleasant lunch with old French friends and her decision to visit her dressmaker while the rest of Paris was tensing up for the riots, which Stewart was covering for *Newsweek*.

While the riots fizzled out, my mother was making productive use of her time doing something that would have pleased Joe: "While Stew was at the Place de la Bastille this afternoon I was at Balmain's . . . Awful not to have seen the proletariat out demonstrating in blue overalls, but one has seen it all before. There was no cutter so we seized the scissors and made me Nureyev-Balmain [by which she meant a kind of improvised gypsylike costume] and Cinette and Denise held the pins."

After replenishing her wardrobe, she was apparently drawn back to the birthplace of her first illicit romance. She sent a flurry of long letters to her mother from her little room on the top floor, which she always took at the hotels St. James and D'Albany on the Rue de Rivoli, facing the Tuileries Gardens, where she had taken us as children. In reassuring terms, she described to her mother a casual dinner at the British embassy: "It has recovered from Lady Riley's abstract pictures. Nice warm Mary Soames has brought it back to what it should be— Hoppners and Lawrences on the walls and gleaming silver on the table, English footmen in green and yellow liveries."

While Stewart was reporting on the riots, my mother managed to cover other world events as if she were working on her own journalistic assignments. She then tells her mother that she had seen their old New England friend Henry Cabot Lodge Jr., who was handling the peace negotiations with the Vietnamese. The Lodges "were as usual so very nice—Cabot a bit bored but funny and relaxed. Says the North Vietnamese treat him as if he was General [Wilhelm] Keitel and they were [Walter] Bedell-Smith at the Rheims surrender in 1944—their contempt is trying . . . Now off to Liliane de Rothschild's to listen to General De Gaulle's speech. Must stop to dress by candlelight."

Having caught up on U.S. negotiations with the Vietnamese, my mother reconvened with Stewart for their flight from Paris to Cairo, though once again she adhered to her own agenda by economizing on her seat. She reported to her mother about the flight, emphasizing her standard habit of economizing. Stewart, she wrote, had said "it's too silly of me to fly tourist class and he sits locked away in first class, but I spent too much of your glorious cheque in Paris. Tourist class was full of interest, where I met a charming French savant next to me, M. De Watcher of the Department of Egyptology at the Louvre, who I had seen lecturing on Tutankamon." She had enough money of her own, but typically wanted to make her mother feel that she had made the difference.

Writing from Shepheard's Hotel in Cairo, my mother tried to resurrect the Cairo her own mother had known before World War I:

> The Sporting Club at Gezira seemed most familiar . . . little touches of colonial Egypt are everywhere . . . I can see the restaurant where we dined last night, which is in fact a converted crusing ship from your day—I think it must be the one Mr. Morgan [Edwin Denison Morgan, DeLancey Jay's father-in-law] took as it is big and grand, the brass gleams, the lamps have shades of pleated pink silk, fringed, and I longed to be headed for the upper Nile. No time for that, alas . . . Tomorrow, in theory, we go to Jordan, but if President Nasser decides to receive Stewart we will stay.

My mother had been bristling at the bossiness of her two male companions as they started to give her instructions before leaving Paris. In her last letter to me from Paris she observed that "they have stopped being boulevardiers and are back in the 60th Rifles. I do so hope for a band at Orly, naturally playing the Marching Song from the Bridge Across the River Kwai." Her determination to follow her own agenda was high-lighted by her refusal to abide by Stewart's warnings not to visit the legendary Petra, an archeological site in southwestern Jordan, described by John William Burgon as "a rose-red city half as old as time." Stewart had argued, "'You're over 21, if you want to put your head in the cannon's mouth you can.'" Mother snapped back, "'Alright, Stew, you've added a paragraph to my book,'" to which he replied. "'What book?' 'It's called DON'T YOU KNOW, you shouldn't go to Petra.'" Arriving in Amman, she ignored Stewart's cautionary advice, and quickly procured the blessing of Sir Philip Adams, the British ambassador, who gave her access to a palace car. She then set off with her *Guide Bleu*, an old French guidebook, exclaiming to us in her letter, "What fun!"

The trip to Europe and the Middle East without Joe was lib-erating for my mother. She realized that she had a network of close friends on whom she could rely. She also reveled in her in-dependence. By the time I started business school in 1971, my mother's letters began to reveal serious doubts about her mar-riage to Joe. If she was confiding in me, she must have been con-fiding in others as well.

Despite the deep fractures in the marriage, politics could still hold them together on a social level. Though Joe had not voted for Richard Nixon, he rallied to the new administration, telling his old friend Ellsworth Bunker (who was ambassador to Viet-nam) that he felt "much encouraged" and "very glad" that Nixon had been elected instead of Hubert Humphrey. Joe and my mother were especially excited by Nixon's new relationship with China, an area of the world that Joe knew well.

In the spring of 1972 my mother attended a small dinner at the White House with President Nixon, Henry Kissinger, treasury secretary John Connally, and several others. She took the opportunity to query Nixon about his recent trip to China and was particularly interested in how Nixon thought Mao "measured up" to the European giants she had known, including Churchill and de Gaulle. She wrote me a long letter detailing Nixon's response. Of Nixon himself she wrote: "The President is not attractive, but that night I found him appealing—I've always thought him clever. But appealing—what an odd word to use— I read today that a poll of visitors to Mme. Tussaud's waxworks exhibition in London consider him the most feared, even ahead of Hitler or Mao or Jack the Ripper! But he was so bouncy."

But even while outwardly collaborating with Joe, that same spring my mother was voicing her concerns to me more openly than ever before. In April she wrote to me in California about the upcoming summer, requesting

> any observations you have on Joe from what you see of him in June. He seems to me perfectly okay during the daytime but from 8 P.M. on, rather more argumentative, combative, and unable to pursue normal conversation than usual. Dialogue has for ages been difficult, don't you agree, but it seems to me even less easy now. I have a feeling that he would be greatly relieved if I told him that I was removing myself from his life, when I broach this (I do it during the daytime) he says, very nicely, that is my decision. My decision is, if you agree—and I want your opinion after you have felt out the atmosphere, [is] to be deliberately selfish for the first time in my life (like most people, I am often selfish, but it goes against my training and nature to be deliberately selfish) and make no decision, because it suits me, for Granny's sake, to remain in Washington. This is hard on Joe.

What could I answer when she asked me about whether dialogue with Joe was more difficult now? In reality Joe could often hear things I told him that my mother could not. I had my own hands full with statistics and linear programming at Stanford, which was mostly unintelligible to me, and I seriously wondered if I was going to graduate.

If the uncertainty about separation was hard on Joe, that was nothing compared with how hard my mother could be on herself. The following year she experienced one of the most anguishing losses she had ever known: the death of her beautiful childhood friend Elise Duggan. Elise had known much sadness. In the summer of 1935, Elise's older brother had shot himself behind their house on Long Island. And her first marriage was a very unhappy one. So when Elise married a wealthy Frenchman named Pierre Bordeaux-Groult in 1952, my mother must have felt the excitement of her old friend joining forces with her and at last finding happiness in Paris.

The Groults had moved in 1957 into a handsome eighteenth-century house on the Rue du Bac that was large enough to display Pierre's important collection of paintings. Elise had suffered from asthma, but her death in 1973 involved deep emotional problems that I never fully understood. In a letter from a spa town in France the previous summer, my mother had written to Marietta Tree about her "confused impressions" when the Groults suddenly arrived from Switzerland, Elise "gasping for breath" and with "a terrible weight loss." It seemed Elise's asthma was compounded by "a terrible fear of being left," thus leaving her totally dependent on her husband, Pierre. "He said one or two things last night that worried me about the effect on him of the strain . . . it's so complicated."

My mother felt somehow responsible for not being able to save Elise. She had visited the Groults that summer, and in late

July she wrote Marietta: "[M]y sense of loss re Elise is as if you had been killed in an automobile accident, compounded by my own stubborn, selfish sense of having failed her, and I still wake up sweating in the night reliving the month of June." Trying to explain Elise's death to Marietta, she wrote, "I am gradually understanding that someone who had such very high standards re her duty to her family and friends did not really want to live a half-life, and that it was better that she died." I felt there was more to this story and it probably involved Pierre. But this dread of succumbing to a "half-life," whatever that exactly may have meant, may well have been a catalyst contributing to my mother's final decision to leave Joe.

At our house in Northeast Harbor the following month, as we were walking around the gravel driveway, Mother told me in a matter-of-fact voice that she felt like she had been living Edgar Allan Poe's "The Pit and the Pendulum" and that unless she escaped she would be crushed by the iron blade. It was unlike my mother to use such dramatic language. It woke me up to how much she must have been suffering. I had long felt Joe's obsession to control all aspects of her life, but this image of suffocation made me realize how desperate she had come to feel.

Still, I was taken aback by her profound sadness at what she claimed was her own failure. I had only seen a glimpse of that sadness. My mother had no experience with grieving; her impulse was always to maintain her composure and move on as rapidly as possible. She commented briskly that she had "failed," and turned back into the dark little library where she had started collecting old letters for her first book, *To Marietta from Paris, 1945–1960*. She had finished that letter to Marietta describing Elise's death a year earlier: "This afternoon I am going into more letters, I find it therapeutic and you have always helped me no end."

It would be misleading to gloss over my mother's painful divorce from Joe and fast-forward to the eighties, when she had established herself as an author and was living harmoniously a few blocks away from 2720 Dumbarton Avenue. That is exactly what happened, but the transition was predictably painful. My mother spent the first four years after her divorce living alone in a rented apartment at the Watergate Hotel. She lived directly under the flight path of Washington National Airport.

Although she had taken the initiative to leave Joe, my mother found it hard to understand why he initially treated her so coldly. He slunk into a shell whenever they saw each other, which was relatively frequently since they had so many friends in common. Both were hurt and confused, and both had an almost adolescent incapacity to cope with loss.

The separation did not affect my relations with Joe, and as I too was in transition, moving back from California to New England and starting my business career, I was not often in Washington. When I was there, however, I visited Joe. He would drop his head into the palms of his hands and ask why he irritated my mother so much. Like his regular refrain of "Am I an alcoholic?" this question was impossible to answer.

Soon after they separated in 1973, my mother wrote to me about their last encounter as a couple:

> Joe [and I] dined and I will not be seeing him often again. After all, he does not feel responsible for me, for, as he said, I am what I am— do call him if he can help. I enjoyed the total rejection, (he was looking at his watch all the time) as now I am sure he does not worry about me, and my rage and suppressed fury at having loved him & fought for him, politically, emotionally, viscerally was a waste of 14 years, and I can be cross. Healthier, no?

Was she asking for permission to be "cross"? I had never seen my mother openly angry, so I couldn't imagine her having the emotions described in the letter. The questions in her letters were so often rhetorical that I had long since given up trying to answer them in writing.

One of my mother's Manhattan friends suggested that she might find solace in a small pet. I was surprised at first that this old friend seemed to be forgetting how much my mother detested animals. But it then sank in that the friend was desperately looking for anything that might help. It took this absurd suggestion for me to realize that my mother was floundering and in tough shape.

After Mother left, Joe made no effort to hide his depression. His brother Stewart was being treated for leukemia, which had been diagnosed two years before, and the Nixon administration was foundering under the Watergate scandal. My sister wrote to cheer him up: "I just won't let you house of usher yourself out of existence—if there's going to be a third world war, keep on fighting against it in your columns—but be an open man, listen, remain open to opposing views." Despite the occasional acrimony between Joe and my mother, I was not surprised by how much time they spent together. I knew that they still loved each other but simply could not live under the same roof.

During those years, Kate and I were still living in Boston. We went to Washington for Thanksgiving in 1975, and Joe joined us. It was one of the grimmest Thanksgivings of my life. My mother was almost exclusively focused on smoothing over the ghastly news about the death of a close friend's young daughter. Clearly the girl had either shot herself or been murdered, and the well-known family did not want the death investigated. My mother wanted Joe to help her cover up the story through his connections, but even he seemed uncomfortable with the idea. I loathed the parents involved and felt sickened by my mother's behavior. Her automatic response to unpleasantness was to try to gloss over it.

Despite the lovely view over the Potomac, and the evocative stories Joe would tell about seeing young men swimming off Roosevelt Island when he had arrived in Washington forty years earlier, there was a modern concrete-fortress aspect to the Watergate complex that clashed with the image of my mother. It felt almost as if she was hiding out until she figured out the next chapter of her life. In fact, my mother used her small top-floor nest—immaculately maintained by her French maid, Mimi—as the cradle of her new career. She stayed there until my grandmother Jay died in December 1977 and then moved into her house on Twenty-ninth Street. My mother never bought her own house; she remained in my grandmother's house until she died.

Author at opening of new offices of the *Camden Herald*, Maine, 1993

fifteen

Facing Demons

It is only by risking our persons
from one hour to another that we live at all.

—WILLIAM JAMES

S AM WAS SEVEN when we moved from Boston to Camden, and Sybil arrived in October 1978, during our first fall in Maine. We lived at 69 Chestnut, a Norman Rockwell street of white picket fences that was featured in the movie *Peyton Place.* Our house overlooked Camden Harbor, which was filled with windjammers, expensive yachts, and lobster boats, although today I wonder how many lobster boats are left. The neighborhood made me compulsive about raking all the leaves from our front yard.

Having forced Rusty Brace to honor his offer, Dick Salton-stall and I took equal ownership of the 150-year-old *Belfast Republican Journal* in January 1979. Peter Scully, a Harvard friend who knew both of us from Harvard's Spee Club, told me then that the biggest problem he foresaw with our partnership was that we were so alike. At the time, I couldn't understand Peter's comment. On the surface Dick and I were opposites. Dick, with his boyish face and knitted ski cap, his love of animals and the outdoors, reflected an innocence that contrasted with my more sardonic outlook. He usually carried a thermos of specially brewed coffee and a roll of paper towels, and would often walk into our corporate lawyer's office with an old knapsack containing fresh green beans from his garden.

Dick's father had spent his whole career on State Street in Boston as a shrewd investor and money manager. Dick complained to me that Richard Sr. had no hobbies outside his work. Dick, in contrast, had countless hobbies: writing, photography gardening, sailing, canoeing, and others. On his first night in our Camden house, before he moved his own family to Maine, he slept on the living room floor in his sleeping bag. Even though he was a decade older than me, he seemed the same age, if not younger.

One of our first moves at the paper was to move our headquarters back into the center of town. My real estate instincts kicked back into gear, and I found a handsome flatiron building that had been built for the Belfast National Bank a hundred years earlier. We retrofitted it into a newspaper office, with darkrooms in the basement, advertising on the first floor, editorial and production on the second floor, and offices for Dick and me on the third floor. Dick took on the role of editor in chief and handled all editorial matters, and I was the general manager, overseeing the business side, including personnel. Except for meeting once a week with his editorial "troops," as he called them, Dick didn't like to spend much time in the office; he preferred to be always on the go.

While in our lawyers' Portland offices in December, I received a call from Russell Wiggins, former editor of the *Washington Post*, who owned the neighboring *Ellsworth American* and had advised me on the Belfast acquisition. He said that as a fallback we should try to buy the *Bar Harbor Times*, which he thought might be for sale. So we ended up acquiring that newspaper from an old Bar Harbor family shortly after winning our negotiations against Brace and taking over the *Belfast Republican Journal.*

Though we enjoyed going out for drinks in the evening, Dick's quirkiness increasingly irritated me, as I felt that among other things, it placed all the difficult decisions of making the papers profitable on my shoulders. While Dick was traveling around Waldo County with his two little dogs, taking scenic photos, I was left in the awkward position of being the bean counter and having to fire people who were earning $3.75 an hour. With a partner whose unearned income exceeded the gross revenue of our two papers, I had a difficult time accepting my role as the hatchet man. Without fully realizing it, we were both testing ourselves, putting ourselves out in rural communities that looked on us like young city slickers. It was intensely invigorating work, but in some ways limitless in its scope. This unconscious drive to redefine ourselves on our own terms contributed, at least on my part, to the dissolution of our partnership.

If we had just stayed with the two papers in Belfast and Bar Harbor, the story might have ended differently. But our challenge to Whitney Communications yielded another dividend in the spring of 1981. Several years earlier the company had partnered with Walter Cronkite to purchase the *Camden Herald.* They had been badly losing money on it, and I suspect they felt that even if they turned it around, the upside was too modest for an aggressive investor. So Walter Thayer offered to sell the paper to Dick and me as something of a peace offering after the company's scrap with Joe, and we accepted the offer.

By May 1981, therefore, by coincidence as much as design, we were minor newspaper moguls in mid-coast Maine. The momentum we had built made us think about continuing to expand our chain by buying Russell Wiggins's paper in Ellsworth. But after meeting with my lawyers, I realized that I would be digging myself in deeper with Dick and that I needed to be on my own. So I initiated a move to dissolve the partnership and take sole ownership of one of our three papers.

There were some rough spots in the lawyers' offices during negotiations in Portland, but since we basically liked each other, we soon settled on an agreeable plan. I would own the Camden paper, and Dick would get the Belfast and Bar Harbor papers. So on Monday, May 11, we ended up shaking hands and drove home in the afternoon.

The papers would be going to press on Wednesday evening. During the day on Tuesday, Dick and I worked shoulder to shoulder in our renovated offices on the top floor of the old bank building in Belfast. Dick's office held a wooden stand-up desk where he liked to write and had a small window looking out on Belfast Harbor. My office had a conference table in it, and as I was packing up my files we joked briefly about the key man life insurance policy that his lawyer had required. Dick told me he had managed to obtain the insurance despite the fact that he took medication for his heart, a health condition I had never known about.

That night around eleven, when I was in bed with my wife, we received a call from Belfast. A newspaper staffer told me that Dick had been found lying dead next to his desk. In his old Underwood typewriter they found a story he was working on for that week's paper: it was a description of our partnership separation.

A few days after Dick died, I walked into the Belfast state liquor store, and the salesman there looked surprised to see me. He said that after reading the paper, he assumed I was dead. I was shocked to realize that it could so easily have been me. I also felt, despite what people tried to tell me, that for someone as sentimental as Dick, the process of putting the dissolution of our partnership into words on a page might easily have triggered the heart attack. It is a feeling I have never entirely shaken.

Earlier that spring Kate had found an ad for a handsome farm about fifteen miles inland from Camden in the town of Union on the St. George River. It was in this remote and lovely valley, the locus of Ben Ames Williams's 1940 classic *Come Spring*, that we started to face our demons. Fairview Farm, with its lovely hardwood floors and moldings, was surrounded by open fields running down to the river, on which we could canoe up to the Sennebec Lake. I planted a number of Norway maples along the road and fruit trees around the house to provide some privacy.

Fairview Farm had a huge old barn across the road from the house. Most of the timbers were sound, but the roof and parts of the foundation needed work. The local farmers told me they didn't need the barn for their hay, and Kate and I didn't have any animals except our cat, Walter, so without any usage it would have slowly fallen apart.

I hired a man with whom I traded the cost of taking the barn down against the value of the lumber. He used it to build a house on Isleboro. With a couple of leftover boards from the barn, I built with my own hands a bus shelter for my kids, who took the public school bus each morning. This made the locals laugh. It was rather an eyesore and reminded them that we were ex-urbanites. Our neighbor Bliss Fuller, who owned the John Deere dealership in town and had grown up in our house, called the shelter "Patten's condo."

Because I went to work in Camden each day, I was partly oblivious to my wife's sense of isolation. Kate was attentive to the children but never became interested in gardening or fixing up the house, as I was. Maybe this is what conjured for Kate the image of *The Mosquito Coast,* Paul Theroux's novel about the mad father who drags his family from Massachusetts to the Amazon jungle to provide the natives with an ice-making machine.

Indeed, in retrospect, my bus shelter was not unlike the mad father's ice-making machine. After a few years I accepted the fact that the shelter was not a masterpiece, and with my friend Tom Wasson's help we took my creation in one piece to the local dump.

I had started smoking pot when I worked for the First National Bank of Boston, but now that I was surrounded by people who grew it locally, I started to use it more regularly. I would smoke lying in the tub in the downstairs bathroom, which was decorated with handmade Mexican tiles and looked out over Hardy's apple orchard. I thought it might help me produce more brilliant editorials, but discovered that it made my writing even more convoluted. Still, pot was a way to put the high-pressure engine of my mind into neutral, letting me coast and not worry about the next appointment.

I would smoke alone during the week or with friends in the valley on weekends, often in my garden, generally trying to hide it from my kids. Since the smell of marijuana is difficult to hide, they certainly knew what was happening. They learned that the best time to ask me for money was when my eyes were red.

But when I wasn't stoned, I was easily irritable. One evening in the spring of 1981, soon after Dick had died, Kate took an interminable amount of time to say good night to a friend who was staying with us. It was a minor thing, but I screamed at her. She told me that if I didn't get help, she would leave me. On my next trip to work on my apartments in Boston, I had dinner with some friends, who referred me to a psychiatrist on Beacon Street.

Though I initially planned only to see my psychiatrist, Richmond, for a few months, I ended up seeing him all through the 1980s. I would combine my visits with my real estate projects and, starting in 1983, with visiting Sam, who was a day student at Dexter School in Brookline and living with Kate's sister and her family. Though I resisted the idea at first, Richmond became my friend; later he would become a mentor to our entire family.

Through therapy I began to recognize my tendency to beat up on myself. This insight was totally new to me. Wasn't I *supposed* to be putting constant pressure on myself? If there wasn't some fire to put out somewhere, *something* must be wrong. And if there wasn't a fire on the horizon, it was my job to start one. If there was a simple way and a complicated way of doing something, I inevitably took the complicated route.

In the early summer of 1983 my friend Alberto Raurell, who had been the best man at my wedding, was shot in a holdup in Mexico City. We had roomed together at Harvard, and he had played a role in restoring the beautiful summerhouse we had owned on Vinalhaven in the late seventies. He was a museum director and had been running the Tamayo Museum in Mexico City. I flew down to this vast, unruly city to look into his death and found myself in an unnerving world that reminded me of Joseph Conrad's *Heart of Darkness.* Coming so soon after Dick's death, Alberto's left me shaken. I was grateful that I had someone like Richmond with whom I could share my grieving.

In retrospect, much of my work with Richmond involved the long-overdue grieving for my father's death. Learning little by little to trust him more, I made good use of Richmond's Kleenex box. He had read my mother's *To Marietta from Paris, 1945–1960* and said he had loved it. He liked to refer to my father as a "prince," and listened with immense patience and good humor to my ramblings.

By around 1984, my mother-in-law, Kitty, noticed something unusual about our family Christmas card that pictured us in front of our farm: I was smiling. Kitty observed that I looked at ease, something I had rarely displayed in all the years she had known me.

Other people noticed small changes, too. Heather Harland, who ran a kitchen equipment store, told me I had looked scary and angry when she first saw me on the streets in Camden. Lynn Allen, the receptionist who welcomed Dick and me when we bought the *Camden Herald,* and who also lived in Union, wondered whether I was the same person who had walked in the door in 1981.

But I could still be really immature. Once after a trip to Boston, I couldn't resist buying a rubber snake at Jack's Joke Shop and bringing it back to the farm. One evening I left it on my six-year-old Sybil's bed. When my daughter saw it, she screamed and ran in tears to her mother.

In the fall of 1984 I was driving through the town of Winterport with my three children. We were on the way home to the farm after a long day in Bangor. It was dark in the car, a black Volkswagen with a small backseat. I asked them about a dramatic movie they had seen that afternoon. In response I heard a voice from the backseat. It was my fourteen-year-old son, Sam. He'd picked up some new language from the film. "Dad, you were abusive," he said. He also said he realized that I had been a verbally abusive father, because I had now changed.

I was surprised by both his statements and by the fact that he had actually said them. In a way, it was easier to accept the idea that I had been abusive than that I had changed, perhaps because this second remark only pounded in the truth of the first one.

Looking back, I now see that my son was being incredibly gentle with me. With Richmond's help I had started to become aware of my anger and sadness, but there were still times when I snapped at Kate and my two older kids. I remember making Eliza cry when I drove her to school once, and being terribly impatient with Sam when we went sailing together. I often made sarcastic jabs that were reminiscent of my mother's, or wrestled with the kids in a brutish way. Once when I was trying to find a word to describe my behavior to Richmond, he suggested "abrasive."

Camden schooners in the inner harbor, Camden, Maine

An Episcopal priest friend of mine in one of my men's groups noted that I looked for what he called the "rawness" in life. Perhaps that is why I delighted in a world where when a stranger meets your wife, he says openly, "Nice to meet the boss!" Or a neighbor might introduce himself by telling you that his wife left him after a tree trunk fell on him a few years ago. I relished this rough honesty and lack of concern with appearance.

I have always had more admiration for a skillful chain-saw operator or backhoe laborer, where one mistake can easily be fatal to them or others, than I've had for Harvard professors or corporate lawyers, who can hide their mistakes in more reams of paper. Consequently, in staffing my newspaper, I drew in part from the ingenuity of these locals.

Nobody embodied this collaboration more effectively than Ken Bailey, a local Camdenite, who was also a licensed Maine guide and who gradually helped bring the *Camden Herald* down to earth as he rose through its ranks in the middle eighties. I met Ken as he was fitting shoes for a customer in his father's store on Main Street. I had heard of this young selectman's community spirit and skill with people, though more than once it was hard to overlook some of his Republican politics. But sometimes we ran opposing editorials before elections.

After Ken eventually became editor, he often infuriated my liberal friends, but his editorials resonated with local merchants. I was content to shut up, as our advertising sales skyrocketed. The *Herald* won the top prize for general excellence from the Maine Press Association under his guidance and continued to garner a dozen or so other journalistic prizes each year. I was also learning to appreciate the benefits of not stirring up trouble.

While valuing my relationship with "locals," I was aware of their penchant for politely watching us "flatlanders" charge off the end of a cliff. Once our paper challenged our competitor to a basketball game that was held in the Camden-Rockport High School gym. Though I had never played the sport, I participated on our team. It was not until the half-time break that a student in the stands came down to quietly inform me that I was wearing my shorts backward.

But while the paper had started to blossom, I inwardly continued to wrestle with issues related to my low self-esteem. On one real estate trip to Boston in February 1986, I had just finished reading Richard Meryman's *Broken Promises, Mended Dreams*, about a woman going through an alcohol rehab. That afternoon I tried to get wasted in the Combat Zone before taking my plane back to Maine, but somehow I couldn't get a buzz. On the way home it dawned on me that I was like some of the people in the book—an addict and hooked on pot.

The next day I went to Belfast and joined a twelve-step program. I quickly got a sponsor. When one day I called this man, a doctor, and apologized for disturbing him at work, he answered that by calling him for help I was in fact helping him. I was bowled over by the honesty, lack of judgmentalism, and spontaneous support I found in this program.

Though I bridled at first at the simplicity of the slogans, I ended up taking at least two of them to heart: "different strokes for different folks" appealed to my love of individuality and need to evolve in my own time frame; the idea of "progress, not perfection" helped me go easy on myself. Next to the impossibly high standards of success I had grown up with, it's hard to describe the comfort I found in this fellowship—founded on spiritual principles but embodied in action and changed behavior.

I also grew through the meetings to confront the ingrained idea of "terminal uniqueness." The word "terminal" evoked that chilly Calvinist idea of double predestination that hung over me as a child, well camouflaged by mother's outward modesty. It was the same notion that Duff had expressed to Diana from the trenches of northern France: "Thank God we are not like other men." What I was learning was the opposite: Thank God I *am* like other men. It was not so much a startling discovery than the confirmation of something I had suspected years ago but had never allowed myself to integrate into my life.

Kate and I left our farm that winter and rented a house in Camden. In October we bought a house on Mountain Street, and in November Sam was expelled from Concord Academy and came home to live with us. Sam had turned Groton School down, partly because he was not attracted by its emphasis on sports, but had started to experiment with alcohol too enthusiastically at Concord. By that summer of 1986 my marriage had begun to feel shaky. Kate was clearly unhappy.

We went to see her counselor, Amy, and Kate admitted that I had profoundly changed, but the issues were complex. I was never exactly sure what was causing her unhappiness, but I sensed that even after I quit pot and sought help in controlling my anger, I was still a burden for her. I felt that her counselor gave her the confidence to admit things she would have been reluctant to say to me alone.

Even though some of her habits often irritated me, I still loved Kate. She was a loving and tender mother to our children. I organized a trip to Paris over the Christmas holidays. We brought the kids and, since Kate felt fragile, also a babysitter, and we all stayed at the Hotel Duc de Saint-Simon on the Left Bank. One day we rented a huge Mercedes and drove to the small town near Amiens where my old governess, Mazelle, was living and took her out for lunch. It felt as if I was trying to give her one last look at us as a family before she died—or before our family did. Kate's face in the family photos shows that she was not enjoying herself.

During our last December together, I decided that the 1986 *Camden Herald* Christmas supplement should focus on the theme of "family." I introduced it by borrowing the well-worn phrase from *Casablanca,* "Round up the usual suspects!" And I did. Joe contributed a column about choosing the right food for Christmas; my mother offered some memories of Christmas in Paris in 1946; my mother-in-law, Kitty Bacon, wrote about Christmases at Wheatly, the Long Island estate where my mother and Bill Patten were married; and Anne and Kate each contributed essays—Anne's about a transient Christmas in Haiti, and Kate's about being helped by a friend at Zayre's department store in her search for the perfect Cabbage Patch doll for Sybil.

In late January 1987 Kate threw a butter dish at me in our kitchen when I told her I was going to spend a weekend with my sister in Utah. If she felt abandoned, she had some cause, because I was also looking for a break from the marriage. I returned to live at Fairview Farm, which we hadn't yet sold.

Looking back at my little blue Featherweight diary for 1987, I see the trying events of a complicated marriage all compressed into one horrendous year: separations, reconciliations, deaths, births, blowout fights, and the beginning of our legal divorce process. It was one of the most anguishing years of my life.

The day I paid our income taxes, Friday, April 10, my sister, Anne, gave birth to a daughter, Julia. I wrote in my diary: "Divorce Inevitable." On Thursday, April 16, I recorded: "Terrible Day," "Feeling Shitty." I picked up the divorce papers and noted: "Kate tells the girls." The following weekend I took Sam and Eliza to stay with my mother. We dined with Joe on Sunday, and on Monday I drove the kids with Joe and my mother to the National Aquarium in Baltimore. My parents favored expediting the divorce.

When I got home, nine-year-old Sybil asked me if Joe and my mother would still be alive when she reached Sam's age. (He was sixteen at the time.) It seemed that she was acting out the trauma of the divorce quite openly. She was learning how to ride horses at Hill 'n' Dale Farm, and her teacher told me that she had asked Sybil why she talked so much. Sybil answered, "Talking is my life!"

Eliza, who was in seventh grade in the Camden public school system, was making high honors in her class and excelling in sports. Sam was getting ready for a trip to Brittany in France through an exchange program sponsored by the Putney School in Vermont. The children's time was equally divided between their mother and me. I would make up what we called "Johnny stories" to tell the kids before they went to bed. I took them on trips and stayed closely involved with their schools.

After the separation, Kate started to spend time with the older, very WASPY Forrester Smith. This infuriated me, even though she claimed it was not a serious relationship. In my diary in May I wrote, "Why the fuck is Kate so angry?" I couldn't get my mind around what had failed in our marriage. I was puzzled when one of my brothers-in-law, Chris Crockett, wrote me a long, thoughtful letter in which he said that he felt that when Kate and I were together we "diminished each other."

That month I had a brief relationship with an athletic friend of my sister's who lived on Ward's Island in Toronto. We had a wonderful weekend biking around the city and exploring its wonderful ethnic neighborhoods, and she visited me in Union. But I still held out hope of patching things up with Kate. We briefly reconciled around the time of her birthday in early June. I took her out to dinner; we spent some time together. At one point she asked me, "Why do we need catastrophes to make it?" and she cried gently.

After spending the weekend with Kate and realizing the extent of her unhappiness, I began to absorb the fact that our chances of getting back together had mostly evaporated. Still, Kate drove me to the airport the next week when I had to fly to Washington to pick up my mother to drive her to Maine for the summer. Kate had a bumper sticker on her car that irritated me; it read, "Shit happens!" It felt like she was advertising our private turmoil.

In late June my aunt Tish Alsop told me that Joe had lung cancer but that I was not supposed to know. She said he did not want the doctors to operate and wanted to tell people in his own time. I was staying with my mother-in-law in Vermont at the time and wrote in my diary, "Heaviness of heart, Feel like crying. Must (for now) keep it concealed. Even from Joe."

By the end of the summer we had sold our farm in Union, and Kate had started dating a lawyer named Bob Perkins. I had bought 37 Mountain Street, a cozy house with a mansard roof under Mount Battie in Camden. It became my refuge over the next decade, as well as a second home for my children. I wrote in my diary, "Ready for divorce!" The house was conveniently located on the same street where Kate was living, and we shared equal custody of the children. Sybil, who had a role in a community theater performance of the musical *Oliver!* that year, boldly noted that she saw more of me now than she had before.

I had just moved into my new house in early September and was waiting for Kate to make up her mind about legal custody arrangements for the kids when we had a disturbing confrontation. She had made a decision about the children that I thought was irresponsible. While not unprovoked, my physical reaction, in total sobriety, scared even me. Something inside me started to break apart.

I confronted Kate and her friend Bob Perkins in his house. When I arrived, the front door was unlocked. I walked into the living room, punched the lawyer hard in the face, and while screaming at my wife, smashed the panes of glass on either side of the front door as I was leaving. In the antiviolence classes I now teach in prisons, I recognize that my rage had taken me to that zone we call a blackout, or what an inmate recently described to me as a "cranial explosion."

That night I went to stay with a friend in a neighboring town. When I got back to my job in Camden the next day, I heard that down at Ayer's Fish Market on Main Street I was already known as "Sugar Ray Patten." Hitting a lawyer was not seen as such an act of infamy in this town. But I found that Perkins, whom Kate later married, was suing me for assault and battery and for trespassing.

As I stood in front of the judge's high bench in the Rockland Superior Court a few weeks later, it struck me how the road to recovery is a rocky one. Later I felt some humiliation at having my children see my name prominently displayed on the front page of our competitor's newspaper. I ended up paying a fine of four hundred dollars.

Kate rejected a mediation settlement, and we were dragged through two more interminable years of interrogatories and other legal maneuvers. It was a frustrating, prolonged process, and we were not divorced until 1990. In the meantime, I lived with a Camden schoolteacher named Barbara, who had two boys about the same age as my children. She was a bright and dynamic person whom I cared for greatly; we went on mountain hikes, ski trips, and sailing cruises with all of our children.

During those early years of the separation I felt immense support from friends and family. My mother-in-law, Kitty, had come to stay with us in Camden the first Christmas that we were separated. Before she arrived, she called me at my office to tell me that she wanted to bring a pony for my daughter Sybil. This entailed driving six or seven hours over country roads from her farm in Vermont. I knew Sybil would be utterly delighted. As Kitty discussed details, tears began streaming down my face. I had no control over them. A friend, Throop Wilder, was waiting to see me outside my office. I slipped past him to the men's room to wash my face, hoping he would not see me.

By the end of the 1980s, Richmond had become a mentor to our whole family, and in different ways helped all of us. On the day Sam graduated from Dexter School, Richmond noticed from his seat on the podium how sad my daughter Eliza looked as she sat in the audience. He soon found a way to initiate help for her. I worked fruitfully with Richmond until he died suddenly on his way back from Bermuda in 1992.

A few years after I had started seeing Richmond, my mother gave a dinner party in Northeast Harbor that put my mental housecleaning efforts in an ironic perspective. It was a larger dinner than usual, so we had two dining tables. Eliza helped my mother draw up the seating arrangement on an old piece of cardboard. At one table my mother sat Lord (Peter) Carrington, the former British foreign secretary, on her right, and Douglas Dillon, Kennedy's secretary of the treasury, on her left. Carrington was on his way back from an important meeting in Canada. I had Lady Henderson, the wife of British ambassador Sir Nicholas Henderson, on my right, and my godmother, Marietta Tree, on my left.

For some strange reason, during the course of dinner I confided in Marietta that I had been seeing a psychiatrist in Boston. I knew that she, unlike my mother, understood the benefits of therapy. My mother often asked me, with barely disguised irritation, how much longer I was planning to be seeing Richmond. On the other hand, Marietta asked me, "How often do you see him?" "Once every two weeks," I replied. "Oh, that's not nearly enough," my godmother said. "I saw one myself for years. You should see him at least twice a week!"

Joe Alsop with Alexandra and Arthur Schlesinger, 1980s

sixteen

A Partnership Restored

I think he's the best host in Washington.

—MY MOTHER REFERRING TO JOE IN A
1981 ARTICLE IN THE *WASHINGTONIAN*

M̲Y CHILDHOOD FRIEND David Sulzberger, who had known both my mother and Joe for more than forty years, mourned their divorce and told me he didn't see why they couldn't work out their differences. In a way, they did. The bitterness didn't last long. For the better part of fifteen years—from 1974 to 1989—my mother and Joe enjoyed a deep sense of companionship a few blocks from each other without the strain of sharing a household.

To some degree the air was cleared when my grandmother Jay, who was close to ninety years old, died in 1977. I came down from Maine for the burial service. I remember driving to the cemetery in Rye, New York, near the historic John Jay homestead, in a rented limousine with Joe, my mother, Anne, and her husband, George. There was no sense of overwhelming sadness in the car. I felt that my mother had been beaten down by my grandmother Jay and that Joe had never had any love for her from the beginning. Joe would say that what kept my grandmother alive so long was that by the terms of the divorce, for as long as my grandmother lived, Joe had to pay my mother a form of alimony. He saw it as her revenge.

My mother and Joe continued to share in the vast network of friends they had collected over the years. She would pick Joe up in her car to take him to the many dinner parties to which they were jointly invited. Often he would find his own way home, something he was skillful at doing, luring his chauffeur in for a "tiny night-cap."

He had sold 2720 Dumbarton Avenue soon after retiring in 1974 and took a long-term lease on a house on N Street that belonged to friends. His new house was less than a ten-minute walk from my mother's house on Twenty-ninth Street.

Perhaps their most intimate moments were the strolls they would take around the city. In the fall of 1984 my mother wrote me, saying, "Joe and I take long walks observing real estate— always the prime Washington topic, and you wouldn't believe the number of rich people who are doing over houses." They would visit sites like the bronze statue of Henry Adams's wife by Saint-Gaudens, and Joe would expound on its unique history.

In the late eighties my mother wrote to me about a day she spent with Joe, typically detaching herself from the issue of homosexuality:

> Then it was lovely, six foot tall Alexandra Schlesinger who adores Joe
> and he her down from New York for lunch, full of funny stories and
> gossip . . . the taxi drivers had stayed at home in order to protest the
> "Gays" who had descended a hundred thousand strong on the city
> the day before for their mass marriage ceremonies . . . Despite the
> logistical difficulties Joe and Alexandra returned (from the National
> Gallery AND the Sackler Museum) to N Street in highest spirits;
> I had to desert them in order to entertain Brooke Astor's young

English butler. Brooke is abroad, but wanted to give her devoted
Paul a cultural treat in the nation's capital and as instructed by her I
was ready with guide books and maps. He is delightful, but I could
not but think it an odd coincidence that he had chosen this particular
weekend to make the trip.

Joe had not lost sight of the world at large. He still made
Zeussian pronouncements about politicians and great events
from his low leather chair next to the fireplace in his living room.
"It's been my observation that you go on living like a young man
until suddenly you're an old man," he once said. "It's a bore.
There's absolutely nothing to recommend old age." Joe had begun working on his memoirs in 1987 with the help of a young
friend, Adam Platt. They were published under the title *I've Seen
the Best of It*, in 1992, two years after his death.

My mother started writing books almost immediately after her
decision to leave Joe in 1973. Her late-blossoming career as an
author owed much to the encouragement of Marietta Tree.
Many of the letters published in *To Marietta from Paris,
1945–1960* in 1974 were ones that Marietta had kept during my
mother's years in Paris. Although the bulk of the letters in the
book were actually written to my grandmother Jay, my mother's
editors at Doubleday saw Marietta's name as a marketing asset,
and Marietta graciously assented to the marketing of her name.
The first book party was held at Marietta's lovely house at
123 East Seventy-ninth Street in New York.

Perhaps the most enthusiastic review of *To Marietta from
Paris* was one published in the British *Evening Standard* by Lady
Antonia Fraser titled "So chic, so true, so sad . . ." The daughter
of an earl, and the acclaimed author of *Mary, Queen of Scots* and
The Warrior Queens, Fraser presciently discerned the "talent of a

born descriptive writer." She also commended the "gallantry" of Bill Patten and Susan Mary, which provided a "counterpoint to the jolly junketings of the rest of the book." With her own sophisticated background, Fraser could appreciate the genuine style of a woman who embodied what she called the "historical high life."

But it was not the "high life" per se that appealed most to my mother. It was being close enough to the action to report firsthand about it. Her literary models included war correspondents like the nineteenth-century William Howard Russell, who covered the major conflicts of the period for the *Times* of London. His legendary dispatches about the Crimean War, the Indian Rebellion of 1857, and the American Civil War were in her library.

To Marietta from Paris brims with political gossip, but unsurprisingly my mother offered little titillation. When it came to scandal, Susan Mary was a master at self-censorship. One day, not long after the book's publication, on a plane coming back from Barbados, my mother and I ran into her old friend Louis Auchincloss. Author of *The Embezzler* and *The Rector of Justin*, Auchincloss was best known for his novels about WASP society. As we stood waiting to deplane, he congratulated my mother on her book, and then asked her with a mischievous grin why she had left out the best parts.

My mother had hardly finished the book when she took off with Tish Alsop, Stewart's wife, in February 1975 to visit her cousin Charlie Whitehouse, who was then serving as the American ambassador to Laos. Her letters home are a rich combination of strategic insight and descriptive local color, a mix of reporting, opinion, and anthropology that is reminiscent of Russell.

She described several dinners with the leaders of the Communist organization Pathet Lao, "a dour lot, accompanied by silent wives who look as if they had just left the caves in the

North." She took a helicopter trip to interview General Vang Pao, "a Montagnard hero who has six wives and 28 children," and to visit a hospital in the jungle, "run incredibly by a nurse I knew at DC General, who told me she was quite happy in her lonely life." She also was able to relax and appreciate the Somerset Maugham romance of Southeast Asia: "Return sweating to shower and sit on the lawn watching the sun set over the Mekong and drink Martinis to sound of faint pagoda bells from Thailand on the other side of the river."

Recognizing that the days of Western colonial dominance in the Far East were numbered, my mother ends this particular letter observing: "Charlie is withdrawing the American presence quietly and efficiently, one passes many little villas covered with signs 'For sale or rent.' Driving by the French Embassy one notices a Victorian statue of a man in a wide brimmed felt hat, this is Pavie who wandered down the Mekong and took Laos for France. Would it have been better if he had never come?"

My mother approached the past with the same zeal for primary sources that characterized her social life. She was accustomed to conversing directly with presidents, ambassadors, and generals to get the best fix on contemporary events. Gaining access to primary archival material was a hallmark of her historical work. In 1975 she took a whirlwind five-day trip to England to examine documents for her second book, a biography of Lady Sackville-West. There is a rare note of exhilaration in her tone as she writes from England, along with the customary apprehension that I was accustomed to whenever she talked about her accounts at the Fiduciary Trust Company or Joe's health. She wrote:

If, by a miracle, the pilot makes it to Sissinghurst I will lose my three huge suitcases, empty now, but hopefully to be filled with precious Sackville diaries & letters for my book. If, another miracle, they are not stolen by a rapacious Englishman, I shall in any case have broken

Ashton Hawkins and Susan Mary Alsop at a book party for *Yankees at The Court*, New York, 1986

my back, as it is well known that there are no porters in England. Suppose that I actually make it to Boston, I will not only be ruined by excess baggage charges, but the inhabitants of Boston lie waiting, eager for their chance at my weighty loot. Final thrust—and it's my Achilles heel—for it could be true—I make it to Northeast Harbor and the documents are without interest.

It turned out that her doubts about the papers and her own skills were unfounded. A reviewer of *Lady Sackville: A Biography* wrote, "Besides brains, a good heart and a lively eye for the way people behave, Susan Mary Alsop is qualified for the biographer's vocation by her civilized values. There is more than a touch of the 18th century in her sophistication."

In her third book, *Yankees at the Court: The First Americans in Paris,* my mother tackled historical events and actors closer to home. She focused on Paris between 1775 and 1785, when her ancestor John Jay, working with Benjamin Franklin and John Adams, secured French support during the American Revolution. Her book was distinctive in that it concentrated on the Old World's perspective on the revolution and on the influence of female relationships on the leading political figures of the times. She told the *New York Times*' social columnist Charlotte Curtis, "I thought I wrote a serious book. I don't want you to get the impression it's Judith Krantz."

My mother's fourth book, *The Congress Dances: Vienna 1814–1815,* was described by *Newsweek* as "an epic of amorous dalliances with far-reaching effects . . . which reads as though the author were present during the 1815 Congress of Vienna, after the defeat of Napoleon." It was in this book that she so artfully portrayed Talleyrand's niece, the twenty-one-year-old lovely and discreet Dorothea, Duchesse de Dino, who played a pivotal role as the aging diplomat's hostess at the Kaunitz Palace on the Johannesgasse. Who knows whether my mother gave herself the luxury of identifying with Dorothea? She had certainly earned the right to do so.

As many reviewers observed, my mother wrote sympathetically rather than cynically about political leaders. She had a firsthand appreciation of the challenges they faced. She was mindful of Prussian general Gebhard Leberecht von Blucher's remark after beating Napoleon at Waterloo in 1813: "May the pens of the diplomats not ruin again what the people have attained with such exertions."

My mother never made a fuss over the task of writing, even when she was struggling with deteriorating eyesight. My sister and I would often remind her that she had become a great success on her own, an accomplishment made all the more remarkable because it came later in life. But Mother was not one for receiving compliments, and I have often wondered whether her success gave her any real joy. Her fading eyesight made it difficult to continue the research needed for her historical books, but I always got the feeling that she believed she still hadn't accomplished enough.

In her letters in the eighties my mother kept me posted on the "larger world," although she observed with disappointment that the players were losing some of their sizzle. Writing about a dinner at Joe's with the George Shultzes, the Ellsworth Bunkers, Kay Graham, Evangeline Bruce, and Charlie Whitehouse, she confessed:

> I was thrilled to be included in such a distinguished party and expected pyrotechnics of brilliant conversation, but it didn't turn out like that. Henry [Kissinger], who would have been the catalyst, was kept at work, Ellsworth has become sadly old and deaf, the Secretary of State is a nice man but he was in a mood to relax so he told me about playing golf at the Annenbergs. Charlie drove me home, both of us feeling a little flat as we had agreed to remain perfectly sober in order to learn all about the Middle East, Central America etc.

My mother respected Kay Graham immensely as a woman who had achieved success on her own, and I felt that over the years, especially after my mother had left Joe, the respect was increasingly reciprocated.

Sometimes I felt a little like Don Quixote ranting in my provincial newspaper about the injustices of the world while my mother was smoothly papering them over in the nation's capital. In 1989 I wrote an impassioned editorial reprimanding Maine senator Bill Cohen for endorsing his alcoholic colleague John Tower as secretary of defense. Cohen called me from the Senate floor to argue that he had taken many long flights with Tower but had never seen him drunk. I later discovered that Cohen was enjoying cozy dinners at my mother's house.

Susan Mary with children of Congressman
William Moorhead, 1980s

In addition to her writing, my mother continued to cultivate
new friends in each new administration. Her adaptability was
Darwinian. In 1981 a photo of her sitting in her living room appeared on the front page of a *Washingtonian* article reporting that
Nancy Reagan regularly slipped out of the White House for
"quiet lunches with five ladies of refined taste, good breeding,
and impeccable social standing." Proudly calling themselves
"The Bright Old Things," the lunch group also included my
mother and two close friends—Marion Oates "Oatsie" Charles
and Lorraine Cooper. Oatsie and Lorraine embodied a mixture
of Southern warmth, irreverence, and quick wit that comple-
mented my mother's Yankee seriousness.

The writer of the article identified Susan Mary Alsop as the most "cerebral" of the bunch. But she was brilliantly self-effacing; none of the women in the article were as quick to credit their husbands with their success. My mother attributed her position to her ex-husband, Joe, for "introducing her to the right people." She continued, "I'm in the lucky position of having been married to Joe and am still on excellent terms with him. I think he's the best host in Washington." The reporter suggested that Joe's success as a host may have been due to my mother serving as his hostess. "'Isn't that odd?'" my mother mused, as if—the reporter concluded—"she had just spun one of the juiciest yarns of the week."

In his memoirs, *A Long Life,* the writer Nigel Nicolson, the younger son of Harold Nicolson and Vita Sackville-West, and the author of the acclaimed biography of his parents, *Portrait of a Marriage,* noted: "In Washington there was Susan Mary Alsop, who wrote Lady Sackville's life and in whose house in Georgetown I stayed several times, marveling at her ability to bring together politicians, writers, artists, journalists and museum people in a way that even Lady Colefax never managed in London."

Joe was genuinely proud of my mother's achievements as a published writer. Her books did not compete with his on the level of academic seriousness, so her success did not threaten him and was a key factor in making their relationship a full partnership; she continued to be an asset in his world. He had happily attended her book parties, and I never heard him say a negative word about her books.

While Mother was churning out her books, Joe was beavering away on his own writings. After twenty years of research, Joe's epic work, *The Rare Art Traditions: The History of Art Collecting and Its Linked Phenomena Wherever These Have Appeared,* finally emerged in print in 1982. My mother often complained about how long it took him to finish it; she had spun off several books in the meantime.

As its subtitle indicates, the theme of Joe's massive study was art collectors. It told the history of art collecting and its reliance on the "fairly grubby men of money"—from the Medicis to John Paul Getty—and documented the byzantine relations of the art market to patrons, collectors, and historians. This project kept Joe in touch with the global academic scene and allowed him to capitalize on his own far-reaching areas of expertise, from pre-historic man to the complex intrigues of the Renaissance and even more abstruse examples of human peculiarities. The bibliography alone was more than fifty pages long.

While finishing his magnum opus on art collecting, in 1982 Joe produced a handsome coffee-table book with nice pictures on Franklin Delano Roosevelt, whom he pronounced, "the greatest President of this century." He said the book "wrote itself, family gossip." With "an insider's natural grasp of the family, its background, its secrets," wrote Susan Bolotin in the *New York Times*, "he's found a showcase for his talents" as a storyteller.

In 1983 I made a photo album for Joe's seventy-fifth birthday with a mixture of clippings, cartoons about "parents who programmed my success," menus, old letters (including a 1970 one from me to the *International Herald Tribune* defending Joe), reprimands from Harvard teachers, speeding tickets, party invitations, my children's report cards, laudatory reviews of my mother's books, and other memorabilia. He must have been surprised to see the full-page photograph of Duff and Diana Cooper that I also enclosed. I knew he idolized the Coopers, but still it makes me wonder today whether if in some part of my reptilian brain I had not already known about my connection with Duff. He thanked me for the present but never asked why I had included the Coopers.

In the middle eighties, after I had separated from Kate, Joe called one evening to commiserate about the trials of being responsible for one's own laundry. He suggested I marry the girl I was seeing, the daughter of a prominent WASP family. I was touched by his expressions of concern. But maybe Joe had faded a little in my mind as well, because I remember listening to his advice with a kind of bemused curiosity.

Although Joe had been complaining that his world was "dead as the auk" for a long time, the phrase gained gravity as I began to hear about his visits to the hospital. After keeping it a secret for more than a year, in June 1988 he told me that his lung cancer had not been arrested and that he didn't think he would be around much longer. As I listened, I visualized him walking invincibly into Georgetown Hospital seventeen years earlier when Sam was born.

The following summer I took a month's vacation in the Ardèche with my children and worried that Joe might not be there when I got home. But he was. I visited him in the hospital. He told me then of a dream he had had of being on a transport ship with Israeli commandos. It fit so perfectly with his love of strong, brave men—and particularly his admiration for the fighting prowess of the Israelis—that I was happy for him. My own son, Sam, was starting at Georgetown University that fall, in part thanks to Joe.

It was my aunt Tish who called on a Monday morning in late August to tell me that Joe had died. I left my office and went for a walk, but discovered a little to my surprise that I was not in tears.

After Joe's funeral, I went to his house and walked around the empty rooms with my girlfriend. As I looked at the bookcases that rose from floor to ceiling in various rooms, I felt some of his loneliness. I talked with Gemma, his housekeeper, who had decided to move up to Twenty-ninth Street to take care of my mother. She told me that she was the one who had found Joe lying by his bed in his study. Gemma said he had been moaning, "Is there a God?"

Given her own unsentimental character, I suspect that Gemma was telling the truth, as peculiar as it might seem to some who knew of Joe's disdain for spiritual topics. But Joe knew the Hebrew testament well, referred often to the book of Job, and I always felt that what he portrayed as his preference for the literary beauty of its works was in fact a lively curiosity about the existence of God and an afterlife.

In fact, this reluctance to talk in depth about religious questions, both in the family and socially, was a habit my mother and Joe instinctively shared. My mother told me once that she had read the Bible from cover to cover while living with Joe, but it was the kind of thing you did alone in bed without making a big deal about it.

The sadness I felt was that after everything Joe had done for me, after all the hours he had spent plotting ways to help my education, career, and social life as he saw best, we had never talked about the big things: his loneliness, his homosexuality or my illegitimacy, his anger or mine, or any of the basic things that defined us as humans. I felt we had missed the chance to be really close.

But thinking back over those evenings when we were alone together with his very weak scotch and soda at his side, I realized that our relationship had never been on an even playing field. He always controlled the conversation. His shield was always up around him. And though I loved him, I believe that shield is largely why I did not cry when I heard he had died.

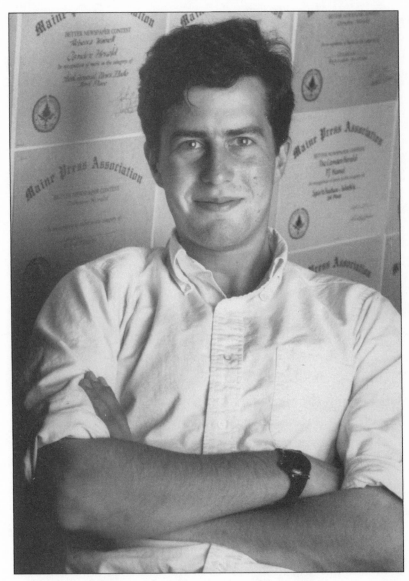

Sam Patten as a reporter for the *Camden Herald*, Maine, 1994

seventeen

Leaving Lotus Land

I continued picking out people I knew until I realized I
knew practically the whole audience. The song was almost
over, but I sang those last three lines the loudest and happiest orphan. In Camden, I could never feel like a real orphan.

—REFLECTIONS OF SYBIL PATTEN, GRADE 8, ON HER ROLE IN

OLIVER! ON OPENING NIGHT AT THE CAMDEN OPERA HOUSE, 1993

B Y THE EARLY nineties my weekly newspaper work at the
Camden Herald had come to feel a little repetitive. I still found
some challenge in the various crises that we needed to overcome
each week and in the interesting characters we unearthed in the
process, but after almost twenty years of the same Wednesday-
night printing deadline, somehow the world had shrunk down to
dangerously small horizons.

Perhaps because I was more concerned about editorial matters than most publishers and even wrote regularly for the paper, I never gave myself enough credit for having rescued a
money-losing business. Much of the early years had felt like
a fight for financial survival. Yet by the early nineties we were
strong enough to fend off a new weekly shopper launched right

under our noses by two experienced journalists from the *Washington Post*. Their venture folded in a few years, and its owners moved away.

The success of the paper mirrored in a way my own recovery. In the early days I was preoccupied with taking stands on local issues and digging out what I saw as the essence of the community. But after about five years I had matured beyond "Patten's Revenge," as one of my friends called it. I had learned a little about swimming *with* the current instead of against it. The "old-timers" in town saw that I could trim my sails and endure longer than they expected.

But now, fifteen years later and looking ahead, I worried about a number of intractable obstacles. On a strategic level I could see that a well-financed chain owned by the *Bangor Daily* had me surrounded and blocked my newspaper's growth opportunities. On a more personal level, my children were now grown, and the joys of seeing them every day were over. The idea of reporting about the schools where they had grown up and studied filled me with sadness.

In the spring of 1996 I took a mini-sabbatical to Europe. I spent three months based in France, but also included a bike trip in Crete in May, a week in northern Portugal with my daughter Eliza in June, and a mountain hike with friends in the Dolomites in July. The overall experience galvanized me to act on what I had been thinking about ever since my divorce was finalized in 1990. Maybe walking down the old Parisian boulevards that Duff had ridden down reminded me of all the other worlds out there; the time had come to move on. So I started talking to people who had previously expressed interest in buying the *Camden Herald*.

I also knew I needed to continue to take risks and build on my dreams. Starting in 1994 I had begun to take classes at Bangor Theological Seminary, which I found fascinating. It was a merciful thing that Joe was dead when I started commuting to Bangor, an hour and a half inland from Camden. I didn't enroll in order to make him turn over in his grave, nor consciously to make my mother uncomfortable. Rather, I saw in my ministry studies a launching pad to a range of new opportunities. But after my spring in Europe I realized I couldn't continue to follow a ministerial path and be a publisher at the same time.

The process of selling the *Camden Herald* started early in the fall of 1996. Largely through the help of my attorney, Joel Martin, and accountant, Brad Hodson, both of whom could see the big picture and move things along, the process went smoothly. Though I would have preferred to sell to an independent owner, the best price came from a chain and one of my chief competitors, the owners of the *Bangor Daily*.

Then in September my life was transformed when I attended a dinner party held by my cousin Joe Alsop and his wife, Christiane, in Prides Crossing, Massachusetts. Seated next to me was Sydney Camp Hayes, an outgoing and youthful-looking forty-one-year-old music composer in a magenta dress. She was separated from her husband and living nearby with her young daughter.

Through that fall, as negotiations for the sale of my paper continued, Sydney and I spoke often on the phone. Those early encounters remain etched in my mind with rare clarity. One weekend I helped Sydney and her bubbly, red-haired eight-year-old daughter, Cassy, load firewood into her Jeep. It seemed clear that I was falling in love with the relationship between mother and daughter as much as anything. Though Cassy seemed ebullient, there was also a remarkable maturity in her conversation.

As I spent an increasing amount of time with them, I felt a confusing mixture of envy and admiration for the way Sydney treated her little daughter. She listened to her, tried to explain to her why she required certain things from her, and showered her with tangible signs of praise and love. I watched Cassy's tendency to gravitate gracefully toward center stage with awe. She delighted in meeting new people and in enlivening any group she could find. At times I felt jealous at the way this little creature seemed to be, as the French say, *"si bien dans sa peau"*—so comfortable with herself—without any conceit.

One morning I woke up in Sydney's condo in Prides Crossing and heard shrieks of laughter coming from the kitchen, the beautiful notes of a little girl and her mother sharing some story. Since I tend to be grouchy until my first cup of coffee, I marveled at this astonishing and incredibly joyous sound. It defied all the typical little squeaks and groans, commands and rebukes I associate with the stress of getting ready for school.

I learned that Faye Dunaway would be playing the role of Maria Callas in *The Master Class*, and I invited Sydney to attend the play with me in Boston. Halfway through the performance, as the lights dimmed and the live voice of Maria Callas was piped into the theater, Sydney placed her head on my shoulder.

She had just launched *The Yellow Dress*. It is a one-woman, educational play focused on dating violence, which Sydney conceived and wrote the music for. It has become a national success in schools and colleges across the country and as of this writing has been performed before more than a million students.

In January 1997 I took Sydney and Cassy to a beach on the Nicoya Peninsula off the west coast of Costa Rica. The native women stopped in their tracks to admire the color of Cassy's red hair. We spent a delightful week on the beach and exploring the nearby rain forest. Meanwhile, my three children watched us with interest. Previous romantic jaunts away had usually spelled doom for my relationships. This one broke the pattern.

In April I took Sydney on her first trip to Washington to visit my mother. I thought it would be better for us to stay at the

Jefferson Hotel opposite the White House than at my mother's house in Georgetown. My mother was as gracious as always, but I discovered a feeling I had never experienced before: I really didn't care what my mother thought of Sydney.

Sydney brought Cassy to meet my mother over lunch at the Ritz-Carlton in Boston later that spring. I had warned Cassy not to talk too much, telling her that my mother wasn't crazy about small kids. Yet in reply to one of my mother's polite questions, the nine-year-old launched into a detailed account of a biography that she was reading on Queen Elizabeth I. I could see my mother coming alive—as when two formidable cerebral forces start to gravitate toward each other.

By Memorial Day of 1996, Sydney and Cassy and I had moved into a little cottage in Brookline, not far from Andover Newton Theological School, where I could earn my few remaining master of divinity credits and serve as an intern minister at First Parish, a Unitarian Universalist church on Walnut Street. The following year Sydney and I went to New Hampshire to witness Sybil graduate from Proctor Academy, and a month later we traveled to Palo Alto to watch Eliza graduate from Stanford University. Sam had started working in a staff role on oil projects in Kazakhstan. It seemed that we were all setting out on new stages of our lives.

Since graduating from Georgetown University in 1993, Sam has been involved in international work, with a base in Republican politics. He initially worked for Republican senator Bill Cohen from Maine and then helped his successor, Susan Collins, win his seat in 1996. He was married two years later and became the father of Max Patten, who was born in Maine on March 29, 1999. After three years working in Moscow for the International Republican Institute promoting democracy, Sam volunteered in 2004 to take a position in Baghdad to help the Iraqis organize for their first free election.

Susan Mary Alsop, Sybil Patten, Kitty Bacon, and Eliza Patten at Sam Patten's Georgetown graduation, 1993

Initially both of my daughters were drawn to Manhattan. Sybil received her undergraduate degree from New York University in 2002 and moved to Brooklyn, where she teaches English as a second language and writes theater. Eliza graduated from New York University Law School in 2001 and obtained a Skadden fellowship to represent indigent parents in child welfare cases and to work on public policy to improve foster care. She married Obediah Ostergard, a gifted restaurateur, in August 2002. She and Obie and their two children, Sophie and Cyrus, have made their home in Berkeley, California.

In the summer of 1998 Sydney, Cassy, and I moved to Iron Horse Farm, which had a beautiful big barn on open fields on the side of Mount Wachusett, in the town of Princeton, Massachusetts, where Sydney had been raised. On weekends I worked with a tractor and chainsaw clearing the fields. I now managed the arts and theology program at Andover Newton, and I commuted from Princeton. To get hired, I had used in my interview the metaphor of the power of dance to transform a man's life, as embodied in the 1996 film *Shall We Dance?* the inspiring story of a Japanese businessman who breaks away from his deadening daily commute to his dreary job to learn ballroom dancing.

Life at Iron Horse Farm was quite isolated but often serene. One spring morning on our farm, I was about to get into my car to drive to work in Boston when I saw Sydney running across a field in her nightgown, pulling a kite behind her. It made me realize and cherish her ability to love the beauty of the world around her and get lost in the feelings of the moment.

On November 24, 1999, Sydney and I were married in Lancaster, Massachusetts. With family so scattered, we had just two witnesses, my friend Ruth Zimmerman and Chris Crockett, for the service in the handsome First Church of Christ. The church had been designed by Charles Bullfinch in 1816 for my Thayer ancestors. We also had two ministers—one appropriately Unitarian, from that church, and the other Congregationalist, who was a friend.

I left the seminary in Boston and for three years served as the minister of a small rural church in Hubbardston, Massachusetts, not far from where we lived. Sydney played the piano for the congregation, and Cassy would sit with the kids in the front row and raise her hand when I made a mistake in my sermons. I never felt totally comfortable wearing a black robe, but the rural congregation, which was made up mainly of mothers and children listened patiently to me.

Then, on a spring fling near Carcassonne, France, in 2000, Sydney and I found a beautifully restored house in the valley leading to Bagnères-de-Luchon in the Pyrenees. The house is nestled under a mountain called the Pic du Gard, which is in the foothills of the Pyrenees about fifteen miles away from the big mountains to the south. Our garden has palm trees, kiwis growing

Bill and Anne Patten in the Pyrenees, France, 1960

from the arbor, roses in front of the house, and a variety of flowering trees. From our bedroom windows we look out over the village, south down the valley of cornfields, and even in summer we can glimpse the snow-crested peaks of the Maladeta range beyond Luchon.

I remembered these mountains from the summer of 1960 after my father died and my mother had rented a house near Biarritz. At the end of the summer she drove us to see some of her friends on the Mediterranean, and I can still remember noticing the unexpected silhouette of the mountains from the backseat of my mother's Jaguar. Looking back at the family albums, I see now that in 1960 my mother took us to visit the great abbey of St. Bertrand de Comminges perched on a hill just a few miles from our house. She must have driven us down by the Garonne River close to our house, where fifty years later many of the monkey prints and French furnishings she collected have come back to settle.

Somehow these mountains fit into my interior landscape. One evening, with Thomas Merton's *Seven Storey Mountain* at my side, we visited the town of Prades and, as we strolled around its little streets, came upon the house where Thomas Merton was born. I had not been looking for his house, but I couldn't help thinking of the amazing parallels in our lives. Merton, a motherless American boy born in France, was sent to French schools, lost his father while in an English boarding school, and spent his college years as a riotous bohemian. Like me, he returned to his native country after a lonely and truncated European childhood.

In some ways Sydney's fluent French and piano concerts in the local churches have enhanced my feeling of coming home. She appreciates the charm of the French countryside, and her joie de vivre has contributed to our making a wonderful variety of generous-hearted French friends. The baker who drives his

Sydney Patten and Sybil Patten, Ore, France, August 2007

van down the lane in front of our house each morning offers the same *pain au chocolat* that my mother gave me as a treat when I got good grades. And the clock on the church above us rings out the hours to bring the farmers home for the midday and evening meals. The gentle pace and beauty of this world brings the past into my daily life and replenishes us for our work at home.

Closing our house in the Pyrenees at the end of each summer, I feel nostalgia that is almost the opposite of the exhilaration I felt as a child when we packed our bags in Paris to go to my grandmother's in Maine for the summer. As a boy, Maine was where I could escape from my Little Lord Fauntleroy childhood of gray flannels and European sophistication. On Mount Desert Island I was able to get my hands dirty. I could play capture the flag with my cousins during the day in Somesville, and in the evenings I could experience the thrill of holding girls at the Kimball House dances. Whenever we leave the United States for France now, I feel much of the same anticipation, and the liberation, that I felt fifty years ago when I left Paris for America.

For my thirtieth Harvard reunion, in 2000, as Sydney and I were living on our farm in Princeton, I submitted the following update:

Last Five Years:

BLESSINGS:

1. Sydney
2. Being a grandfather
3. Bald Mountain Maple Syrup

CHALLENGES:

1. Leaving Maine (1997)
2. Calvinism (still)
3. Slowing Down (again)

DELIGHTS:

1. Working the fields at home.
2. Watching *Shall We Dance?* (the movie)
3. Returning to France in the summers

Reception after Susan Mary Alsop's funeral; left to right standing: Anne Milliken, Molly and Katie Crile, Sydney Patten; sitting front: Sybil Patten, Julia Milliken, author; sitting rear, Annabelle Milliken, Eliza Patten-Ostergrad holding daughter Sophie; Washington D.C., September 24, 2004

eighteen

The Long Good-bye

My funeral will be so boring for you!
—MY MOTHER TO MY SISTER AND ME

TWO OF THE major pillars in my mother's life disappeared within two years. Joe Alsop died in 1989 and Marietta Tree in 1991. As Joe was dying, my mother jockeyed for position among the women around him, his sister, Corinne, and his far more tactful sister-in-law Tish. But Marietta kept her terminal illness a secret; only my mother and a couple of family members knew about it during her last few months. I visited my mother in Northeast Harbor a few times in Marietta's final summer, and she looked utterly drained.

Her old friends relied on my mother's great loyalty and discretion; she once told me about having to decline a particularly tragic request. She had been staying at a resort in Florida with her friend Evangeline Bruce, who by this time was mostly blind. One day Evangeline asked Mother to go down to the beach with her to cover for her; she planned to take a lethal dosage of pills and swim out alone into the ocean.

Death was an unspoken topic, and people like Marietta and Evangeline understood that my mother handled it with the discretion of a decorated veteran and could be counted on to manage with a minimum of fuss. She had, of course, earned her spurs helping Diana with the aged Duff while still coping with my father's lingering death, and then standing by Joe in his last years. I always had the feeling that death was her most faithful companion.

Even as her friends grew ill and passed away, until near the end of her life my mother continued to be one of *Architectural Digest's* most prolific contributors. As far as she was concerned, she was a journalist and author, not a socialite. She always strove to be productive. A *Washington Post* piece reported that it "tweaked author Susan Mary Alsop to be called 'fashion doyenne of Washington.'" Around this time I began to become aware of what a notable figure my mother had become in Washington.

All through the middle eighties and nineties, Mother documented the dying world in which she and Joe had thrived for so many years. She wrote pieces for *Architectural Digest* about the houses of her famous American friends, among them Lady Bird Johnson, Ethel Kennedy, and Kay Graham. She traveled to Europe to write about homes like the Bordeaux-Groults' fine house on the Rue du Bac in Paris, where her childhood friend Elise had lived, or Spaso House, home of the American ambassador, in Moscow. She also wrote about the Travelers Club in Paris, where Duff Cooper and Bill Patten had spent many hours. She wrote pieces on Teresa Heinz's ski house in Idaho, Brooke Astor's summerhouse in Maine, and on historic houses like Henry Clay Frick's in Pittsburgh and the Rockefeller estate at Pocantico Hills in New York state. With her indefatigable sense of curiosity, my mother retraced her life on both sides of the Atlantic.

Though she had grown up in this world of wealthy people, in a way my mother was also an outsider and constant reporter on it. A 1988 *U.S. News & World Report* article titled "The Social Olympics" included my mother with champions like Jacqueline

Kennedy, Brooke Astor, and Barbara Walters. But Mother was an anomaly on the list. She adored her friends, but "Social Olympics" was not her sport.

When Malcolm Forbes arrived at Northeast Harbor each summer on his huge yacht, *Highlander*, my mother usually looked for an excuse not to attend his ritual cocktail party. One summer she turned to me in the living room and asked bluntly what lie she could give him this year, as she couldn't remember the lie she had given him the previous year.

Financially she was a pauper next to most of these figures. She drove herself around in an old Honda Civic. When she flew, it was always economy class. Perhaps it was this lifelong habit of frugality combined with our living so far apart that had made her icon status creep up on me. Part of her fiscal conservatism came from of her father's Huguenot heritage, and part came from her mother's Scotch Presbyterian side, and this attitude was reinforced by her intellectual hunger. The one animal she seemed to enjoy embodied this quality: she loved and collected pictures of monkeys, the most cerebral of animals.

But it was not my mother's fame that kept us apart. When I visited her from Maine, she met me in her red room, cigarette and drink in hand, struggling heroically to find a connection. She certainly knew how to look like she was listening, but the little gushes of flattery gave her away. They landed on me like raindrops, familiar and haphazard, reminding me that I was as invisible as ever. Even the handwritten notes she would leave on the stair landing, thanking me for coming to see her, felt like sad little life buoys flung out to a departing ship.

When I was planning to go down to Washington, the more she would ask me on the phone, "Who would it interest you to see when you come down?" the more pathetic it sounded when I replied, "No one, I just want to see you." It felt disingenuous, and maybe it was. Her question was partly an unspoken reminder that I did not know many important people. But she was gracious to the friends I did have in D.C., always engaging my old classmates like Rob Morgan or David Bruce.

Her drinking and all the behavioral dodges that went with it didn't help. I always felt I was letting her down when I declined offers to join her for a cocktail. But in a way it was more our lively conversation—that ancient bridge that had linked her so effectively to my fathers—that betrayed us. We could always find something to talk about; the words papered things over too quickly. We were both good conversationalists, too good. Even as a middle-aged man what I needed was to touch her, to feel her skin. The early nineties were something of a second childhood for me, but as an unmarried person I felt more vulnerable, more alone than ever in her presence.

I had somehow been inoculated from the hope of ever getting physically close to my mother, no doubt stemming from my childhood with her in Paris. I began keeping a small diary a couple of years after I was sent to Beachborough. On January 1, 1961—the year after my father's death and seven years to the day after Duff died—I started my diary by describing the day's visit to St. Firmin with my mother and the Sulzberger family.

That afternoon David Sulzberger and I got the family Studebaker stuck in the mud. We were short on beds that night, so there was some doubling up. I recorded in my diary on January 2: "Sleep in the same bed as Mum. Wake up & help w/depannage [repair service] of the car from the mud with a garage jeep. Boat having been stuck in the weeds is released by gardener. Leave for Paris . . . have dinner with Mummy."

It was the only time I shared a bed with my mother, and I remember it vividly. She tossed and turned without saying a word. Her exasperated sighs and physical machinations made it clear that she wanted to avoid any contact with my body. I struggled to find a place in the bed where my limbs would not risk touching hers. That night was the first time I felt that my body might somehow be selective. I wondered how my presence could cause her such obvious discomfort.

Throughout my life, if I tried to hug my mother, I found my arms folded around a skeleton. She didn't seem afraid of my touch, just unresponsive. As she became increasingly ill and fragile, my sister would give her back rubs and insist on lying next to her on her little bed. I envied Anne's confidence.

I tried to reach my mother through letters and literature. Even before I learned about Duff's being my biological father, I tried to suggest to her the benefits of talking more honestly about our various issues. In June 1990 I wrote to her about one of the famous Bloomsbury children's memoirs, Angelica Garnett's *Deceived with Kindness*. Like me, Angelica, the niece of Virginia Woolf, had discovered her true father later in life. In my letter to my mother I noted that "the author's fascinating parents were in a sense creations of their own making, not real people— and that can be hard for kids who as a rule gravitate to authenticity the way plants do to sunlight." I naïvely hoped my mother might see how Angelica, as she admits in her book, had struggled with the help of a therapist to come to terms and accept the deceptions she had grown up with.

In the same letter I wrote: "You, like Joe, children of lonely childhoods, really succeeded in making something out of yourselves that took you far from the dark, dreary, narrow confines of your Avons and Bar Harbors. But the pressure to do this did not leave room for much else." My words surely sounded pedantic, and her lack of response didn't surprise me. Instead she would ask me, barely masking her impatience, how much longer I planned to see my shrink.

Meanwhile, I saw my mother devoting energy to rescuing wealthy personalities she didn't even know. In 1990 I noticed a letter from my mother to the *Bar Harbor Times* welcoming the

Family lunch outside, left to right: Sybil Patten, Susan Mary Alsop, Anne Milliken, author, John Milliken, Molly Crile, Camden, Maine, 1995

arrival of Mr. and Mrs. Robert Bass of Texas: "It seems harsh and unfair to suggest that he and his family are regarded with hostility by old-timers in the community . . . I do not know Mr. and Mrs. Bass personally, but as a summer resident of the island since 1925, I can assure you that I welcome new blood." That she would write this letter on behalf of perfect strangers as a favor to a powerful Washington lawyer friend felt like a personal blow in contrast to her inability to connect with me.

In 1995, after the intervention, my mother decided she wanted to spend Christmas with me in Camden. This was an unprecedented event; voyaging to Maine in the dead of winter was not something she did unless her summerhouse had been broken into or there had been some other emergency. I was touched by her making the effort.

Many of us change in our parents' presence, and I am no exception. When my elderly neighbor Dorothy Seits, a deeply spiritual person, stopped by my house a few days before my mother's arrival, she found me wrestling on the floor with the Christmas tree decorations and snarling like an animal. Like my own children, she found there was no reason to linger.

I picked my mother up at the Portland airport, and on the way to Camden we stopped at a bakery in Bath for coffee. She told me she had brought me one of her last important pieces of jewelry, a lovely emerald and diamond brooch. There was a sudden moment of panic when she couldn't find it, but she returned from the ladies room with a look of relief on her face. She had secured the brooch with a safety pin to her underwear, and I guess her underwear had slipped down.

That was the only moment of real relief I remember from my mother's visit. My daughters and ex-wife rallied around and played card games with her in the kitchen. But there was no way of overcoming the penitential undertone of her presence. I couldn't even keep her physically comfortable. With her thin frame, she was always cold. Although when I would ask her if she was comfortable she insisted that she was wonderfully warm, she later sent me two portable electric heaters as a thank-you present.

My mother was not drinking that Christmas, but she was clearly white-knuckling through the holidays and living for her cigarettes. On the Sunday morning before Christmas, we arrived at church too early, and she refused to sit and wait. The strain on my mother that week was palpable, and without being able to talk about it in any meaningful way, I felt helpless, angry, and sad.

In my diary I tried to describe the hollow feeling inside me: "Is it my aloneness or my aloneness from her?" In truth the two feelings overlapped. I thought of the vacant look in my mother's eyes as she sat as a young woman on Duff's lap at the Volpi Ball

Frances Fitzgerald, Sam Peabody, Marietta Tree, Blueberry Ledge, Northeast
Harbor, Maine, 1980s

in Venice forty years earlier. I wondered whether Duff had been
able to fill some of that emptiness in her.

Loyal friends like Marietta's brother, Sam Peabody, were
faithful summer guests during the last decade of my mother's
life, but it was not a happy time, and she was depressed about her
lack of physical energy. Thanks to my sister, my mother received
superb care from live-in nurses, who fed her, cleaned the house,
and did their best to control the cigarettes and booze she had at
her disposal. One big fear we had was that she would set fire
to her sheets, as she often smoked while lying in bed. Fortunately, the nurses slept in her room, attending to her every wish.

When by August 1998 it became clear that the intervention
was not going to keep her from drinking, Anne wrote our
mother a forceful letter:

Mummy, we had a two almost three year haven. You came back to yourself. Engaged, honest, funny, no holds barred fantastic Susan Mary. Now, the disease has kicked in, the remission is over. We're losing you again . . . You shake when you pour your tea. You are lying about your drinking . . . Mama, I know you hate being told this. You are uncomplaining. You have emphysema. You are brave and you are lonely.

A sign to me of the effects of my mother's drinking were some uncharacteristically critical remarks she let slip about Nancy Reagan. In the early nineties she was quoted as referring to the former First Lady as a superficial person. I remember some of her friends being a little shocked by her newfound candor.

Still, my mother kept the old flags flying as long as she could. The last words of Sidney Blumenthal's 1996 article "The Ruins of Georgetown" were aptly hers. She summarized the end of an epoch: "We're all so old or dead. There's almost no one left. Just the Fritcheys and Kay and me, if you like. You see, they've all died. You see, they're gone. So on, and so on."

In 1997 Mother and my son, Sam, were walking to a friend's house for dinner one Sunday evening when three young men attacked them and tried to grab my mother's pocketbook. She wouldn't let go of the purse. Sam finally got it away from her to let the muggers take it, but not before he was stabbed in the chest. My mother was quoted in the paper making a light joke of the incident and my son's protective behavior. Sam survived, but my mother's cavalier remarks enraged me.

I wrote her the next year to tell her that Sydney and I were getting married that November in an informal ceremony in Lancaster. I took the opportunity to reinforce Anne's letter:

When Anne writes that "we don't bull shit" she is appealing better than I can to the blood line that links us. It's called straight talk and

(as exhausting as it is) it's what has made us at this late date a family
. . . A superb family, thanks in large part to your huge streaks of
generosity . . . As I told you in Northeast, you have accomplished SO
MUCH in your life to feel proud about, that I can only pray that you
do a little.

Anne and I had enlisted the help of a substance-abuse expert
at Georgetown University Hospital. He visited my mother but
was experienced enough to see that behind her thinly veiled
good manners she was not about to take the recovery program or
any twelve-step meetings seriously. The following spring Anne
wrote another blunt letter:

> Do not kid yourself: your drinking took you to Georgetown Hospi-
> tal. You were in detox, mum, not for flu but for having abused your
> body, lost your mind, not made sense, lost your bodily controls. Alco-
> holics lie. You lie about your not drinking, you lie about pills you take
> and don't take. It's part of the disease . . . Take on Dr. Flynn as a re-
> source instead of a waste of time. Stop feeling sorry for yourself. Get
> real! You are not the only one in the world with this disease, you can
> get help.

It had been four years since our intervention on her, and
though she now substituted wine for scotch and vodka, she had
been drinking and smoking for the last three years. She had clearly
beaten all the averages already, but with most of her close friends
gone, her loneliness was palpable. When I was in the room with
her, I, who had never smoked cigarettes, would smoke one just to
numb the sadness.

That summer of 1999 I chose not to stay with her for my
birthday on July 4, a ritual that she never seemed to enjoy anyway. I explained: "It is simply too grim for me to be in a house
where you are serving alcohol to yourself—against doctor's

orders and the pleas of both your children . . . Strangely perhaps, it is less the actual booze that makes my remaining hairs stand up on end, it is the lying, the dishonesty and all the ancient associations involved."

She responded: "I love you very much and deeply regret that I have made you so unhappy. Your allegations are grave, and as you are a very fair man, surely you will see that I have a right to ask you to answer my questions . . . What ancient associations? What deceit? . . . I am your loving and devoted, Mother." This submissive tone was deeply familiar, and I knew it ended the chances of an honest, perhaps angry, exchange.

In response to my daughter Sybil's concern about my being too hard on my mother, I wrote my daughter: "Over the last few years, as I hope you've sensed, I've reached some new feelings of love for my mother. Love mingles with sadness . . . I sincerely hope she may feel some of this 'rapprochement,' but I have no idea. You and her other grandchildren are a great consolation to her, as you know, and I'm grateful for the concern you show her . . . But as far as birthdays are concerned, Granny is the opposite of your mother, for whom birthdays are really important."

All of this time my mother was quietly coping with incipient blindness. Her cataract operations were complicated by glaucoma. Toward the end of her life she was virtually blind in one eye and could read only with a magnifying glass. Her principal consolation was a constant diet of books on tape, and a range of mysteries and historical biographies.

In her eighties my mother slowly started to slip into dementia. Luckily, a new summer resident and recent friend of hers, Charles Butt, lent her his private jet to fly back and forth from Maine during her last few summers. By the summer of 2002 she was spending nearly all of her time in her bedroom that looked out over the ocean. She would spend most of her days listening to her books on tape, and at times even seemed unresponsive to visitors who came to see her. Some, like her goddaughter, Frankie FitzGerald, would read to her. There was also a little TV in the room.

In August that year the engine on a sloop I had chartered broke down, so Sydney and I spent a week with my mother in Northeast Harbor. One evening we went into her bedroom to say good night, and she said with a doleful look, "Isn't it too bad about the crisis?" We asked her what she meant, and she told us there had been a revolution in the White House, that George W. Bush was hiding in the basement, and that her friend General Colin Powell had taken over the country.

We returned later in preparation for Eliza's wedding near Blue Hill, Maine. My sister was also in Northeast Harbor with her daughters. I stayed with my mother, and Anne would come over every day from her in-laws' house on the other side of the harbor. In September my mother was still strong enough to be driven to Eliza's wedding. It was her last summer in Maine. Both my sister and I had moments when we wished that death would take her out of her misery.

One evening before she had her dinner, I made my mother an unusually strong scotch and soda, which she drank without demurring.

Was I trying to kill her? My mother had always told me she did not want to linger in pain, and, more important, she had never lingered in life, always among the first to arrive at a cocktail party and one of the first to leave. I had inherited this compulsion to be always under the pressure of the clock, and I hated it. But I knew it was at the very essence of her being. So in a way, perhaps I *was* trying to kill her.

Around 11 P.M. she summoned us to her bedroom to announce that she was dying. Anne came rushing over with her

Susan Mary Alsop at her granddaughter Eliza Patten's wedding, Brooklyn, Maine, August 2002

husband and daughters, and we all sat around my mother's bed in tears. I sheepishly told my mother she was not going to die, but I felt too guilty to admit to anyone that I had poured her such a strong drink.

Occasionally she would let out short, high-pitched screams that we could hear from another room. I noticed them more clearly in her Georgetown home. They didn't come from physical pain, though. They sounded to me like a final release of anger, almost like the million pent-up complaints and sadnesses that she had suppressed for eighty years.

Amazingly, my mother held on for another two years. In the spring of 2003 her doctor recommended hospice care. Sitting in her little Georgetown garden that May, I wrote in my diary, "As SMA dies I find a new-found sense of peace . . . also the idea that peace is ok, that it is not some shallow form of self-delusion, that it is real and leads to something called enjoyment, that it is not BORING."

During the last month of our mother's life, my sister and I and our families gathered once again at Twenty-ninth Street in Georgetown. My mother's doctor, who was also a Carmelite nun, suggested we hold a service for her, since all of her grand-children were there. We stood around her bed with the nurses who had lit candles and with Stewart Alsop's widow, Tish, and we read some prayers. Each of the grandchildren shared their feelings for her. We listened to the song "Don't Cry for Me, Argentina." I thought it might remind her of her sister, Emily.

After we had lunch and departed, my sister went back to Mother's room to let her know that everyone had gone. She stirred, and with her eyes still closed, asked Anne, "Is there any cake left?"

Not knowing how much longer Mother would linger, I returned to join Sydney in our house in the Pyrenees. My mother battled gamely for two weeks, though she did mention the idea of suicide to her doctor. She stayed in her little bedroom on Twenty-ninth Street, and in her last conversation on the phone with Sydney a few days later, she said, "I love you." I felt that she was thanking Sydney for being with me.

Dr. Christina Puchalski speculated half seriously that maybe my mother was hanging on with such tenacity because, as a polite hostess, she didn't want to leave the party before all the guests had gone. My mother's doctor gently explained to her that it was all right to let go and move on to a more peaceful place. Anne was there in the room for that talk and remembers that Mother looked up toward her and said, "Tell her to go away, she's being a bloody bore."

In the afternoon of August 18, 2004, my sister called me at our home in the Pyrenees and said, "I have good news." Our mother's little body had finally given up.

Earlier that day Sydney had performed in a piano and flute concert in our house. When I introduced the performers to our guests, I had mentioned that my mother was close to death. I said that I could feel her spirit hovering above us and perhaps coming home to France. After Anne called, I walked out alone into the garden across the street and looked up at the stars. I felt that—at last—my mother was not so far away.

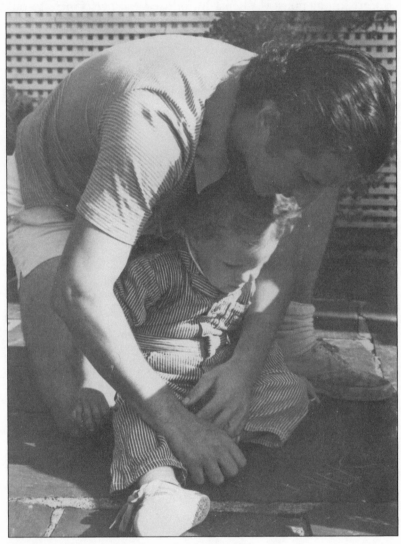

Bill and Sam Patten, Los Altos, California, 1973

nineteen

Looking at the Box

My Life is in the hands of any fool
who makes me lose my Temper.
—JOSEPH HUNTER

A FTER JUST A year of spending summers and various holidays at our home in the Pyrenees while returning to renovate our farm on Mount Wachusett, Sydney and I started to feel overwhelmed by the sizable work that these two rural properties required. So in 2001 we decided to sell the twelve-acre farm and move to a more manageable house in nearby Worcester, where Sydney was born.

The city had flourished from 1850 to 1950 as a major industrial center. It had been a global leader in barbed wire, abrasives, looms, steel rolling mills, and a wide variety of machine tools. Today many of the old factory buildings are closed and in a state of decay. The once bustling downtown is now vacant on weekends.

When people ask me if I'm retired, I reply, "I'm in real estate." Reassuring to the questioner, this is my quick and easy answer, and though it in fact has been my consistent occupation over my lifetime, it is only partly true and is certainly not what drew us to Worcester. If I mention that I'm also a part-time minister, I usually get a glazed look. It doesn't fit with a person who owned a newspaper for two decades and can afford a vacation home in France.

In fact, my major focus over the last five years has been working with men on antiviolence education both in prisons and in the community. This is an old calling of mine. I had looked into it in 1973 after being inspired by a progressive new commissioner of corrections appointed by Massachusetts governor Michael Dukakis. But my father's friends had advised me against it, so I went into banking instead. A combination of factors, perhaps more self-confidence and the ability to resist ancestral expectations, has brought me back to this less common kind of work.

The year after we moved to Worcester I started a nonprofit organization aimed at helping men find ways to change their lives, an idea modeled by the Men's Resource Center (MRC) in western Massachusetts. I was inspired by one of its founders, Steve Botkin, who more than twenty years ago helped build up a unique organization offering various types of self-help groups for men of all ages, including antiviolence programs. The Worcester initiative has taken its own direction, and I continue to serve on its board. For a number of years I worked part-time as a paid staff member of the MRC of Western Massachusetts, in Amherst.

Today I spend more of my time in a state prison in Shirley, a few miles across Route 2 from the cemetery in Lancaster where Bill Patten and my mother are buried. The prison itself is hidden from the busy two-lane Route 2, which runs from Boston directly west. You enter the prison grounds by driving down a limited-access road into a shallow valley that was once settled by Shakers.

Built in 1998, the Souza-Baranowski Correctional Center is a gray, boxlike fortress standing behind rolls of sparkling barbed wire. As a maximum-security prison, it houses a large number of "lifers." Some of these men, many of them young, will die behind these walls. More than one in four will never meet with a parole board. For many, it is a life without hope, a slow version of the death penalty.

Approximately a third of my students are lifers, while several others have been convicted of second-degree murder, which entails a life sentence but offers the prospect of parole after fifteen to twenty years. I was unprepared for the acute importance that inmates attach to their families; even those who are serving life sentences have desperate hope of being reunited with their children. Now their hope reminds me of the hope I had nourished when my mother first entered the rehab facility at St. Mary's in Minnesota.

In one class, my partner, a veteran volunteer named Ron Kearns, draws a box on the blackboard and asks the men to list the qualities that society expects in a man. Their answers conjure the stereotypical American male norms of our culture: strength, independence, self-reliance—in short, the Rambo machismo pounded into us from childhood.

The constraining image of a box resonates with the inmates each time we use it. My own box contains the contrasting styles of manhood embodied by my three fathers: the British upper-class ideals of chivalry for Duff; Rector Peabody's exhortation of Christian manliness at Groton for Joe; and my father Bill's graceful and independently crafted acceptance of physical vulnerability.

Two of my three fathers recreated their own versions of the male box. Duff and Joe remind me of inmates who admit to you that their crime was induced by alcohol and yet affirm with a grin that even after a decade or two of sobriety behind bars, they can't wait until the day they are released to go out on a glorious bender.

Like many inmates, Duff and Joe enjoyed above-average intelligence. It fed a certain arrogance and unwillingness to conform to the rules that the average person is expected to follow. Neither Duff nor Joe could wait in line patiently; both were used to gaining shortcuts, most often through friends in high places and family connections. For Duff, the shortcuts led to women's beds; for Joe, who struggled more, they helped bolster what he called his Proustian cork-lined room—a custom-designed ambiance like 2720 Dumbarton Avenue, which he created and controlled.

Their anger, nevertheless, never left them. Both men were notoriously hotheaded and given to temper tantrums. Churchill never forgot Duff's explosive temper. Joe's old Harvard classmate Charles Bohlen, who was so used to Joe's making scenes and storming out of his house only to receive flowers and notes of apology the next day, described Joe as an "emotional hemophiliac." It was as if Joe sometimes tested out his tantrums on those he could count on forgiving him.

These outbursts were expressions of a cosmic outrage. Part of it came from the injustice or insanity of the world as they saw it. Joe witnessed the former at Groton, and Duff experienced the latter in the trenches. And his old standby, booze, as Duff openly admitted, often sparked his eruptions. Joe, inflamed by feelings of betrayal or being mocked, would denounce the wobbly knees of a friend over Vietnam or bully a waiter in a restaurant for his incompetence. Self-pity was often at the root of his tantrums.

Both Joe and Duff benefited from the creative ability to avoid what Nietzsche called the sickness of the middle class: the tendency to transform rage into resentment. Through their voluble outbursts they bypassed the more socially accepted but odious forms of passive-aggressive behavior. And through their profound love of books and their writing they found productive outlets—Joe in his polemical columns, and Duff in his speeches and whimsical prose writings. But even the availability of these diversions did not relieve their underlying rage. It was not pretty to witness, Duff exploding with his "veiners" and Joe with his public outbursts. Both images remind me of an expression I often heard in Maine: when someone gets angry, they get "ugly."

Even without fully understanding how much of it was, as Richmond put it, my sadness turned inward, much of my own lifelong rage was drained during the ten years I worked with him. A number of people who had known me when I arrived in Camden in the late seventies noticed the change. Still, my physical aggression in the home of Kate's boyfriend in 1997 proved that I was far from cured.

Today people look puzzled when I tell them about this incident. Though I still get angry, I try to use the same tools that I teach batterers to reduce the chance of violence. I have learned to take time-outs when I feel my blood pressure rising, a designated period of time when I go for a walk and cool down. I focus on my warning signs, physical symptoms, such as a flushed face, that accompany rising anger.

A deeper and more inbred way of channeling my anger is through my almost fanatical need for honesty. The straightforward talk of the men I work with in prisons satisfies some urge inside of me, some visceral response to the half-truths of my mother and, to a lesser degree, of Joe. Straight talk contributes to the joys I find in what my parents would call the simple or common people I engage with most of my days, whether in real estate or prison ministry. The more highly educated or emotionally sophisticated the group I work with is, the more difficult it is to drop façades and find any real honesty. The only Harvard student I ever saw in one of my batterer groups was an intelligent and articulate young man who was so deeply self-defended that he reminded me of my mother.

My mother's anger was deeply muffled behind her rigid good manners. I never witnessed an honest howl of rage from her until I heard the little guttural shrieks that erupted from her bedroom in the last two years of her life. She had lived most of her life in her head.

I feel some of this same impulse to apprehend the world through my intellect. I notice it driving down the road with

Sydney when she cries out at the sight of a nasty piece of road-kill and I detach emotionally from it. On the other hand, I will react angrily to a lousy movie that my wife shrugs off as a minor disappointment.

Ever since I resigned from banking in 1974, I have been drawn to work that offsets this tendency to intellectualize the world. Real estate work mainly involves down-to-earth decisions about people and economic trade-offs. My antiviolence work aims far more at raw emotions than cerebral rationalizations. What we teach at the MRC are mainly basic behavioral skills, such as learning to listen or to empathize, and the process takes root more in the heart than in the head.

In 2002 I was trained to be a facilitator of batterer intervention classes in different communities around the state. Most of these programs involve two-hour classes once a week for forty weeks. Usually sent to us by the courts, the participants are men who have been arrested for acts or threats of violence. "Batterer" is actually a faulty label, since we sometimes deal with men who have never hit anyone but who have used other forms of abuse—verbal, sexual, or economic—to intimidate and control their partners.

I also work farther west along Route 2, in Athol. It is a hard-scrabble, machine-tool community built around a railway line that runs through a deep ravine. The older kids remember when the Millers River changed color regularly, depending on which factory was dumping which chemical into it on a particular day. In the eighties most of the factories closed down and are now decaying shells. The town is reputed to have the highest per capita level of traumatic brain injury of any town in Massachusetts.

Most of the men I work with were in one way or another terrorized as children. Rob's mother shoved a broken bottle into his chest, Willy's father smashed his ribs, and John's mother was arrested for driving her car onto the pavement to run him and his children over. When he was only eleven, Cubby, who is illiterate and bipolar, dragged his father out of a barroom which he'd been shooting up. Cubby then fought with the U.S. Marines in Iraq until he was discharged for threatening to kill one of his own officers.

Many of the men carry serious physical ailments the way Harvard freshmen in my day carried a squash racquet—without much concern. One has cancer, another degenerative brain disease, several are depressive and suicidal, another has a cracked backbone, which he shrugs off as he lugs shingles up ladders to replace roofs.

I am often asked why I find this work so rewarding; indeed, that's a question I ask myself. At best in the batterer program we can expect to significantly change the behavior of only about one-third of the men with whom we work, and to marginally influence another third. But seeing real changes in even just one or two men is rewarding. In addition, these men give me something important: there is something in them that I see in myself, something broken that gets healed a little bit every time I venture down into that ravine called Athol.

In many ways it is the voice of my son, Sam, that leads me to my work with these troubled men. Through Sam's democracy work around the world, risking his life in Iraq, he has been perhaps the most idealistic in my family. He has an inner gentleness that reminds me of his grandfather, Bill Patten, as well as a bravado façade that reminds me of Joe Alsop.

In her last years my mother used to say "Sam" when she was calling for me. In a funny way, it was a relief to hear her call for my son. It was his political work in the international arena that drew her to him; Sam was living in her world, and I was glad for her that someone in the family was carrying on that tradition. But although I admire the drive to serve, embedded in my mother's family all the way back to the Jays, it is something else that compels me to do the work I do. It is Sam's voice from the backseat of the car in 1984, calling me an angry father. It is that little reminder of my own abrasive behavior in the past that leads me to Athol and into the prisons.

Cassy Hayes and Bill Patten, Chestnut Hill, Massachusetts, 1997

twenty

Meeting
the Stranger

I was an old man when I was twelve; now
I *am* an old man, *and it's splendid.*
—THORNTON WILDER

DurING MY YEARS in Maine I had built a second family among my friends in the mid-coast area. When I returned to Camden after the St. Mary's episode in the fall of 1995, I shared my news about Duff's being my real father with four of my best male friends. We met regularly and talked about the central issues in our lives—the pressures to perform, our vulnerabilities, our relationships, our work.

Jeff and Brian were Maine natives; the former had owned the local grocery store, and the latter was the son of the town's blacksmith. Tom, who had been raised on a farm in New Hampshire, was a school superintendent, and George, who came from a Greek immigrant family, was a businessman. We enjoyed one another's company, and I suspect we discussed our personal struggles more candidly than most men do.

When we met at my house, we sat in the living room, which doubled as a library. One wall was lined with bookshelves, while another featured a large, gold-framed portrait of an unknown American ancestor and his golden retriever that I had found in my grandmother's basement. The evening I told my four friends about Duff I pulled down a copy of his memoirs, *Old Men Forget*, from the bookshelf and passed it around. The guys looked at the photos of Duff as a boy at Eton and dressed in his various uniforms as a member of the British cabinet. They laughed and agreed that my resemblance to Duff was unmistakable.

But when I started to explain who Duff Cooper had been, that he had been a hero in the First World War, that he had stood up to Hitler before the Second World War, and that his wife had facilitated his infidelities, my friends seemed to lose interest. I knew they cared about me, but it was clear that Duff didn't capture their imagination.

"Christ!" I thought. How could they not be intrigued by his colorful life or even a *little* impressed by his accomplishments? Duff had lived on the front steps of twentieth-century history, and these guys couldn't care less. Was I overidealizing him? One reason I like native Mainers so much is that they show little or no deference to pedigree or the high and mighty. Still, I found my friends' unresponsiveness surprising.

I grew to realize that the level of entitlement embodied by Duff and his world was faintly repugnant to my friends—though they would not have felt the need to tell me that. What my friends could relate to in a positive vein was that I now had a better chance for a longer life. Both Bill Patten and his father had died in their early fifties. Duff had lived until his early sixties, and his death most likely was accelerated by his nonstop heavy drinking, a habit his doctors had warned him about.

My buddies in Camden each had qualities that reminded me of Bill Patten—above all, his preference for low-key, peaceful approaches to life. I often thought they would be better suited to study for the ministry than I was, and in fact George was taking some classes at the seminary with me. These men were all devoted fathers, and in their own ways they reflected some of the greatness I found in Bill Patten.

I have been chasing my father for my whole life, whether gravitating back to Boston in 1973 or settling into Fairview Farm in 1982. When I once asked him where he would prefer to live if he could live anywhere, he said his dream would be to live on a saltwater farm. And of my three fathers, only Bill would have understood the mundane satisfaction of building a bus shelter from old boards. Only Bill could really have grasped my joy in working with my own hands, however amateurish the result.

My quest for recognizing the influence of my three fathers has perhaps inevitably been a rambling one. I have felt torn between Bill's gentle Christian conformity and the iconoclastic restlessness of Joe and Duff. I have bounced back and forth between the inclusive world of Unitarianism and the hard-driving world of real estate. I have wondered what I was doing preaching about forgiveness from a pulpit on Sundays when on Monday I am showing no forgiveness to tenants who are late with their rent money.

And part of me is still angry about the deceptions of my mother. As I look back at my parents' glamorous world, part of me still bridles at the image of my invalid father being trotted around Paris and London as Mother's "well-dressed Yank." As I come to the end of this story, I have come to feel more sorry for the deceiver—my mother—than the deceived—my father—because I can sense her pain more vividly.

I hear the brisk clip-clop of my mother's heels crossing the parquet floors of the dining room at 2720 Dumbarton Avenue as she heads out of the house or to Joe's office to deliver a message. I still see the grimaces she made turning the steering wheel to get into a tight parking spot. I see her grimly donning her rubber bathing cap before plunging into the frigid Maine waters off Indian Point. She is my brave little soldier.

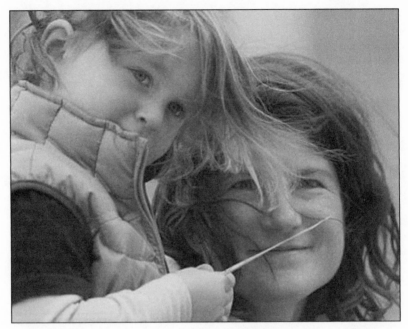

Sophie Morgan and Eliza Patten-Ostergard, Berkeley, California, 2008

The incessant curiosity of my three-year-old granddaughter, Sophie Morgan Patten-Ostergard, her ability to recover quickly from falls, and her intense energy all remind me of my mother. Even at her age she likes to clean up messes in the kitchen, help her parents pick tomatoes in the garden, and bring order to her little world.

Yet the social world my mother climbed into fifty years ago is one that I will never fully understand. Last summer I met an old Scotsman in the hospital in St. Gaudens, near where we live. When I mentioned my own Scottish connection and the name of Duff Cooper, the old man recognized the name and said, "Oh well, of course, he was part of the aristocracy," as if he were talking about some remote African tribe.

These upper-class Englishmen like Duff Cooper and Gladwyn Jebb were the stars of a small society that is often defined by its capacity for emotional detachment. The late-night stream-of-consciousness letter my mother wrote to Sir Gladwyn Jebb the spring that my father died is a reflection of this world. Her coolly rational advice to the young couple who had fallen so passionately in love reminds me how she herself focused on men outside her reach, men who appeared regularly on the front pages of international newspapers, men who were safely beyond the reaches of the intimacy she claimed to miss with my father, men who were almost certainly never to leave their wives for her.

Was Duff right in believing that my mother fell for the image of him rather than the man? Probably. But who was this man, anyway? Who was Duff behind the persona of the artful conversationalist, the literary wit, the restless lover, the warrior and poet? I am grateful to my half brother, John Julius, for having published Duff's private diaries. Duff conveyed in his *Old Men Forget* the picture of a man who was happier than he really was. But the diaries make him sound, God forbid, even introspective and unsure of himself.

On January 9, 1938, at the apex of his career, he writes: "During recent weeks I have been suffering from a lack of confidence which is new to me and depressing." He admits, "My political ambitions have dwindled. I always wanted to be Prime Minister. I want to be no longer. I got near enough to see the position without its glamour." Duff would not have wanted these private feelings published, but this vulnerability, for me, makes him more interesting.

Despite all of his bravura and claims to pleasure, in the wake of one of Diana's rare moments of distress at his womanizing, Duff borrowed from the poet Robert Browning to remind himself: "What I seem to myself, do you ask of me? No hero I confess." There was something about having survived when most of his friends had perished that he could not articulate except perhaps in his diary, and then only by inference.

Those who had died, young men he had loved, they were the real heroes. Writing in his diary about the guests at his bachelors party before marrying Lady Diana in 1919, Duff observes: "I could easily replace the eleven living with eleven dead[,] all of whom—at least eight out of the eleven—I should have loved better."

Though I respect Duff for his heroism at Munich and his capacity to sacrifice his career to benefit his country, his intimate writings have given me empathy for his simple struggles as a man, which, in the end, I find more important. Instead of the image of the insouciant rake that most people form from his diaries, I see an undersized fellow who tried and failed to control his drinking but said to himself, "What the hell, let's make the best of it," knowing how incredibly brief life is on this earth. And he did so in part after recognizing his own weaknesses.

Joe Alsop's vulnerability was far more transparent to those around him. Even growing up in his house, I was aware of his desperate need to prove himself as a man, reflected in the small things like avoiding soft suede shoes, or the big things like denigrating "second-rate" occupations such as teaching. I accepted the economic benefits like the English-made clothes, but the snob values were impossible to digest.

It was more difficult to distance myself from Joe's contrarian habits. I shared some of his rabble-rousing qualities in my early years as a newspaper editor and in my temptation to stoke controversy. Yet I could never take it to Joe's level if I tried. In one famous episode after attending the opening of the film *My Fair Lady* in Washington, Joe declined to take the bus to the reception with my mother, Marietta and her husband, his brother

Stewart, and the rest of the crowd. Instead he jumped into the nearest limousine, oblivious to the hundreds of fans clamoring on the sidewalk. Faced with its occupants, Audrey Hepburn and Mel Ferrer, Joe acted as if he didn't know them. In response to Hepburn's attempts to make polite conversation, he grumbled something about the poor quality of the movie. While it's hard not to be awed by such chutzpah, I think it left him more alone in the end. Who can create their own reality to such an extent without paying a price?

Perhaps I was saved by Joe's overbearing tenets about the merciless nature of history and the dark tendencies in human behavior. My Unitarian Universalist beliefs in the inherent goodness of humans would make Joe turn over in his grave.

My sister told me recently that my mother had not revealed the truth about Duff because Duff and she had decided that they had never known a "happy bastard." Knowing my mother, for whom the idea of personal growth was totally foreign and the notion of happiness highly suspect anyway, my fate was sealed. As long as she lived I could never shake the feeling of being somewhat pitiable in her eyes.

After a few sharp reminders in the nineties, my mother finally started to address me as "Bill" instead of "Billy," something Joe had done on his own two decades before. To me, "Billy" embodied the unconscious denigration she tried so hard to hide but could not. It seemed to me only fair that after my father had died I should have the chance to assume the name by which he was mostly known.

Recognizing the galaxies that separate me from the world of my parents, I decided that winter of 1996, after learning about my connection to Duff, to take a short leave from my life in Maine. Initially I had arranged to study theology at Oxford, but when

David Sulzberger offered me his apartment on the Left Bank in Paris, my friends told me to accept it. I put the *Camden Herald* in the hands of three women, and with the blessings of the seminary I started my mini-sabbatical.

During my little tour of Europe, I was staying in Paris and couldn't resist returning to the grounds of the Chateau de St. Firmin, Duff and Diana's country house in Chantilly, for a visit. I took a commuter train to Chantilly and got a taxi to drop me across the river in the hamlet of St. Firmin.

I slipped through the front gates of the Chateau de St. Firmin and found a young gardener raking grass near the driveway. He said that the Hermès family now owned the property. I explained my interest and asked if I could look around. The owners were away, so he told me to go ahead.

I walked to the lawn in front of the house, where I hoped to be able to take some photographs of the ponds and the paths leading to the great avenues of the Chateau de Chantilly directly across the way. I had spent hours sailing toy boats in the first pond at the base of the upper lawn.

The grounds were painstakingly manicured. What looked to be quarter horses were grazing beyond the ponds in the distance. The atmosphere was very polished and had little of the relaxed elegance perfected over centuries by English aristocrats like Lady Diana and her ancestors. So I was not surprised when several maids in black-and-white uniforms came rushing from the shuttered house and announced crossly that I was trespassing on private property. The house, they said, belonged to a famous family, and the path to the chateau was closed to the public. I took some pictures and left.

Who was this stranger trespassing?

A couple of years later something unexpected happened in a class I was taking on writing sermons. The topic for my first assignment was the story of the two disciples on the road to

Emmaus not recognizing Christ—the stranger—after Christ had risen. As I stood up and spoke, I remember my teacher and classmates sitting up in their pews, almost as astonished as I was by the sudden clarity of what I was saying.

My voice came alive in that classroom as I described the strangers we meet in our everyday life. Somewhere in the back of my mind I was being moved by the unexpected truth I had discovered about my own origins. I pictured the desolate back-country road I took each week from Camden, cutting inland from Belfast up toward Bangor, running through Swanville, past rusty old trailers and rural shacks. I felt that my words about the journey on that road could be describing the travels of the stranger in any one of us—the lonely, ragged passages we all encounter. And in my case, the stranger I had met along this road—was both my father Bill Patten and me.

I ended my practice sermon with Derek Walcott's poem "Love After Love":

The time will come
When, with elation,
You will greet yourself arriving
At your own door, in your own mirror,
And each will smile at the other's welcome.

— notes —

CHAPTER ONE—THE BUTLER OF ST. MARY'S

My copy of *Don't Tell Alfred* by Nancy Mitford (London: Hamish Hamilton, 1960), is an original copy given by "Mildred Jungfleisch" (Susan Mary Patten) to Evangeline and David Bruce, October 28, 1960, with handwritten note from my mother explaining who the other characters in the book represent in real life—for example, British ambassadress is Diana Cooper, American ambassadress is Evangeline Brice, Dior don is Isaiah Berlin, and so forth.

50 Maps of Washington D.C.: Hot Embassies, Power Hostesses, Ghosts, Think Tanks, Political Scandals, Media Hot Spots (New York: H. M. Gousha, 1991).

Letters from author in Camden, Maine, to Connie Murray at Freedom Institute in New York City on September 18, 1995, and various letters to his mother at St. Mary's at Fairview Medical Center in Minneapolis in late October 1995 and to John Milliken in Salt Lake City, Utah, dated November 5, 1995.

CHAPTER TWO—YANKEES AT THE COURT

Title of this chapter inspired by book *Yankees at the Court: The First Americans in Paris* by Susan Mary Alsop (Garden City, NY: Doubleday, 1982).

Physical descriptions of Peter and Susan Jay taken from their diplomatic passports.

Information on the McCooks from *The Fighting McCooks: America's Famous Fighting Family*, by Charles and Barbara Whalen (Bethesda, MD: Westmoreland Press, 2006).

Professor Richard B. Morris quote on John Jay taken from catalog of Jay family paintings and documents prepared by Gail Galloway, curator, and Susanne Owen, assistant curator, Supreme Court of the United States.

Quote by John Adams about John Jay taken from December 9, 1971, speech given by Otto E. Koegel, first president of the board of trustees of the John Jay Homestead.

Comparison of John Jay and Alexander Hamilton and descriptions of the Jays' frugality taken from *Memorials of Peter A. Jay for His Descendants,* compiled by his grandson John Jay and privately printed in 1929. Peter Jay (1776–1843) was the eldest son of John Jay and Sarah Van Brugh Livingston.

Notes

Copy of 1792 letter from Alexander Hamilton to Sarah Livingston given to me by my grandmother.

Several letters from Peter A. Jay at Eton in the early 1890s to his mother in Paris.

The title of Duke de Mouchy was a French peerage held by members of the cadet branch of the Noailles family. The founder of the branch, Philippe, Comte de Noailles (1715–1794), was the younger brother of Louis, 4th Duc de Noailles and a marshal of France. He received the Spanish title of Prince de Poix in 1729, and later that of Duke de Mouchy, also a Spanish title, when upon the birth of his first son the title of Prince de Poix became a courtesy title held by the heir. My contemporary's full name is Antoine-Georges-Marie de Noailles, Prince de Poix, who will become Duke de Mouchy when his father dies.

Letter from Theodore Roosevelt, The White House, Washington, D.C., to Augustus Jay, Esq., Newport, Rhode Island, dated October 17, 1902.

Letter from "HG" (Hugh Gibson), dated "September 4, 1922," from the Legation of the United States in Warsaw.

Letter from "Buck," dated "Twenty something, September 1925, Friday that's certain" from the Legation of the United States in Montevideo.

Letter of March 31, 1941, "The Late de Lancey K. Jay" to the editor of the *New York Times,* by Grenville Clark.

Recollections for My Family, by Edwin D. Morgan (New York: Charles Scribner's Sons, 1938).

The Last Romantic: A Biography of Queen Marie of Roumania, by Hannah Pakula (New York: Simon and Schuster, 1984).

CHAPTER THREE—AN INCIDENT AT SEA

The *Pan America* was among the first of four German-built 535-class transports converted to passenger ships by the United States Shipping Board in July 1921. They belonged to the Munson Line, which after World War I began a passenger and freight service from New York to the east coast of South America.

Peter A. Jay's appointment appeared in several U.S. newspapers, including the front page of the *Christian Science Monitor* on March 18, 1926, under the heading "Jay Is Named Ambassador to Argentine, Elevated by President Coolidge from Post in Rumania," with a photo of him.

The accounts of Emily Jay's death appeared in several Buenos Aires newspapers—*La Nacion, El Diario, Critica, La Prensa, La Razon*—in the week before Christmas 1926. The appendicitis operation was done by a Dr. Dowling, a friend of the Jays, but the lethargic encephalitis (inflammation of the brain) that apparently led to her death was treated by a Dr. Mariano Castex. The reports speculated that a medical error was involved, but the doctors made no comments. The immediacy of Peter Jay's decision to resign fueled speculation about a possible investigation.

News of Emily's death appeared on December 20 in the *New York Tribune,* on December 22 in the *New York Times,* and later in various Newport, Rhode Island, newspapers (Peter Jay was born in Newport). On December 30 the *Times* reported the Jay family sailing from Argentina and wrote: "Although Mr. Jay announced that he has not presented his resignation, merely going home for a long leave of absence, the belief here is that he will not return to Buenos Aires." The *Boston Herald* headline included "Secretary Kellogg Expected to Ask Him to Reconsider." All of these reports mentioned that the family was bringing Emily's body back with them.

CHAPTER FOUR—THE SMELL OF FEAR

Information on the history of Breakwater comes from *A Century in the Life of Breakwater*, by Rev. Edwin A. Garrett, III, president, Bar Harbor Historical Society.

Letter from William S. Patten at Holbrook, Cabot & Rollins Corp. in Boston, to Rev. Endicott Peabody at Groton School about Bill's records at Fay School, dated April 24, 1922.

The following correspondence, the comments of his teachers, and the Groton School yearbook 1927–1928, were made available to the author courtesy of Douglas Brown at Groton School:

> In reminiscences of their class, the 1927–1928 yearbook refers to "Joe Alsop's books with long labels and small print."

> Letter from Reverend Peabody about Bill's poor grades and doubt of "his ability to continue with this Form" to Mr. W. S. Patten, dated December 19, 1922.

> Letter from Reverend Peabody recommending Bill repeat first form to Mr. W. S. Patten, dated June 20, 1923.

> Letter from Reverend Peabody about Bill's being withdrawn from Groton School for a year and returning for his fourth form year to Mr. W. S. Patten, dated July 4, 1925.

> Letter from Reverend Peabody about "a general consensus of opinion that he is not getting hold of himself intellectually . . . and has fallen badly behind his class" to Mr. W. S. Patten, dated October 29, 1925.

> Letter from Reverend Peabody about how "Bill ejaculated 'God' in class the other day. This is not simply a case of profanity which is reprehensible," to Mr. W. S. Patten, dated December 18, 1925.

> Letters from Anne Thayer Patten at 234 Beacon Street, Boston, to "Mr. Peabody" at Groton School about Bill's education having "suffered from a constant change of teachers and methods" and efforts "to inspire him to do better."

"3 O'Clock in the Afternoon" essay written by eight-year-old Susan Mary Jay.

Foxcroft School, grade report on Susan Mary Jay, December 8, 1934–1935.

Undated letter from Susan Mary to her mother about first visit to Bill Patten's mother in Lenox, Massachusetts.

Description of modeling for *Vogue* with Babe Cushing from introduction to *To Marietta from Paris, 1945–1960*, by Susan Mary Alsop (Garden City, NY: Doubleday, 1975).

Numerous letters from John Alsop, mainly from Smith Barney & Co. in New York, and congratulatory letters from his brothers, Joseph and Stewart, to Susan Mary on her engagement to Bill Patten.

Letter of congratulations from Monroe Douglas Robinson in Westbury, Long Island, to Susan Mary in Bar Harbor, Maine, dated August 3, 1939.

Letter of congratulations from D. K. J. (DeLancey Kane Jay) in Windsor, Vermont, to Susan Mary at Breakwater in Bar Harbor, Maine, on her engagement, dated July 31, 1939.

Two letters of congratulations and advice from Martha Cross on Fishers Island, New York, to Susan Mary in Bar Harbor, Maine, on her engagement, postmarked July 4 and July 15, 1939.

Letter of congratulations from Albert Kornfield at 1148 Fifth Avenue, New York, to Susan Mary in Bar Harbor, Maine, dated August 10, 1939.

Letter of congratulations from Archie Alexander at The Cove, Beverly, Massachusetts, to Susan Mary in Bar Harbor, Maine, dated August 12, 1939.

CHAPTER FIVE—THE MAKING OF A WARRIOR

Letter from Susan Mary at 21 Square du Bois de Boulogne, Paris, to Marietta about "Billy looks like me but in character is so like his father," dated "Good Friday" 1950.

Duff Cooper: The Authorized Biography, by John Charmley (London: Weidenfeld & Nicolson, 1986).

The Arms of Time: A Memoir, by Rupert Hart-Davis (London: Hamish Hamilton, 1979).

The Duff Cooper Diaries, 1915–1951, ed. John Julius Norwich (London: Weidenfeld & Nicolson, 2005).

Mrs. Jordan's Profession: The Actress and the Prince, by Claire Tomalin (New York: Knopf, 1995).

The Return to Camelot: Chivalry and the English Gentleman, by Mark Girouard (New Haven, CT: Yale University Press, 1981).

The Perfect Summer: England 1911, Just Before the Storm, by Juliet Nicolson (New York: Grove Press, 2006).

Old Men Forget: The Autobiography of Duff Cooper (Viscount Norwich), by Duff Cooper (London: Hart-Davis, 1953).

A Durable Fire: The Letters of Duff and Diana Cooper, 1913–50, ed. Artemis Cooper (London: Collins, 1983).

Men Who Marched Away: Poems of the First World War, ed. I. M. Parsons (London: Chatto & Windus, 1966).

The Bullet's Song: Romantic Violence and Utopia, by William Pfaff (New York: Simon & Shuster, 2004).

Notes

The Pity of War, by Niall Ferguson (London: Allen Lane, 1998).

Europe's Last Summer: Who Started the Great War in 1914? by David Fromkin (New York: Knopf, 2004).

The Ghost Road, by Pat Barker (London: Viking, 1995).

CHAPTER SIX—DANGEROUS LIAISONS
The Face of Battle, by John Keegan (London: Jonathan Cape, 1976).

Diana Cooper, by Philip Ziegler (London: Hamish Hamilton, 1981).

Louise, ou, La vie de Louise de Vilmorin, by Jean Bothorel (Paris: Bernard Grasset, 1993).

Recollection of Duff in 1947 from interview with Mrs. John Alsop in Old Lyme, Connecticut, 2005.

Letter from Stewart Alsop in England to his parents in Connecticut, April 1944.

Description of Duff coaxing a boat of women at fancy dress party in George Granville Sutherland-Leveson-Gower, *Looking Back: The Autobiography of the Duke of Sutherland* (London: Odhams Press, 1957).

CHAPTER SEVEN—STANDING UP TO HITLER
Harold Nicolson remark about Duff's resignation from Nicolson's *Diaries and Letters, 1930–1939,* ed. Nigel Nicolson (New York: Atheneum, 1966).

Interview with Henry Kissinger in New York City, March 16, 2005.

Letter to editor about Chamberlain promising "peace in our time" in 1938 from Bernard J. Forletta of Shrewsbury to *Telegram & Gazette* in Worcester, Massachusetts, March 8, 2005.

Description of Hitler from the second volume of Diana Cooper's memoirs, *The Light of Common Day* (London: Hart-Davis, 1959).

Troublesome Young Men: The Rebels Who Brought Churchill to Power and Helped Save England, by Lynne Olson (New York: Farrar, Straus and Giroux, 2007).

Churchill visit to Coopers in Marrakesh in December 1943 described in *Churchill: Taken from the Diaries of Lord Moran: The Struggle for Survival, 1940–1965* (Boston: Houghton Mifflin, 1966).

Macmillan, Harold, *War Diaries: Politics and War in the Mediterranean, January 1943–May 1945* (New York: St. Martin's Press, 1984).

Comparison of Diana Cooper's beauty to Napoleon's sister Pauline, Princess Borghese, from Cynthia Gladwyn's *The Paris Embassy* (London: Collins, 1976), a history of the house on the Rue Saint-Honore.

Reflections of Cassandra in *Daily Mirror* on Duff Cooper's death taken from a privately printed volume of collected French and English newspaper and radio obituaries given to the author by John Julius Norwich.

Notes

Bob Boothby: A Portrait of Churchill's Ally, by Robert Rhodes James (London: Hodder and Stoughton, 1991).

Anthony Eden, by Robert Rhodes James (London: Weidenfeld and Nicolson, 1986).

CHAPTER EIGHT—KEEPING THE FIRE LIT

Susan Mary's letters are from *To Marietta from Paris, 1945–1960* unless otherwise noted.

Artemis Cooper remark about Paris from *Paris after the Liberation, 1944–1949,* by Antony Beevor and Artemis Cooper (New York: Doubleday, 1994).

Letter about transporting a bidet from Paris to Oxford from Susan Mary to Gladwyn Jebb.

Reply about *Don't Tell Alfred* from Nancy Mitford at Chatsworth in Derbyshire to Susan Mary in Paris, October 30, 1960.

Letter about Camaro acceleration from Susan Mary to author at Harvard, May 21, 1971.

Letter from Joe Alsop in United States to Susan Mary in Paris about Marietta and Desmond FitzGerald, April 1947.

Bill Patten's ignorance of author's paternity from conversation with Charles F. Adams in the fall of 1996.

Physical description of Duff and Cocteau quotation from *Louise, ou, La vie de Louise de Vilmorin,* by Jean Bothorel (Paris: Bernard Grasset, 1993), pages 158 and 160, author's translation.

The Congress Dances, by Susan Mary Alsop (New York: Harper & Row, 1984).

CHAPTER NINE—THE SAD BRAVE SMILE

Sulzberger, Cyrus, *My Brother Death,* dedicated to "Bill Patten, who understood the problem and faced it gallantly" (New York: Harper & Brothers, 1961).

Reference to Bill Patten as "a well-dressed Yank" in letter from Evelyn Waugh to Nancy Mitford in *The Letters of Evelyn Waugh,* ed. Mark Amory (New York: Penguin Books, 1980).

Letter from Bill Patten in Paris to Susan Mary in Washington, about missing her and taking care of Billy, summer 1949.

Letter from Bill Patten in Paris to Susan Mary in Washington, about visiting Coopers in Chantilly and Duff having a "veiner," summer 1949.

Letter from Bill Patten in Paris to Susan Mary in Washington, about Duff Cooper forgetting dinner invitation, summer 1949.

Letter from Susan Mary in Paris to her mother in Washington about her first Christmas tree and Billy kissing people, December 17, 1950.

Notes

Letter with "life is hellish without you" from Bill Patten in Paris to Susan Mary in Washington, spring 1955.

Letter with "cannot wheeze and be romantic at same time" from Bill Patten to Susan Mary on French Liner in New York, September 1955.

Letter from Bill Patten in Paris to Susan Mary Alsop in Naples about taking Anne to movies, spring 1958.

Letter with "sad brave smile" from Bill Patten on the French *Flandre* to Susan Mary in Paris, June 30, 1959.

Letter about visit to Beachborough from Bill Patten in Paris to Susan Mary in Maine, June 1959.

Letter with "reminder you are married" from Bill Patten in Maine to Susan Mary in London, July 1959.

Letter with "have faded from world picture" from Bill Patten in Maine to Susan Mary in Paris, July 1959.

August/September long letters from Susan Mary in Maine to Gladwyn Jebb in Europe:

>August 3, about ordeal of summer resorts, Bill and her mother bickering

>August 7, reports from Walter Lippman, Rockefeller versus Nixon, and Bill's Boston friends coming to visit

>August 15, fantasy about Venice "antidote to Kansas poison," "miss someone in Europe day and night"

>August 24, Franco-British relations, dinner with Sumner Wells, Bill "slowly dying of smothering"

>September 1, reading his letters secretely on hikes, seen as "hard-boiled because I am so damned cheerful"

Letter from Susan Mary in Paris, to Marietta Tree, November 5, 1959.

Letter about Bill's funeral from Gladwyn Jebb at British embassy to Susan Mary, March 29, 1960.

Letter of condolence from Gladwyn Jebb at British embassy to Susan Mary, April 8, 1960.

Letter about "fear and loneliness in Bill's eyes" from Susan Mary at Le Castellet, Var, to Gladwyn Jebb, spring 1960.

Letter about Bill Patten from Lord Salisbury to editor of the *London Times* of April 6, 1960.

Letter of condolence from Isaiah Berlin in Italy to Susan Mary in Paris.

Letter from Susan Mary to Gladwyn about Cynthia being "without dislike or jealousy of me," May 19, 1960.

Letter from Susan Mary to Gladwyn about anonymous couple's affair and opening Duff's after-death letter about Billy and Eton, May 31, 1960.

CHAPTER TEN—NABBING MY MOTHER

Taking On the World, reviewed by David M. Kennedy, on cover of the *New York Review of Books*, February 25, 1996.

Crusaders, Scoundrels, Journalists: The Newseum's Most Intriguing Newspeople, ed. Eric Newton (New York: Times Books, 1999).

Letter to author about value of asking questions from McGeorge Bundy in New York, September 17, 1966.

Taking On the World: Joseph and Stewart Alsop–Guardians of the American Century, by Robert W. Merry (New York: Viking, 1996).

John Dean's indignation about being called slug in his book *Lost Honor* (New York: Harper & Row, 1982).

A. J. Liebling description of Joe Alsop from David Remnick's review of Liebling's works in *New Yorker*, March 29, 2004, 58.

I've Seen the Best of It: Memoirs, by Joseph Alsop with Adam Platt (New York: W. W. Norton, 1992).

David Brinkley's memories of Joseph Alsop from 1989 National Public Radio newscast.

John Julius Norwich's report to Susan Mary about his letter of support to Alsop on his marriage to her and his attempts to speak to author about same in letter to her from Norwich at Stansted Park, Rowlands Castle Hants, January 14, 1961.

Letter about Bill Patten's life not worth living to Susan Mary in Paris from Joseph Alsop, spring 1960.

Letter from Joseph Alsop in Washington to Evangeline Bruce in Europe, spring 1958.

Letter about marriage proposals from Susan Mary in Hossegor, France, to Gladwyn Jebb, dated June 28 but more likely July 28, 1960.

Three separate letters from Susan Mary in Hossegor in August to Gladwyn Jebb about not wanting to marry Alsop, Anne being "wildly nervous," Alsop's reports on the Kennedy presidential campaign, "Jack is best of the crop," Alsop proposing LBJ to JFK campaign, his visit to Hyannisport.

Letter about "Live all you can" from Arthur Schlesinger Jr. to Susan Mary from Wellfleet, Massachusetts, July 2, 1960.

Letter from Pam Berry in United States to Susan Mary in Paris, September 1960.

Letter from Susan Mary in Paris to Marietta Tree about having "fallen in love" with Alsop, November 1960.

Letter from Susan Mary in Paris to Marietta Tree about problems with Anne written from "Anne's room at a clinic where she had her appendix taken out four days ago" and her decision to marry Alsop in December.

Undated letter from Joe Alsop to Susan Jay about decision to marry her daughter sent to author by his mother in October 1974.

Letter of congratulations to Susan Mary from C. L. Sulzberger in Paris, December 27, 1960.

Letter of congratulations to Susan Mary from Mrs. C. E. Bohlen in Washington, December 8, 1960.

Letter of congratulations to Susan Mary from Stewart Alsop in Washington, December 26, 1960.

Letter of congratulations to Susan Mary from Philip L. Graham in Washington, December 23, 1960.

Letter of congratulations to Susan Mary from her goddaughter, Frankie Fitzgerald, in United States.

Letter of congratulations to Susan Mary from Charles Stockton in Boston.

Letter to Susan Mary about Joe inventing marriage from his mother, Mrs. Cole, March 12, 1961.

My Brother, Theodore Roosevelt, by Corinne Roosevelt Robinson (New York: Charles Scribner's Sons, 1921).

CHAPTER ELEVEN—IN CAMELOT'S COURT

Letter of condolence on death of Susan Mary to author from Dudley Fishburn in U.K., September 1, 2004.

Quote about "patients supposed to be in love with their psychiatrists" from obituary of Joseph Alsop by Henry Fairlie in *The Independent*, August 30, 1989.

Description of Joe Alsop on Martha's Vineyard in portrait of Lillian Hellman, from Rosemary Mahoney's *A Likely Story: One Summer with Lillian Hellman* (New York: Anchor Books, 1999)

Consequences of exposure for Joe Alsop from interview with Henry Kissinger, March 16, 2005.

Author's phone conversation with Peter Duchin in 2005.

Schlesinger, Arthur M., Jr., *Journals 1952–2000* (New York: Penguin, 2007), 75–76, 212.

The Best and the Brightest, by David Halberstam (1972; New York: Random House, 1992), 499.

Heymann, C. David, *The Georgetown Ladies' Social Club: Power, Passion, and Politics in the Nation's Capital* (New York: Simon and Schuster, 2003). Joe Alsop held a leading role in this club.

Seymour M. Hersh reference to Joe Alsop being JFK's "favorite reporter" from Hersh's *The Dark Side of Camelot* (New York: Little, Brown, 1997), 243.

Notes

Letter from Susan Mary to Marietta about Miss Armstrong's swimming in Joe's pool, August 10, circa 1972.

Letter from Susan Mary about dinner with Kennedys at the White House to author at Groton School, September 1962.

Comment about Joseph Alsop "giving and getting pleasure" from *Personal History*, by Katharine Graham (New York: Random House, 1998).

Comment about Joseph Alsop being too "boy-stood-on-the-burning-deckish" from *Alice: Alice Roosevelt Longworth, from White House Princess to Washington Power Broker*, by Stacey A. Cordery (New York: Viking, 2007), 457.

"Remembering Jackie," interview with Susan Mary Alsop, *New Yorker*, May 30, 1995, 35.

CHAPTER TWELVE—MAKING THE CLUB

Letter about "keeping low posture" from Joseph Alsop in Washington to author at Harvard College, 1967.

Author's interview with Dean Acheson in Washington at his home, fall 1969.

Letter from Joseph Alsop in Washington to Bill Patten in Boston, circa 1937.

Alastair Forbes remark about Joseph Alsop and Lord Salisbury from review of *I've Seen the Best of It*, by Forbes in *The Spectator*, June 6, 1992.

Joseph Alsop letter about "liking Bob Silvers enormously" to author in Brussels, February 18, 1971.

Letter about Alsop doing his research in Washington on Bronze Age from Miss Puffenberger to author at Harvard.

David Halberstam's note about young Joseph Alsop arriving at Groton from his commencement speech at Groton School reprinted in August 1992 issue of *Groton School Quarterly*, ceremony attended by author and his mother and daughter Elizabeth Patten, who was in the graduating class.

Gore Vidal's recollections of his last visit with Joseph Alsop at his home on N Street in Washington from his "Reflections on Glory Reflected," *Threepenny Review* (Spring 1991).

A Bright Shining Lie: John Paul Vann and America in Vietnam, by Neil Sheehan (New York: Random House, 1988).

James Reston quote about Joe being cruel was in context of vicious remarks Joe was making about some of the younger reporters in Vietnam who worked for the *New York Times*.

The Paper: The Life and Death of the New York Herald Tribune, by Richard Kluger (New York: Alfred A. Knopf, 1986), 413.

Letter from Susan Mary to author in Brussels about Rod Knoop's visit with Joseph Alsop, January 18, 1971.

Letter from Susan Mary to author in Brussels about John Kerry's "star quality," April 25, 1971.

CHAPTER THIRTEEN—LAUNCHED BY JOE

Letter from Joseph Alsop about clubs to author in Wigglesworth Hall at Harvard, 1966.

Various letters from J. Alsop to author at Harvard about his orders to London tailor, social events, driving accidents, and suggestions about thesis on Acheson, 1966–1970.

Letter from J. Alsop on trip to Saigon to author about marriage on the rebound, fall 1969.

Letter from J. Alsop to author about sticking it out at Stanford Business School, January 3, 1972.

Letter from Susan Mary Alsop to author following joint visit to Yosemite, California, 1972.

Covering letter from J. Alsop to author about letters to Andre Meyer and Douglas Dillon in New York on behalf of author, March 8, 1973.

Letter from J. Alsop about "perfect solution" of moving to Maine, October 24, 1978.

File containing all correspondence, legal briefs, and newspaper articles concerning Patten and Saltonstall negotiations for acquisition of the *Republican Journal* in Belfast, Maine, 1978–1979. Includes December 14, 1978, letter from Joseph W. Alsop in Washington to Walter N. Thayer, president of Whitney Communications Corp. and Thayer's reply of December 28, 1978.

CHAPTER FOURTEEN—MOTHER BREAKS AWAY

Letter from Susan Mary to author in Washington about how depressing to know so many ambassadors and about assault outside house, March 6, late sixties.

Letter from Susan Mary in Washington to author about Stew dancing the Watusi, 1960s.

Letter from Susan Mary in London to author about Joe visiting British prime minister, 1968.

Letters from Susan Mary in London to her mother about Pompidou and Alain Delon sex scandal and Hood wanting to marry her, March 6 and 7, 1969 (to be passed around family).

Letter from Susan Mary in London to author about night with Lord Harlech, July 6, 1968.

Letters from Susan Mary in Paris to Joseph Alsop about having seen it (the riots) all before, Anne's wedding presents, and her visit to Balmain's, March 10, 12, and 16, 1969.

Letters from Susan Mary in Paris to her mother about dinner at British embassy, seeing Bohlens, Groults, Blakes, Mouchys, etc., March 9, 12, and 14, 1969 (to be passed around the family).

Letter from Susan Mary to author about planning visit to Petra over Stew's objections, March 17, 1969.

Letter from Susan Mary in Cairo to her mother about the Sporting Club, March 21, 1969.

Letter from Susan Mary to author about dinner with President Nixon and Connally, 1972.

Letter from Susan Mary to author in California about problems with Joe, April 1972.

Letter from Susan Mary in Washington to Marietta Tree about feeling that she had failed Elise Bordeaux-Groult in Paris, July 20, 1973.

Letter from Susan Mary in Evian-les Bains to Marietta in Siena about Elise, August 20, 1972.

Letter from Susan Mary in Washington to author in California about separating from Joe, 1973.

Letter from Anne (then Crile) to Joseph Alsop from Robert Merry's *Taking On the World*, 519.

CHAPTER FIFTEEN—FACING DEMONS

Sources include author's various personal diaries and his "Smythson Featherweight Diary" for years 1980–1995.

CHAPTER SIXTEEN—A PARTNERSHIP RESTORED

Letter from Susan Mary in Washington to author in Maine, 1984.

Letter from Susan Mary in Vientiane, Laos, to author in Charlestown, Massachusetts, 1975.

Letter from Susan Mary in England to author in Charlestown, Massachusetts, 1975.

Letter from Susan Mary in Washington about dinner at Joe's to author in Maine, 1980s.

"Mitford Originals," review of *To Marietta from Paris,* by Philippa Toomey, *New York Times,* March 18, 1975.

"So chic, so true, so sad . . ." Antonia Fraser's review of *To Marietta from Paris, Evening Standard,* March 16, 1975.

"Inner Sanctum Celebration, 200 'Best Friends' and Susan Mary Alsop," by Donnie Radcliffe, *Washington Post,* October 16, 1978, B–1.

"Lunch with Nancy," by Charlotte Hayes, *Washingtonian,* November 1981.

"Alsop Holds Court," by Donnie Radcliffe (on book signing of *Yankees at the Court* at Francis Scott Key Book Shop in Washington), *Washington Post,* May 21, 1982, B–3.

"The Alsop Chronicles: Susan Mary and Elegance Amid the Strains of Life," by Paul Hendrickson, *Washington Post,* June 2, 1982, Style section.

"New York Is the Social Olympics" *U.S. News & World Report,* February 8, 1988.

"Georgetown on Their Minds," *Town & Country,* May 1992.

"My World Is as Dead as the Auk," profile of Joseph Alsop by Adam Platt, *Forbes FYI,* 1993.

James Atlas, "Victoriana," review of *Lady Sackville: A Biography, Time,* October 9, 1978.

Rachel Billington, "Vita's Mother," review of *Lady Sackville: A Biography, Financial Times* of London.

CHAPTER SEVENTEEN—LEAVING LOTUS LAND

Sources include author's various personal diaries and his "Smythson Featherweight Diary" for years 1996–2000.

CHAPTER EIGHTEEN—THE LONG GOOD-BYE

Letter from author to Susan Mary Alsop, June 1990.

Letter from Anne Milliken to Susan Mary Alsop, August 11, 1998.

Letter from Anne Milliken to Susan Mary Alsop, May 26, 1999.

Letter from author to Susan Mary Alsop, June 20, 1999.

Letter from Susan Mary Alsop to author, June 23, 1999.

Letter from author to his daughter Sybil Patten, June 19, 2000.

CHAPTER NINETEEN—LOOKING AT THE BOX

Pseudonyms used for men referred to in Massachusetts Batterer Groups.

CHAPTER TWENTY—MEETING THE STRANGER

Epigraph taken from *A Christmas Cracker: Being a Commonplace Selection,* ed. John Julius Norwich (London, 1999).

Louis Menand, "Woke Up This Morning: Why do we read diaries?" (review of Virginia Woolf and other diary writers), *New Yorker,* December 10, 2007, 107.

Derick Walcott poem, "Love After Love."

— acknowledgments —

In the course of researching and writing this book, I have relied mainly on letters, memoirs, diaries, and my memories. All of the main characters, except Bill Patten, were published writers and wrote eloquent books about their own lives. In addition, both Duff and Bill were subjects of first-rate biographies. While I am grateful for these books, I have tried to allow the main characters to speak for themselves as much as possible though their own words.

Nevertheless, organizing the material was a daunting challenge. To begin with, I need to acknowledge a number of professional writers who have supported me in a general sense: Alfred Friendly in Washington at the very beginning; and Walter Pincus, David Fromkin, and Dominick Dunne along the way. I am especially grateful to John Ranelagh for his endorsements and Michael Jones for his comments over the summers I spent writing in the Pyrenees. David Sulzberger, one of my oldest friends from Paris days and who knew my parents well, was also encouraging.

The most specific early guidance came from my classmate Ken Emerson, who helped give shape to the long stretch of time covered in this story. Another Harvard classmate, Gil Bettman, also gave me warm support, as did Andrew Schlesinger, who recently granted me access to his father Arthur's journals. Peter Carey's thorough reading at the end was also a major boost.

I am grateful to Betty Meyer and Anne Ladley Mahoney for their comments. And I thank my cousin Sybil Jay's husband, Bill Waldron, for his steady encouragement over the years. I am also grateful to my cousin Elizabeth Winthrop for sending me Derek Walcott's poem "Love After Love." Steve Trudel was kind enough to work with me on personal aspects of this story that I was tempted to avoid.

For additional recollections of my mother I want to thank Muffy Brandon Cabot, Jessica Cato, Tish Alsop, Sherry Geyelin, David Bruce, Jan Wentworth, and Laurie Dunham in Washington and Anne de Rougemont, Anne Marie de

Ganay, Celestine Bohlen, and Avis Bohlen in Paris. For their memories of Joe I thank Arthur and Alexandra Schlesinger, Henry Kissinger, Alfred Friendly and Walter Pincus, Joe's faithful housekeeper Gemma Pozza, and his nephew and namesake, Joseph W. Alsop VIII.

For memories of Duff Cooper I thank his son, John Julius Norwich, his old friends Lady Kitty and Frank Giles, and my aunt Gussie Alsop. For memories of Bill Patten I thank Phoebe Milliken, Katharine O'Neil, and Bill Pellegrini. I am grateful to Douglas Brown at Groton School for his archival help and to Scott Marshall for his technical support. And I thank my beloved cousin Kitty Jay Bacon for her memories of her father and my grandfather and her overall generosity of spirit.

Most of the photographs in this book come from my mother's albums. I am hugely grateful to Joe's nephew Joe Alsop for the numerous photos from Joe's collection and especially to Beatrice Adams for her late husband Charles's wonderful photos of the youthful Bill Patten and his Boston friends.

The British ambassadress in Paris, Lady Holmes, and Diana Neill, the embassy's historical adviser, graciously showed me around the embassy residence and the rooms where Duff and Lady Diana lived. Lord Thomas of Swynnerton was good to send me the original letters from my mother to his father-in-law, Lord Gladwyn Jebb.

I have benefited from the criticism of my various men's groups. From the group in Camden, Maine, I am especially indebted to Brian Smith for his reflections, and from the group in Worcester, Massachusetts, I thank the Reverend Mark Beckwith and Scott Reisinger for their comments. Dick Nethercut has been the greatest inspiration in my antiviolence work in prisons in Massachusetts.

It was during a hike up Monadnock Mountain in the fall of 2005 that my neighbor Jim Welu suggested I contact Jock Herron. I am deeply grateful to Jock for his personal interest and editorial guidance over an extended period. Together with Ken Emerson, Jock was fundamental in helping me pull together a long and complex story. Jock with his Tidepool Press and his cousin Ingrid Mach helped me take this project to another level.

At PublicAffairs Lindsay Jones has offered invaluable editorial guidance, and I am grateful to Peter Osnos for his interest and support. I am grateful to their art and production departments for their highly professional help.

Acknowledgments

My oldest comrade, my sister, Anne Milliken, has been there with me since the beginning. Geography has separated us most of our lives, but she has always been there for me in the crunch. Her memories of our mother have been invaluable. I have included in this book recollections that she has shared with me, even some that I cannot substantiate myself. We differ in our memories of certain events, but this is hardly unique among siblings.

Finally, my sincere thanks to my three children, Sam, Eliza, and Sybil, for their forbearance and love. And, above all, deep gratitude to my wife, Sydney, for her patience and joie de vivre.

— index —

Note: The author's father is indexed as Bill Patten; the author is indexed as William Patten.

Acheson, Dean, 215, 238
Adams, Charles F. "Charlie," 61, 164, 246
Adams, John, 24, 295
Adams, Mrs. Charles F., 241
Adeane, Michael, 259
Agnelli, Gianni, 201
Agnelli, Marella, 201
Alcoholics Anonymous, 7, 11
Aldrich, Mrs. Winthrop, 54
Alexander, Dr. Archibald, 23
Alexander, Henry, 23
Alexander, Mrs. Charles B., 54–55
Alexander, Rev. Dr. Maitland, 32
Allen, Lynn, 277–278
Alsop, Christiane, 305
Alsop, Corinne (née Robinson), 170–171, 172, 191
Alsop, Corinne (sister of Joe Alsop), 315
Alsop, Gussy, 94
Alsop, Joe
    and academia, 217–220, 228
    alcohol consumption, 3, 175, 221, 256
    on America's role in the world, 179–180
    on aristocracy, 169, 216
    as author, 218, 298–299
    background, xiii, 169–170
    as Bill Patten's roommate, xiii, 119
    at boarding school, 173
    books, love of, 173, 177, 217, 220, 334
    charm of, 201
    courtship of Susan Mary Patten, 57–58, 182, 184–188
    curiosity of, 171, 226
    death of, 300, 315

depression, 268
    divorce from Susan Mary Alsop, 266–267
    Drink, Eat and Be Thin, 175
    and Duff Cooper, xiii, 179, 299
    entrance into William Patten's life, 167–168, 180–181
    extended family, 172–173, 175–176
    and Franklin Delano Roosevelt, 176, 299
    From the Silent Earth, 218
    and General Claire Chennault, 176, 177–179
    at Groton School, 173, 176, 214, 217, 220, 226–227, 333
    homosexuality, 183, 185, 202–203, 227, 229
    household management, 193–198
    internment in Japanese POW camp, 177, 226–227
    I've See the Best of It, 211, 291
    on Jay family, 25
    and John F. Kennedy, xii, 182–184, 204–207, 208–211
    journalism career, 168–169, 174–175, 180, 204–205, 207
    and Lady Diana Cooper, 179, 299
    love of political power, 225
    love of younger people, 199
    lung cancer, 284, 300
    manhood, style of, 333–334, 344–345
    marital strife with Susan Mary Alsop, 255–257, 263–164, 266
    marriage proposal to Susan Mary Patten, 13
    marriage to Susan Mary Alsop, xi, 181, 189

Alsop, Joe *(continued)*
  and Marietta Tree, 129, 257
  on McCarthyism, 180, 203, 227
  Men around the President, The, 176
  need for control, 257, 266
  168 Days, The, 176
  politics of, 228
  pomposity of, 191, 201, 217
  and Porcellian Club (Harvard),
    213–214, 216, 236, 250
  Rare Art Traditions, The, 298–299
  relationship with mother, 171–172,
    173
  relationship with Susan Mary Alsop
    after divorce, 3, 289–291, 298
  relationship with William Patten,
    220–221, 232–240, 250,
    251–253, 267
  and religion, 301
  retirement, 211
  and Roosevelt family, 172
  scholarship at Harvard, in Bill
    Patten's memory, 164
  and sexual activity of others,
    201–202
  and Southeast Asia, 176–177
  in Soviet Union, 203
  and Stewart Alsop, 168–169, 203,
    231
  on Susan Mary's relationship with
    Bill Patten, 58, 129
  temper, 255, 334
  and war, 221–224
  weight, 175, 215–216
  and William Patten, 167–168,
    180–181, 300–301
  as William Patten's stepfather, xii
  and Winston Churchill, xiii
Alsop, Joe (cousin), 305
Alsop, John, 94, 203
Alsop, Joseph IV, 169–170, 172
Alsop, Joseph W. V. *See* Alsop, Joe
Alsop, Stewart
  on Adlai Stevenson, 182
  on Duff and Lady Diana Cooper,
    95
  and Joe Alsop, 168–169, 231
  on Joe Alsop's sexual orientation,
    203

  as journalist, 180
  leukemia, 268
  on marriage of Joe and Susan Mary
    Alsop, 190
  on McCarthyism, 180
  in Office of Strategic Services
    (OSS), 183
  on Susan Mary Jay's engagement to
    Bill Patten, 58
  trip to Europe and Middle East
    with Susan Mary Alsop,
    257–263
Alsop, Susan Mary (née Jay, formerly
    Patten)
  admiration for Bill Patten, 120
  alcohol consumption, 322–325
  alcohol intervention, 1, 3–4, 5–10,
    322–324
  alcohol treatment, 11–19
  and Anne Milliken (née Patten),
    319, 322–323, 324
  anger, 335
  anorexia, 55, 133
  and *Architectural Digest,* 316
  in Argentina, 43–47
  arrival in Paris, April 1945, 116
  as author, 11, 136–137, 291–296,
    316
  and Bill Patten's career prospects,
    118, 120
  birth of, 34
  at Breakwater estate, 52–53
  in Cairo, 262
  *Congress Dances, The: Vienna
    1814–1815,* 2, 137, 295
  correspondence, 67–68, 115–116,
    117–118, 126, 159–161,
    164–165, 186, 207–208, 265–266
  courtship of by Bill Patten, 62
  courtship of by Joe Alsop, 57–58,
    182, 184–188
  death of, 269, 327–329
  death of Joe Alsop, 315
  death of Marietta Tree, 315
  dementia, 325
  divorce from Joe Alsop, 266–267
  and Duff Cooper, 67, 125–126,
    127–131, 132, 135, 157, 164–165
  engagement to Bill Patten, 58, 63

eyesight, 295–296, 325
at Foxcroft (boarding school),
    55–56
friendship with Duff and Lady
    Diana Cooper, 67–68
frugality, 2, 317
and Gladwyn Jebb, 157–162, 164,
    184–185, 188, 343
health of, 322
introduction to Bill Patten, 58
on Jay lineage, 40–41
and Kennedy family, 206, 208–209,
    210
and Lady Diana Cooper, 128, 137
Lady Sackville: A Biography, 294
loneliness of, 55
loyalty to Bill Patten, 128
    marital strife with Joe Alsop,
    255–257, 263–264, 266
marriage proposals, 13, 185
marriage to Bill Patten, 64
marriage to Joe Alsop, xi, 181, 189
mugging, 323
with new baby (William Patten),
    145–146
and political power, 122, 184
pregnancy, 133
relationship with Joe Alsop after
    divorce, 3, 289–291, 298
relationship with William Patten,
    xiii, 242–244, 317–321, 323–325,
    341, 345
and religion, 301
in Romania, 39
sense of obligation/duty, 131
and sister Emily, 43–49
as socialite, 316–317
and Sydney Patten, 306–307
To Marietta from Paris, 1945–1960,
    xii, 40–41, 58, 186–187, 266,
    277, 291, 292
trip to Europe and Middle East
    with Stewart Alsop, 257–263
uniqueness of, 11
Yankees at the Court, 2, 295
"The Yosemite Incident," 242–244
Alsop, Tish, 284, 292, 315, 328
Ambassadors, The (James), 186
America's Cup, 35

Andover Newton Theological School,
    307, 308
Ankeny, George, 198
Anson, Denny, 80
Apple, Lydia, 239
Architectural Digest (magazine), 316
Arms of Time, The (Hart-Davis), 70
Asquith, Cynthia, 87
Asquith, Herbert Henry, 69, 74, 82
Asquith, Katharine, 81
Asquith, Margot, 82
Asquith, Raymond, 74, 80, 81
Astor, Waldorf, 39
Athol, Massachusetts, 336–337
Auchincloss, Louis, 292

Bacon, Kitty (née Jay), 148, 201, 238,
    277, 286
Bailey, Ken, 279–280
Baldwin, Stanley, 91, 92–93
Bangor Daily (newspaper), 304, 305
Bangor Theological Seminary, 304
Bar Harbor Times (newspaper),
    272–273
Baring, Maurice, 74
Bass, Robert, 320
Battle, Luke, 238
Bayard, Anna Maria, 25
Beaverbrook, Max, 82, 90
Belfast Republican Journal (newspaper),
    249, 250, 271–272
Bergman, Ingrid, 90
Berlin, Aline, 123, 163
Berlin, Isaiah, 90, 123, 135, 162–163,
    232
Bernstein, Carl, 207
Bernstein, Leonard, 206
Berry, Marinette (née Sulzberger), 133
Berry, Pamela, Lady Hartwell, 123, 186
Best and the Brightest, The
    (Halberstam), 207
Bissell, Richard, 183
Blagden, Sam, 234
Blair, Bill, 57
Bland, Dorothea, 69
Blumenthal, Sidney, 323
Bohlen, Avis, 189–190
Bohlen, Charles "Chip," 119, 190,
    203, 238, 334

Bolotin, Susan, 299
Books
  at Breakwater estate, 53
  Duff Cooper and, 110–111, 334
  Joe Alsop and, 173, 177, 217, 220,
    334
Boothby, Bob, 111
Bordeaux-Groult, Pierre, 265
Bothorel, Jean, 124
Botkin, Steve, 332
Bowra, Sir Maurice, 218
Brace, Rusty, 249, 251, 271
Braden, Tom, 258
Breakwater estate, 51–53
Brewster, Kingman, 232
Bright Shining Lie, A (Sheehan), 223
Brinkley, David, 180
Brock, Woody, 213
Brokeback Mountain (film), 227
Broken Promises, Mended Dreams
  (Meryman), 280
Bruce, David, 136, 142, 256
Bruce, Evangeline, 296, 315
Buffet, Warren, 252
Bullfinch, Charles, 309
Bundy, McGeorge, 171, 217, 232
Bunker, Ellsworth, 263, 296
Burden, William A. M., 32
Burgon, John William, 263
Bush, President George H. W., 200
Butt, Charles, 325

Cabot, Muffy Brandon, 55
Camden Herald (newspaper), 273, 280,
  282, 303–305, 346
Capote, Truman, 201
Carrington, Lord Peter, 287
Carter, President Jimmy, 227
Castex, Dr. Mariano R., 45
Castle, William R., 41
Catledge, Turner, 176
Catlin, Ephron, 163
Cecil, Lady Gwendolen, 53
Cecil, Lord David, 122, 135
Cecil, Lord Edward, 53
Cecil, Robert (Lord Salisbury), 87,
  216–217
Chamberlain, Neville, 92, 100, 102,
  104, 107

Chaplin, Charlie, 90
Charles, Marion Oates "Oatsie," 297
Charmley, John, 16, 70, 73, 76
Charteris, Hugo, 80
Charteris, Yvo, 80
Chennault, General Claire, 176,
  177–179, 223
Chiang Kai-shek, 177
China, 264
Chivalry, 72–73, 112, 116, 333
Churchill, Winston
  alcohol consumption, 87
  and Charles de Gaulle, 109
  and Duff Cooper, xiii, 67, 69, 92,
    104, 106, 334
  as First Lord of the Admiralty, 102
  and Joe Alsop, xiii
  on Lady Diana Cooper (née
    Manners), 82
Clarence, Duke of (later King William
  IV), 69
Clark, Grenville, 35
Cocteau, Jean, 121, 124, 128
Cohen, Bill, 296, 307
Collins, Susan, 307
*The Congress Dances: Vienna
  1814–1815* (S. M. Alsop), 2, 137,
  295
Connally, John, 264
Coolidge, President Calvin, 48
Cooper, Artemis, 116
Cooper, Duff
  and Adolf Hitler, 98–100, 103–106
  alcohol consumption, 87–88, 240,
    344
  on Anthony Eden, 103
  appointments during World War II,
    108–109
  background, xiii
  and Bill and Susan Mary Patten,
    67, 157
  birth of, 70
  books, love of, 110–111, 334
  and Charles James Fox, 72
  correspondence with Lady Diana,
    75–76, 77, 81, 89–90
  courtship of Lady Diana, 80–84
  and Dean Acheson, 108
  death of, 16, 112–113

death of friends in war, 80
diaries, 79, 85, 86, 100, 103–104,
    105, 125, 128–129, 131,
    343–344
drug use, 85
early years, 70–71
in French society, 120
friendship with Bill Patten,
    141–143
and General Douglas Haig, 77, 92
and Gloria Rubio, 86
infidelities, 83–87, 125–130, 343
and Joe Alsop, xiii, 179, 299
and John and Gussy Alsop, 94
and John F. Kennedy, xiii
and Lady Cranborn, 87
and Lady Warrender (Dollie),
    85–86
and League of Nations, 108
and Louise Levêque de Vilmorin
    (Loulou), 84, 126–127, 128–129
love of France, 73
manhood, style of, 333–334,
    342–344
marriage to Lady Diana, 88
as mediator between Churchill and
    de Gaulle, 109
and Neville Chamberlain, 102, 104
in Paris, 110
personality, 124
political career, 91, 110–112
and Prince of Wales, 93–94
relationship with father, 71–72
resignation as First Lord of
    Admiralty, 105–106
on romance, 86
and Stanley Baldwin, 93
and Susan Mary Patten, 125–126,
    127–131, 132, 135, 164–165
temper, 334
war experience, 80
as William Patten's biological
    father, xi, xii, 17, 68, 340
William Patten's recollection of,
    16–17
and Winston Churchill, xiii, 67, 69,
    92, 104, 106, 334
in World War I, 72–77
writing career, 91

Cooper, John Julius (Lord Norwich),
    87, 90, 95, 180, 343
Cooper, Lady Diana (née Manners)
    as "accomplice" in Duff Cooper's
    affairs, 125–126, 131
    acting career, 88
    and Adolf Hitler, 98–99
    carelessness, 90–91
    on Charles de Gaulle, 109
    correspondence with Duff Cooper,
        81, 89–90
    courtship of by Duff Cooper, 80–84
    and death of Duff Cooper, 16
    drug use, 85
    and Duff Cooper's resignation, 106
    in French society, 120–120
    friendship with Bill and Susan
        Mary Patten, 67
    insecurities, 95
    and Joe Alsop, 179, 299
    and John F. Kennedy, 209
    and Louise Levêque de Vilmorin,
        84
    marriage to Duff Cooper, 88
    memoirs, 103
    in Paris, 110
    redecoration of Admiralty House,
        100
    sense of entitlement, 95
    social life, 74
    and Susan Mary Patten, 128, 137
    visit to Joe and Susan Mary Patten,
        209
    on Winston Churchill, 109
Cooper, Lorraine, 297
Cooper, Mione, 70
Cooper, Sir Alfred, 69, 70, 71
Cooper, Steffie, 70
Cooper, Sybil, 70
Coward, Noel, 90, 208
Coyne, Kevin, 35
Cranborn, Lady, 87
Crile, George, 260–261
Crockett, Chris, 284, 309
Cronkite, Walter, 273
Cross, Martha, 54
Crusaders, Scoundrels, Journalists
    (Newton), 169
Cunard, Nancy, 82

Curtis, Charlotte, 295
Curzon, Lady, 85
Curzon, Lord, 91
Cust, Henry, 81
Czechoslovakia, 102–103

d'Aulby, Comtesse, 73
Dayan, Moshe, 223
de Bothorel, Jean, 84
de Gaulle, Charles, 109
de Noailles, Antoine, 28
de Noailles, Philippe and Diane, 28
de Perigord, Madame, 137
de Rothschild, Liliane, 123
de Vilmorin, Louise Levêque
    (Loulou), 84, 121, 126–127,
    128–129
Dean, John, 174
Deceived with Kindness (Garnett),
    319
Desborough, Lady, 80
Devens, Charles, 61, 214, 228–229,
    246
Dillon, Douglas, 207, 287
Don't Tell Alfred (Mitford), 135, 137
Dorothea, Duchesse de Dino, 295
Douglas, Harriett, 172
Douglas, Waldo Robinson, 58
*Drink, Eat and Be Thin: The Full Story
    of the Martini Drinker's Diet*
    (J. W. Alsop), 175
Duchin, Peter, 205, 206
Duff, Lady Agnes Cecil Emiline,
    69–71
Duffy family, 245
Duggan, Elise, 265
Dunraven, Lord, 35
Dupplin, Viscount, 70

Eden, Anthony, 103, 108
Embezzler, The (Auchincloss), 292
Erlanger, Rudolph, 214
Erroll, Earl of, 69

Fairlie, Henry, 226, 227
Fairview Farm, 275, 282
Fellowes, Daisy, 126–127
Ferdinand, Prince (later King) of
    Romania, 38

Ferrer, Mel, 345
Fife, Earl of, 69
Finley, John, 220
Fishburn, Dudley, 198–199
FitzGerald, Desmond, 56, 58, 129,
    130
FitzGerald, Frankie, 190, 326
Flanner, Janet, 143
Fleming, Ian, 90
Flower, Herbert, 70
Forbes, Alastair, 216
Forbes, Malcolm, 317
Fox, Charles James, 72
Franklin, Benjamin, 24, 295
Fraser, Lady Antonia, 291–292
Freedom Institute, 5, 8, 9
Fritchey, Polly (formerly Wisner), 6, 8,
    207
From the Silent Earth (J. W. Alsop), 218
Fuller, Bliss, 275

Gardner, George Peabody, 143–144
Garnett, Angelica, 319
Gelb, Leslie H., 227
Geyelin, Phil, 204
Gibson, Hugh, 31
Giles, Frank, 259
Giles, Lady Kitty, 259
Girouard, Mark, 72
The Glorious Adventure (film), 88
Goldman, Guido, 248
Goodwin, Doris Kearns, 97
Graham, Kay, 199, 201, 207, 252, 296,
    316
Graham, Phil, 190
Grant, Eddie, 35
Grenfell, Billy, 73, 80
Grenfell, Julian, 73
Grew, Joseph C., 41
Groton School, 59
    Bill Patten at, 59–60
    code of athletic Christianity, 214,
        333
    Dean Acheson at, 215
    Eliza Ostergard (née Patten) at,
        220
    Joe Alsop at, 173, 176, 214, 217,
        220, 226–227, 333
    Joseph Alsop IV at, 169

and Sam Patten, 281
social codes at, 173, 215, 227
William Patten at, 12, 68, 143, 164,
  191, 226, 232–233
Guest, Ivor, Lord Wimborne, 83

Haig, General Douglas, 77, 92
Halban, Peter, 163
Halberstam, David, 207, 220
Hamilton, Alexander, 24–25, 25–26
Harland, Heather, 277
Harris, Fred, 200
Hart-Davis, Rupert, 70, 86
Hay, Elizabeth, 69
Hay, Lady Agnes, 69
Hay, William George, 69
Hayes, Cassy, 305, 308
Hearst, Willy, 236
Hellman, Lillian, 202
Henderson, Lady, 287
Henderson, Sir Nicholas, 287
Hepburn, Audrey, 345
Hersh, Seymour, 204
Higginson, Francis Lee, 32
Hildreth, Hoddy, 249
History of the Modern World (Palmer),
  98
Hitler, Adolf
  and Duff Cooper, 98–100, 103–106
  and Lady Diana Cooper, 98–99
  and Neville Chamberlain, 104
  opposition to, 103
  and pacifism of Europe, 99, 102
  popularity of, 97–99
  rise to power, 99–100
Ho Chi Minh, 122
Hodson, Brad, 305
Honesty, 335
Hood, Sammy, 259
Hoover, J. Edgar, 203
Horner, Edward, 80
Horses, 32
Humphrey, Hubert, 263
Huxley, Julian, 86

Iron Horse Farm, 308–309
Iselin, Jay, 249
I've Seen the Best of It (J.W. Alsop),
  211, 291

Jackson, Ira, 247
James, Henry, 186
Jay, Augustus (father of Peter A. and
  De Lancey), 27
Jay, Augustus (grandfather of chief
  justice John Jay), 25
Jay, DeLancey, 27
  and daughter Kitty Bacon, 238
  marriage of, 35
  on Susan Mary Jay's engagement to
    Bill Patten, 63
  wedding of Bill Patten and Susan
    Mary Jay, 64
  in World War I, 34–35
Jay, Elizabeth Morgan, 35
Jay, Emily Astor Kane, 27, 28
Jay, Emily Kane, 34, 43–47
Jay, John, 24–25, 295
Jay, Judge William, 25
Jay, Peter A., 27
  in Argentina, 41
  at Breakwater estate, 51
  in Cairo, 33
  career, 24, 118
  correspondence, 28
  death of daughter Emily, 45–49
  as diplomat, xiii, 29
  education of, 29
  end of diplomatic career, 47
  frugality of, 25, 26
  in Japan, 33
  love of horses, 32
  marriage, 32
  and President Taft, 33
  and Queen Marie of Romania, 39
  in Romania, 37–40
  in Rome, 34
  and Roosevelts, 33
  salary of, 25
  in San Salvador, 36–37
Jay, Peter Augustus, 24, 27
Jay, Sarah, 25–26
Jay, Susan Alexander (née McCook),
  21–24
  and Bill Patten (son-in-law), 160
  in Cairo, 33
  death of, 289
  death of daughter Emily, 49
  departure from Paris, 31

Jay, Susan Alexander *(continued)*
    in Japan, 33
    marriage, 32
    and money, 25
    in Rome, 34
    and Roosevelts, 33
Jay, Susan Mary. *See* Alsop, Susan
    Mary (née Jay, later Patten)
Jay, Sybil Kane (later Kinnicutt), 64
Jay, William Jr., 25
Jay Treaty, 24
Jebb, Lady Gladwyn, 110
Jebb, Sir Gladwyn, 124, 157–162, 164,
    184–185, 188, 342–343
Johns Hopkins diet program, 175
Johnson, Lady Bird, 316
Johnson, Lyndon, xiii, 186, 207,
    209
Jordan, Mrs. *See* Bland, Dorothea

Kane, Annie, 51
Kane, John Innes, 51
Kearns, Ron, 333
Keegan, John, 80
Kennan, George, 238
Kennedy, David, 169, 174
Kennedy, Edward, 209
Kennedy, Ethel, 209, 316
Kennedy, Jacqueline Bouvier, 182–183,
    204, 209–210
Kennedy, Joan, 209
Kennedy, John F. (JFK)
    assassination, 210–211
    dinner with Lady Diana Cooper at
        the Alsop home, 209
    and Duff Cooper, xiii
    and Joe Alsop, xiii, 182–184, ,
        204–207, 208–211
    sexual exploits, 204
Kennedy, Joseph, 98
Kennedy, Robert, 204, 209
Kenny, Doug, 236
Kerry, John, 225, 226
Kidder, Dottie, 258
Kinnicutt, Frankie, 63
Kinnicutt, Mrs. Francis P., 64
Kinnoull, Earl of, 70
Kissinger, Henry, 97, 203, 217, 223,
    264

Kitchener, Lord Herbert, 34, 53
Kluge, Richard, 224
Knoop, Rod, 225, 226
Kornfield, Albert, 63

Lady Sackville: A Biography (S. M.
    Alsop), 294
Lambton, Lord Antony Claud
    Frederick, 202
Last Romantic, The (Pakula), 39
Lawford, Peter, 206
The Leisure of an Egyptian Official
    (Cecil), 53
Liebling, A. J., 175
Life of Lord Curzon, Viceroy of India
    (Ronaldshay), 53
Life of Robert, Marquis of Salisbury
    (Cecil), 53
The Light of Common Day (Cooper),
    103
Lippmann, Walter, 217
Lipton, Sir Thomas, 35
Lister, Charles, 80
Livingston, Sarah, 25
Lodge, Henry Cabot, 37
Lodge, Henry Cabot Jr., 261–262
London Times, 106
A Long Life (Nicolson), 298
Longworth, Alice (née Roosevelt), 31,
    201, 209, 211
Lorenz, Konrad, 222
Lyman, R. T., 61

Maclean, Lady Veronica, 142
MacMillan, Harold, 98, 110
MacNamara, Frank, 225
Mahoney, Rosemary, 199, 202
Manners, John, 72, 80
Manners, Violet, 81
Margaret, Princess, 90
Marie, Queen of Romania, 38–39
Marshall, General George, 122
Martin, Joel, 305
Mary, Queen of Scots (Fraser), 291
McCarthy, Joseph, 180, 203, 227
McClellan, George, 32
McCook, Charlie, 22
McCook, Colonel John J., 22, 24, 32
McCook, Daniel, 22

McCook, John (son of Colonel John
    J.), 22–23
McNamara, Robert, 226, 242
Melendez, Jorge, 36
The Men around the President (J. W.
    Alsop), 176
Men's Resource Center (MRC), 332
Merry, Robert, 169, 172, 173, 207,
    229, 256
Merton, Thomas, 311
Miller, Arjay, 242
Milliken, Anne (née Patten)
    alcohol intervention with Susan
        Mary Alsop, 3–4, 5–10
    appendix removal, 187
    birth of daughter Julia, 283
    as a child, 152
    correspondence with William
        Patten, 197
    education, 196–197
    letter to Susan Mary Alsop,
        322–323, 324
    loss of father, 187
    marriage to George Crile, 260–261
    relationship with Susan Mary
        Alsop, 319
    relationship with William Patten, 5,
        15
    and substance abuse by Susan Mary
        Alsop, 324
Milliken, John, 5, 7, 8
Milliken, Julia, 283
The Miracle (play), 89
Mitford, Nancy, 117, 121, 132, 135,
    136, 137
Mondale, Walter "Fritz," 200–201
Monnet, Jean, 240
Morgan, Edwin Denison, 35–36
Mortimer, Vicky, 149
The Mosquito Coast (Theroux), 275
Mouchy, Henri and Marie, 28
Munich Pact (1938), 97, 102, 104
Murray, Connie, 8, 9
My Brother's Death (Sulzberger), 141

Nicolson, Harold, 98, 105, 298
Nicolson, Juliet, 82
Nicolson, Nigel, 298
Nitze, Paul, 238

Nixon, President Richard, 183, 263,
    264, 268
Norwich, Lord. *See* Cooper, John
    Julius

Oger, Mademoiselle (Mazelle), 144
Old Men Forget (Cooper), 340, 343
The 168 Days (J. W. Alsop and
    Catledge), 176
Oppenheimer, Robert, 180
Ormes, David, 247
Ormsby-Gore, David (Lord Harlech),
    260
Ostergard, Cyrus, 308
Ostergard, Eliza (née Patten)
    alcohol intervention with Susan
        Mary Alsop, 7, 8
    birth of, 247
    and father, William Patten, 278
    graduation from Groton, 220
    graduation from Stanford, 307
    parents' divorce, 283
    personal life, 308
    in Portugal, 304
    sadness of, 286
    wedding, 326
Ostergard, Obediah, 308
Ostergard, Sophie, 308

Packard, David, 242
Paley, Bill, 251
Paley, Kate, 239
Palmer, R. R., 98
Pao, General Vang, 293
Parascan, Johnny, 52
Pathet Lao, 292
Patten, Bill
    appointment to embassy in
        Paris, 119
    career, 64–65, 119
    courtship of Susan Mary Jay, 62
    death of, xi, 17, 140
    and Duff and Lady Diana Cooper,
        157
    education, 59–61
    engagement to Susan Mary Jay, 58,
        63
    friendship with Duff and Lady
        Diana Cooper, 67

Patten, Bill *(continued)*
  friendship with Duff Cooper,
    141–143
  funeral, 161
  at Groton School, 59–60
  health, 59–60, 63, 154
  introduction to Susan Mary Jay, 58
  jealousy of, 134
  as Joe Alsop's roommate, xiii, 119
  and Kitty Jay Bacon, 148
  knowledge of William Patten's
    parentage, 134
  love for Susan Mary Jay, 152
  manhood, style of, 333
  marriage to Susan Mary Jay, 64
  in nursing home, 131
  and Porcellian Club (Harvard), 213
  similarities to William Patten,
    340–341
  and Susan Alexander Jay (mother-
    in-law), 160
  Susan Mary Patten's ambitions for,
    118, 120
  during William Patten's childhood,
    117–151
  as William Patten's father, xii
Patten, Kate (née Bacon)
  and Bob Perkins, 284, 285
  divorce from William Patten, 283,
    286
  family of, 225
  and Forrester Smith, 283–284
  introduction to William Patten, 239
  unhappiness, 275, 281–282, 284
Patten, Max, 307
Patten, Sam
  birth of, 241
  career, 307
  and Concord Academy, 281
  at Georgetown University, 300
  graduation from Dexter School, 286
  influence on William Patten, 337
  move from Boston to Camden, 271
  mugging of, with Susan Mary
    Alsop, 323
  relationship with father, William
    Patten, 278
  trip to France as exchange student,
    283

Patten, Susan Mary. *See* Alsop, Susan
    Mary (née Jay, later Patten)
Patten, Sybil
  birth of, 250
  in community theater, 285
  graduation from New York
    University, 308
  graduation from Proctor Academy,
    307
  horse from grandmother, 286
  move from Boston to Camden, 271
  and parents' divorce, 283, 285
  practical joke by father, William
    Patten, 278
  in school play, 13
  on William Patten and Susan Mary
    Alsop, 325
Patten, Sydney (formerly Camp
    Hayes), 305–309, 311–313, 326,
    328, 329, 331
Patten, William
  abrasiveness, 276, 277–279, 337
  alcohol intervention with Susan
    Mary Alsop, 5–10
  at Andover Newton Theological
    School, 307, 308–309
  antiviolence education, 332–334, 336
  and Bill Patten, xii, 117–151
  at boarding school, 11–12, 167, 191
  at *Camden Herald*, 303–305
  career, 236, 246–247
  childhood, 144–147, 312
  children, 278, 304, 337 (*see also*
    Ostergard, Eliza (née Patten);
    Sam Patten; Sybil Patten)
  correspondence with Susan Mary
    Alsop, 14
  and death of Bill Patten, 17, 277
  divorce from Kate Patten, 283, 286
  Duff Cooper as biological father, xi,
    xii, 17, 68, 340
  Fairview Farm, 275
  in France, 309, 311–313
  at Groton School, 12, 68, 143, 164,
    191, 226, 232–233
  and Joe Alsop, 167–168, 180–181,
    300–301
  in the late 1960s, 238
  learning of paternity, 339–341

letter to Susan Mary Alsop,
323–324
in Maine, 271–287, 331
and *To Marietta from Paris,
1945–1960,* xii
marijuana use, 276
marriage to Kate Bacon, 241
marriage to Sydney Patten, 309
and Marietta Tree, 57, 68, 287
meeting of Kate Bacon, 239
move to Maine, 248–251
need for honesty, 335
as newspaper owner, 271–274
in Paris, 155, 157
and Porcellian Club (Harvard),
213–214
psychiatric treatment, 276–277,
278, 287
relationship with Anne Milliken
(née Patten), 5, 15
relationship with Joe Alsop,
220–221, 232–240, 251–253, 267
relationship with Susan Mary
Alsop, xiii, 242–244, 317–321,
323–325, 341, 345
religious studies, 304–305, 307, 309,
346–347
return to Boston, 245–247
sabbatical in Europe, 304, 346
self-esteem issues, 276, 280, 281
similarities to Bill Patten, 340–341
at Stanford, 241–242, 265
and substance abuse by Susan Mary
Alsop, 324
substance abuse (treatment),
280–281
and Sydney Patten, 305–309
"The Yosemite Incident," 242–244
violent outbursts, 276, 285, 335
Patten-Ostergard, Sophie Morgan,
342
Peabody, Endicott, 59
Peabody, Sam, 322
Pearson, Josephine, 25
The Perfect Summer (Nicolson), 82
Perkins, Bob, 284, 285
Pershing, General John, 34
Pierrepont, Nancy, 6, 8
Platt, Adam, 291

Pol-Roger, Odette, 182
Porcellian Club (Harvard), 61, 213,
214, 216, 235, 236, 250
Portrait of a Marriage (Nicolson), 298
Puchalski, Christina, 328

Rabin, Yitzhak, 223
*The Rare Art Traditions: The History of
Art Collecting and Its Linked
Phenomena Wherever These Have
Appeared* (J. W. Alsop), 298–299
Raurell, Alberto, 236, 239, 277
Reagan, Nancy, 297, 323
Recollections for My Family (Morgan),
35
The Rector of Justin (Auchincloss), 292
Reston, James, 224
*The Return to Camelot: Chivalry and the
English Gentleman* (Girouard), 72
Richmond, 276, 278, 286, 335
Robb, Ham, 228
Robinson, Corinne (née Roosevelt),
172
Robinson, Douglas, 172
Robinson, Stewart, 172
Rockefeller, John D. I, 32
Rockefeller, John D. Jr., 52
Roosevelt, Eleanor, 176
Roosevelt, Franklin, 206
Roosevelt, President Franklin Delano,
56, 176, 299
Roosevelt, President Theodore
attempts to democratize Foreign
Service, 37
daughter, Alice Longworth, 211
letter to Peter A. Jay's father, 29, 31
niece, Corinne Robinson Alsop, 170
sister, Corinne Roosevelt Robinson,
172
and war, 223
Rostow, Walt, 217
Rothermere, Lady Ann, 135
Rubio, Gloria, 86, 127
Rusk, Dean, 238
Russell, William Howard, 292
Rutland, Duke of, 81, 88

Sacco, Nicola, 41
Sackville-West, Lady (Vita), 293, 298

Salisbury, Lord, 162
Saltonstall, Dick, 249–250, 251,
    271–274
Saltonstall, Leverett, 250
Schlesinger, Arthur Jr., 186, 206, 210,
    222
Scully, Peter, 271
Seits, Dorothy, 321
Sendak, Maurice, 245
Shall We Dance? (film), 309
Shaw, Nancy Langhorne, 39
Shaw-Stewart, Patrick, 80
Sheehan, Neil, 223–224
Shultz, George, 296
Silvers, Bob, 218
Simpson, Wallis, 93
Slavery, 25
Smith, Forrester, 283–284
Souza-Baranowski Correctional
    Center, 332–333
Stevenson, Adlai, 182
Stillman, Chauncey, 63
Stilwell, General Joseph, 177
Stockton, Charles "Swig," 63, 190
Stuyvesant, Anna, 25
Stuyvesant, Peter, 25
Styron, William, 87
Sulzberger, Cyrus, 141, 164, 189
Sulzberger, David, 235, 289, 318, 346
Sulzberger, Marina, 121–122, 133, 201

Taft, Helen H., 32
Taking On the World (Merry), 169, 207,
    229
Talleyrand, Charles Maurice de, 68,
    92, 112, 137
Thayer, Walter, 251–252, 273
Theroux, Paul, 275
To Marietta from Paris, 1945–1960
    (S. M. Alsop), xii, 40–41, 58,
    186–187, 266, 277, 291, 292
Tower, John, 296
Tree, Marietta (née Peabody, formerly
    FitzGerald), 56–57
    appointment to United Nations
    Commission on Human Rights,
    204
    at Bar Harbor Club, 56
    correspondence from Susan Mary

Alsop, 207–208, 265–266
    correspondence from Susan Mary
    Patten, 67–68, 186
    death of, 315
    divorce from Desmond FitzGerald,
    129, 130
    encouragement of Susan Mary
    Alsop to publish letters, 291
    as hostess of Ditchley, 130–131
    and Joe Alsop, 129, 257
    and William Patten, 57, 68, 287
Tree, Ronald, 56, 130
Tree, Viola, 71

Ultimate Sacrifice (Coyne), 35

Vann, John Paul, 223–224
Vanzetti, Bartolomeo, 41
Vernon, George, 80
Vidal, Gore, 222, 223
Vietnam, 226
The Virgin Queen (film), 88
von Blucher, Gebhard Leberecht, 295

Walcott, Derek, 347
Wales, Prince of (later King Edward
    VIII, then Duke of Windsor),
    xiii, 70, 82, 90, 93
Walton, Bill, 206
War, casualties of, 80
Warrender, Lady, 85
Warrior Queens, The (Fraser), 291
Wasson, Tom, 276
Watergate scandal, 268
Waugh, Evelyn, 86, 121, 136, 157
Wedgwood, Josiah, 107
Welles, Sumner, 65
When the Moon Was High (Tree), 130
Whitehouse, Charlie, 6, 292, 296
Whitehouse, Mrs. Sheldon, 54
Whitney, Jock, 124, 251, 252
Whitney Communications, 251, 273
Whitridge, Janetta, 54–55
Wiggins, Russell, 272–273
Wilder, Throop, 286
William IV, King, 69, 69–70
Williams, Mrs. Hwfa, 82
Wilson, Charles McMoran (Lord
    Moran), 109

Wilson, President Woodrow, 36
Windsor, Duchess of, 85
Wood, General Leonard, 35
Woolf, Virginia, 319

Yamagata, General Aritomo, 33
*Yankees at the Court: The First
    Americans in Paris* (S. M. Alsop),
    2, 294–295
Yosemite National Park, 242

Zane, Tony, 144
Ziegler, Philip, 81, 125–126, 127
Zimmerman, Ruth, 309

William S. Patten is a businessman with thirty years experience in real estate development and venture capital. From 1978 to 1996 he published weekly newspapers in Maine. He has three children, two stepchildren, and three grandchildren. He lives in Worcester, Massachusetts, with his wife and stepdaughter.

PublicAffairs is a publishing house founded in 1997. It is a tribute to the standards, values, and flair of three persons who have served as mentors to countless reporters, writers, editors, and book people of all kinds, including me.

I.F. STONE, proprietor of *I. F. Stone's Weekly*, combined a commitment to the First Amendment with entrepreneurial zeal and reporting skill and became one of the great independent journalists in American history. At the age of eighty, Izzy published *The Trial of Socrates*, which was a national bestseller. He wrote the book after he taught himself ancient Greek.

BENJAMIN C. BRADLEE was for nearly thirty years the charismatic editorial leader of *The Washington Post*. It was Ben who gave the *Post* the range and courage to pursue such historic issues as Watergate. He supported his reporters with a tenacity that made them fearless and it is no accident that so many became authors of influential, best-selling books.

ROBERT L. BERNSTEIN, the chief executive of Random House for more than a quarter century, guided one of the nation's premier publishing houses. Bob was personally responsible for many books of political dissent and argument that challenged tyranny around the globe. He is also the founder and longtime chair of Human Rights Watch, one of the most respected human rights organizations in the world.

• • •

For fifty years, the banner of Public Affairs Press was carried by its owner Morris B. Schnapper, who published Gandhi, Nasser, Toynbee, Truman, and about 1,500 other authors. In 1983, Schnapper was described by *The Washington Post* as "a redoubtable gadfly." His legacy will endure in the books to come.

Peter Osnos, *Founder and Editor-at-Large*